Maitland+20 : Fixing the Missing Link

Maitland+20
Fixing the Missing Link

A collection of essays to mark the 20th anniversary of the final Report from the Independent Commission for World Wide Telecommunications Development, set up by the UN's International Telecommunication Union and chaired by Sir Donald Maitland GCMG.

Authors

Professor Victor Ayeni
Dr David Cleevely
James Deane
Ambassador Astrid Dufborg
Professor Heather E. Hudson
Yasuhiko Kawasumi
Dr Tim Kelly
Shafika Isaacs
Professor Robin Mansell
Dr Gillian M. Marcelle
Dr Nii Quaynor
Devindra Ramnarine
Chetan Sharma
Dr Jean-François Soupizet
Professor David Souter
Professor Tim Unwin
Professor Dr Leonid E. Varakin

Editor

Gerald Milward-Oliver

Published in the United Kingdom by
The Anima Centre Limited
1 Wine Street Terrace, Bradford on Avon
Wiltshire BA15 1NP, United Kingdom
Telephone: + 44 1225 866612
Email: team@theanimacentre.org

British Library Cataloguing in Publication Data
A CIP catalogue record for this book is available from
the British Library

ISBN-10: 0-9551616-0-6
ISBN-13: 0-978-0-9551616-0-5

Typeset in Bookman Old Style 9/12pt
Printed and bound by
Gutenberg Press Limited, Gudja Road, Tarxien PLA 19, Malta
www.gutenberg.com.mt

This book is printed on acid-free paper, responsibly
manufactured from sustainable forestry.

**Copies of *Maitland+20 : Fixing the Missing Link*
can be purchased direct from the publishers.**

- For online sales, go to www.theanimacentre.org/maitland.
- You can also send an order by post to:
  Maitland+20, The Anima Centre Limited, 1 Wine Street Terrace,
  Bradford on Avon BA15 1NP, Wiltshire, England.
  Please specify the number of copies required and include a
  telephone number as well as your own name and full postal
  address. We will then call you to take payment by credit card.
- You can email your order to team@theanimacentre.org.
- Or you can call us direct at +44 1225 866612.

Maitland+20 : Fixing the Missing Link is priced at £30 including
packing and airmail postage worldwide. Libraries, educational
establishments and NGOs qualify for a 30% discount. Substantial
discounts are also available for purchases of more than 10 copies
– please contact the Anima Centre for details.

Dedicated to Thomas A. Watson,
who had the good grace to answer the first ever
telephone call, on 10 March 1876.

———

*"In every age there is a turning-point, a new
way of seeing and asserting the coherence of
the world. Each culture tries to fix its visionary
moment, when it was transformed by a new
conception either of nature or of man. But in
retrospect, what commands our attention as
much are the continuities – the thoughts that
run or recur from one civilisation to another."*

Jacob Bronowski, The Ascent of Man, *1973*

Acknowledgements

Credit for the idea of marking the 20th anniversary of publication of the Maitland Commission Report is due to Richard Simpson, Director General at Industry Canada, Electronic Commerce Branch and John Gilbert, seconded from the Canadian civil service as Secretary to the Maitland Commission and now a telecommunications consultant.

Guidance and help has been generously provided by an editorial group consisting of John Gilbert, Alison Maitland (journalist and daughter of Sir Donald Maitland), Professor David Souter (ict Development Associates ltd and University of Strathclyde) and Myles Wickstead (UK Ambassador to Ethiopia 2000-2004 and Head of Secretariat, Commission for Africa 2004-2005).

Help has also been provided by senior staff at the International Telecommunication Union, and by the Commonwealth Foundation.

None of this would have been possible without the enthusiasm of the authors whose work this is. They are all astonishingly busy people who found the time and the inclination to make their own invaluable contributions, in spite of the imposition of unfairly tight deadlines. Their response is perhaps a measure of the respect still felt for the work of the members, the advisors and back-room staff of the Maitland Commission.

Profound respect and thanks to them all.

Finally, and most importantly, this project is inspired by the energy, enthusiasm and deeply valued friendship of Sir Donald Maitland.

Contents

i

Introduction

It is the job of the writer of the introduction to a collection of essays to act in the manner of the Fool in a Shakespearian drama – bid welcome to the audience, titillate their imagination with some tidbits of what is to come, encourage their commitment to stay the course, and to prepare them for a period of comedy, tragedy and all the emotions that lie between.

For the Maitland Commission, all the world was their stage in 1984 as they set out to map the state of the telecommunications world as it was between rich and poor, industrial and subsistence economy, developed and developing.

The purpose behind this collection of essays is to take the opportunity provided by WSIS and the Commonwealth Heads of Government meeting (which has taken networking as its theme) to pause and reflect on some of the issues raised by Maitland. Nor should they be read without also reflecting on the events leading up to the 2005 G8 meeting in Gleneagles (notably the extraordinarily well written and presented report from the Commission for Africa) and the material produced during the past year assessing progress towards attainment of the Millennium Development Goals.

The contributors to this volume have all been involved for many years in telecommunications development – indeed, some were involved as advisers to the Maitland Commission. They share a passion for communications and they have committed their professional lives to its enhancement. They have been progressing on their own journeys over the past 20 years, alongside the introduction of technologies that have been as, or more, disruptive as the invention of the plough, the steam engine or the factory production line.

We start with some reflections on then and now. David Souter asks what a modern-day Maitland Commission would consider as its brief? He concludes that it would inject some much-needed new thinking into the development debate, just as it did 20 years ago.

Tim Kelly looks at some of the statistics relating to the missing link – and brackets his comments between the work of the Maitland Commission (when the industry was still largely run by state-owned telephone monopolies) and the rise of voice over IP – what *The Economist* heralds as the "death" of the phone business.

Heather Hudson (who drafted some of the original Maitland Commission material) provides a thorough review of progress in the past 20 years, with particular emphasis on accessibility and capacity to use. James Deane argues that we need to focus more closely on the information and voice needs of the poor, rather than on the technology.

Victor Ayeni and Devindra Ramnarine explain how the Commonwealth Action Programme on the Digital Divide (CAPDD) is following some of the same logic – and seeking to help those still marginalised by lack of access to information. A similar tack is taken by Robin Mansell, who stresses that "people's livelihoods do not change because of technology: they change in the light of the way technology becomes embedded in the overall context of the local and the global".

Moving into the actualities of "the local", Yasuhiko Kawasumi (another Maitland veteran) concentrates on rural connectivity, reflecting his role as rapporteur for the ITU's work in this area. And the focus on needs continues with Gillian Marcelle's powerful analysis of one of the poorer regions of the world that can all too easily be forgotten – the Caribbean. She echoes the call of others for development work to be directed at what she evocatively describes as "self expression for the world's majority".

Astrid Dufborg takes the argument further into the detail of our lives, with a concise assessment of the progress being made by GeSCI – the Global eSchools & Communities Initiative. The theme is followed by Shafika Isaacs, who concentrates on the vital issue of empowering women to benefit from the information society, and by Chetan Sharma, whose Datamation Foundation Trust is making an extraordinary difference to women's lives in a north-eastern corner of Delhi. Tim Unwin also looks at those who suffer from the missing link, in particular the disabled – reflecting the success of his Imfundo project, run under the auspices of the UK's Department for International Development (DFID).

And so we change focus again, back from the particular to the more general, with Nii Quaynor's assessment of governance issues, with particular emphasis on the experience in Africa; and Jean-François Soupizet's complex but forthright analysis of the need for greater accessibility.

Returning to the early part of the book's reflection on the legacy of Maitland, we hear from Leonid Varakin – one of the original members of the Maitland Commission – and conclude with a powerful examination of what lies ahead from David Cleevely, another one of Maitland's advisers. He provides a pitch-perfect conclusion to this pot-pourri of thoughts and passions from some of the world's foremost thinkers on the subject.

And so this diversion is complete. At the end of Shakespeare's plays, the Fool returns to draw together the strands of what people have seen and heard. In thanking those who have so generously contributed to this mark of respect for what the Maitland Commission achieved, I would say no more than that the work started by Maitland is not yet ended, but it has begun, and it *will* succeed.

Gerald Milward-Oliver
Bradford on Avon, October 2005

Maitland+20 : Fixing the Missing Link

David Souter

Managing Director ict Development Associates ltd,
Visiting Professor in Communications Management,
University of Strathclyde

1.

Then and now: what would be the remit of a modern-day Maitland Commission?

David Souter

Managing Director ict Development Associates ltd,
Visiting Professor in Communications Management, University of Strathclyde

History moves quickly in telecommunications: even twenty years is a long time in an industry driven by rapid technological change. The Maitland Commission Report, which we celebrate in this publication, was a product of its time – written at the dawn of mobile communications, as the first neoliberal reforms began a trend which has since liberalised and privatised telecommunications across the globe, when the Internet was little more than a glimmer in the eye of computer scientists. How relevant are the questions it asked twenty years ago to current debates about the relationship between communications and development? What would preoccupy a new Maitland Commission if one were appointed today? This essay discusses these questions.

The historical context

The Maitland Commission is commonly seen as the *fons et origo* of discussion on ICTs and development. Speech after speech at the first session of the World Summit on the Information Society cited it and hailed its influence. In many ways, at that summit, it seemed to have acquired canonic status, to have become a text which was cited to give authority by association to viewpoints that were currently being expressed. At the same time, ironically, it was actually rather difficult to obtain a copy of this key text of the digital era outside traditional libraries, though it had recently been made available (if hard to find) on the ITU website[1]. Like most canonical texts, *The Missing Link* has probably been cited more often than it has been read[2].

This suggests two things about the impact of the Commission's report. The fact that it is so frequently cited attests to the nature of its significance at the time: it was the first analysis that identified the possible interactions between telecommunications and development in a systematic and (within the industry, at least) popular form. But it also draws attention to the lack of subsequent analysis of those interactions in the following decade. The Commission did not, in the short term, lead to a major change in thinking either within the telecommunications industry or the development community. Its primary target – "that by the early part of the next century virtually the whole of mankind should be brought within easy reach of a telephone and, in due course, the other services telecommunications can provide"[3] – was very far from being fulfilled. It was not until the late 1990s that ICT businesses and development agencies became seriously interested again in the relationship between telecoms and development. In that sense, therefore, the Maitland Commission's report was far ahead of its time.

To understand this missing link between *The Missing Link* and today's ICT4D debate[4], we need to look briefly at both development and telecommunications sector contexts.

In the development context, it should be remembered that the Maitland Commission met during a period when global commissions made up of international experts and figureheads were fashionable instruments of international discourse. Usually identified by the names of their chairs, these commissions focused on different aspects of international development and governance – most notably the Brandt Commission on North-South issues (which reported in 1980), the Palme Commission on international security (1982) and the Brundtland Commission on environment and development (1987). Each of these major commissions developed a central concept – mutual dependence of North and South, common security, sustainable development – which influenced discourse during the remainder of the 1980s and in some cases beyond. The Maitland Commission did not address as substantial an issue or achieve anything like the prominence of these major international commissions. Nevertheless, *The Missing Link* shared a certain ethos with them and added a small component to their global visions[5].

Development policy, like all other areas of human thought, is subject to the whims of fashion, and the vogue for global solutions gave way during the 1980s to greater focus on more nationally-based approaches to development, accompanied by renewed faith within the international community in economic liberalism. The 1990s have seen something of a reversion to globalism in development thinking, most notably in the Millennium Development Goals and the associated Millennium Project (in some ways a successor to the earlier Brandt Report)[6].

Throughout this period, however, the overriding goals of development policy – poverty reduction; improvements in health and education, opportunity and entrepreneurship; reductions in civil conflict – have been relatively unchanged, as (more regrettably) has the scale of the challenge posed, especially in Africa. There is, perhaps, more emphasis today on governance, environmental factors and gender equity, as well as the new problems presented by the HIV/AIDS pandemic. But the underlying nature of the development challenge that telecommunications or ICTs might contribute to addressing is much the same today as it was in 1985.

The same, obviously, cannot be said of the telecommunications sector. While much of Africa and parts of Asia have stagnated economically, the telecoms industry has grown more quickly and changed more dramatically than any industry before. In 1985, typically, state-owned telecoms monopolies provided a limited range of services (primarily fixed voice telephony) to subscribers that were, in many countries, narrowly confined to businesses, government and wealthy urban residents. Today, in most countries, competitive markets, including multinational businesses active in many different countries, offer a wide range of different services (including three mass market products: fixed telephony, mobile telephony and Internet) to customers coming, in almost all countries, from much wider social and geographic groupings. Telecoms businesses are global, privately-owned, market-oriented and compete with businesses in a range of adjacent markets as telecoms converges with broadcasting, computing and other formerly separate sectors. Mobile rather than fixed lines are the telephones of choice, bringing connectivity to rural areas of most developing countries for the first time during the past five years. Continuing technical and market developments create a context of rapid and unpredictable change. What this industry can do today is immeasurably different from what it could do in 1985, while the people who might choose to do it are very different people, schooled in business not bureaucracy.

Priorities for 1985, priorities today

In short, then, the telecommunications context that the Maitland Commission considered has changed much more than the development context which surrounds it. To see how this might affect the questions asked today, we should start by reminding ourselves of the argument presented in the Commission's report.

The starting point for *The Missing Link* was the *observation* that telecommunications were disproportionately concentrated in a small number of countries. At that time, the Commission observed 600 million telephones worldwide, of which 450 million (75%) were in nine countries. In many areas of many countries, there was no telecommunications network at all[7].

This observation was then associated with *assumptions* about the benefits that telecommunications could bring to social and economic development. These were seen as being general and wide-ranging, as follows:

"Telecommunications play an essential role in emergency and health services, commerce and other economic activity, in public administration, and in reducing the need to travel. There is moreover a clear link between investment in telecommunications and economic growth.

The economic and social benefits an efficient communications system confers on a community or a nation can be clearly perceived. The system can also be used as a channel for education, for disseminating information, encouraging self-reliance, strengthening the social fabric and sense of national identity, and contributing to political stability"[8].

More widespread telecommunications worldwide would also, the report, argued, increase telecommunications traffic and demand for telecoms equipment and other manufactured goods from industrial countries, so contributing to beneficial growth in global trade and prosperity. This point in particular chimed with the 'mutual advantage' thesis at the heart of the then-recent Brandt Report.

The Commission then presented a *critique* of current inequalities in the distribution of telecommunications and the role of the international telecoms community in addressing them. Finally, it offered a series of *prescriptions* – recommendations and suggestions – intended to stimulate investment in network deployment, management and implementation. These included proposals for increasing capital flows, capacity-building, research and technological development, but not specific development applications.

This line of argument is, in fact, very close to much of the current literature on ICT4D, particularly that concerned with the "digital divide". This, too, starts from the observation that communications resources are disproportionately distributed both internationally and within nation-states. It also assumes that ICTs (rather, today, than just telecommunications) deliver social and economic gains across the board: indeed, the paragraphs quoted above could, with substitution of the word "ICT" for "telecommunications", easily be taken from the Declaration of Principles of the World Summit on the Information Society[9]. The present debate identifies and critiques perceived deficiencies within the international development and telecommunications institutions (most notably, of late, through the two working groups set up by the United Nations following the first session of the World Summit on the Information Society: the Task Force on Financing Mechanisms and the Working Group on Internet Governance). And it also offers prescriptions, though these are related to a wider range of development-focused objectives than the more specifically telecoms sector recommendations of 1985.

That the line of argument in 2005 should be similar to that of 1985 is, in some sense, not surprising. The central issue is the potential role which telecommunications (then) or ICT (today) can play in facilitating development objectives. These have not changed substantially since 1985, and nor have the types of contribution that information/communication businesses can bring to them. There are, however, much sharper differences evident when this contribution is unpacked, and these lie in three main areas: in the different modes of telecommunications available in 1985 (principally fixed voice) and in 2005 (fixed, mobile and data/Internet); in the different scope of contribution envisaged (a development from telecommunications to ICTs); and in the relationship between these and potential development applications/outcomes. A word about each of these is relevant before we consider other differences and similarities between the debates of 1985 and 2005.

The change in modes of telecommunications is, in many ways, profound. Fixed telephone networks are built around communication between locations; mobile networks around that between individuals. Fixed networks are costly to deploy, relatively inflexible for users but currently offer higher functionality (especially where Internet access is concerned); wireless networks are cheaper to install, more flexible for users but offer lesser functionality. Users everywhere are migrating from fixed to mobile networks as their primary mode of voice telephony – with over 90% of telephone lines in some countries now being mobile lines[10]. Ownership of mobile telephones is highly desired even in low-income communities, where telephony is highly valued for emergency use and social networking[11]. We now suspect, as a result, that voice telephony networks are likely to prove commercially viable in all but the remotest, least populated and most problematic environments. The new pattern of mobile network predominance may soon be threatened by alternative networks built around the Internet in some industrial countries, but it is unlikely that the preferred mode of communications will revert to one that is location-based rather than personal. This requires new ways of thinking about the relationship between citizens and networks, and the ways in which networks will be used to meet individuals' development choices.

The change in sectoral scope from telecommunications (1985) to ICTs (today) is also profound, but has been underestimated. The World Summit on the Information Society, the "digital divide" debate and the development of national ICT strategies are all predicated on the belief that a wide range of related new technologies and applications can transform development. These technologies and applications include broadcasting, computing and information technology, e-government and e-business, as well as telecommunications. Yet much of the current ICT4D debate has been conducted by telecommunications specialists: a much higher proportion of delegates to the first World Summit on the Information Society, for example, came from the traditional telecommunications sector than from innovative ICT/Internet or from mainstream development backgrounds. Telecoms specialists, not surprisingly, see other ICTs as subordinate to and dependent on telecoms networks.

Development specialists, too, have failed to distinguish sufficiently between the different potentialities of different ICTs, though these are clear enough from the uses made of them by citizens and consumers – with telephony highly valued by the general public for emergency and social use, broadcasting valued for general information and entertainment, and Internet and information technology primarily valued by those with significant resources or specialist expertise (including business people and those managing development programmes) as means of enhancing their productivity and effectiveness[12]. The importance of these demand-side differences has been underestimated by contrast with supply-side (technological and business) convergence. Today's ICT4D debate is, in fact, about a much wider range of resources drawn from many different sectors with different characteristics than 1985's discussion of telecoms, rather than mere widening of how "telecommunications" are defined.

Finally, in this context, conceptual thinking about the relationship between telecommunications/ICTs and development has evolved substantially since 1985. As mentioned earlier, the Maitland Commission report was not followed by extensive further debate about the role of telecommunications in development. The telecoms sector over the following decade was preoccupied with restructuring (liberalisation, privatisation, regulation), globalisation and technological change. The ITU did set up a specialist Development Bureau, but this did not achieve high status within the organisation or engage extensively with other development bodies. Development agencies in general noted the high cost of infrastructure investment, welcomed the stimulation of investment resulting from liberalisation, and urged the private sector to play the lead role in developing what many development specialists still considered luxury services for elite constituencies. And the private sector did invest. Only in the late 1990s did development specialists begin to re-engage with the issues raised in the Maitland Commission report, noting the rapid spread of telecoms access that was beginning to take place and seeing in it (and the ICT applications that could run over telecoms networks) potential for supporting delivery of development objectives.

Around the turn of the century, ICT4D became, for a while, the fastest growing area of development policy, stimulating a range of donor initiatives, a UN Task Force, a World Summit and a welter of national ICT strategies. Some within the development community – and within governments of developing countries – have come to see ICTs as central to the future delivery of development goals. Others, however, are still cautious and unconvinced, their caution increased by the relatively high failure rate of early ICT4D initiatives. Most donor agencies reflect this caution in their overall approach to ICTs in development, usually described as "mainstreaming" – that is, incorporating ICTs as delivery mechanisms in programmes focused on traditional development outcomes such as health and education, rather than establishing them as separate development objectives in their own right.

It would be a mistake to judge the level of support for ICT-related approaches to development from the outcomes of fora led by ICT professionals like WSIS and the International Telecommunication Union's World Telecommunication Development Conference. Global development policy today is dominated by the struggle to achieve the Millennium Development Goals (MDGs) for poverty reduction agreed by the United Nations in 2000. Only one of the eighteen targets within these goals mentions ICTs – the last, generally considered an afterthought rather than a priority[13]. ICTs are mentioned as potential delivery mechanisms in the interim MDG reports published by the UN Millennium Project in early 2005, but they play a minor role[14]. They receive even scanter attention in the 2005 Human Development Report's review of MDG targets and priorities[15]. At national level, MDG implementation and overall development strategy focus in many countries on Poverty Reduction Strategy Papers (PRSPs) – the latest attempt by international institutions to balance donor and recipient priorities for development. ICTs feature in hardly any PRSPs[16], while PRSPs themselves get little attention in national ICT strategies drawn up by communications or information ministries.

Seen from the perspective of telecoms and ICT professionals engaged with development, therefore – for example, from the Geneva preparatory committee meetings for the World Summit on the Information Society – ICTs seem central to current development policy. Seen from the perspective of general development debate, they seem marginal. There is a profound paradigm gap still between the thinking of the two expert groups involved, and no substantive consensus on the value, role or significance of ICTs in development. Much needs to be done before this paradigm gap is bridged and consensus reached.

The ethos of telecoms/ICT/development debate

We will return to this point later. Before doing so, however, it is useful to compare the methodology and analytical character of the Maitland Commission report and the current ICT4D debate. These share a number of common characteristics that in turn point to areas which a new Maitland Commission, or its equivalent, might investigate were it set up today.

The Maitland Commission was established by a telecommunications agency (the International Telecommunication Union) to investigate a telecommunications issue (the disparity in telephone access between rich and poor countries and how this might be reduced). Its focus was on telecommunications rather than development – on the supply of technology and its potential rather than on demand for technology as such or for information and communication in general. This is not a criticism of the Commission or its sponsors: no-one had looked seriously at the implications of differentials in telecoms access before it, and, by focusing sharply on that question, it raised important issues that had previously been overlooked.

Approaching ICT4D issues from a technological, supply-side perspective does, however, have its problems, and these are fundamental to the misunderstandings found today between ICT and development communities. The priority challenges which the world faces – the crises in poverty, health, education, gender equity, governance etc. addressed by the Millennium Development Goals – are development challenges. From a development point of view, technologies – from bicycles to vaccination, transport and electric power to broadcast radio and telecommunications – are means which may contribute towards achieving a range of development objectives, including the MDGs. Their value, from this point of view, depends on their cost-effectiveness, given available resources (financial, human and complementary resources such as, for telecoms, transport for equipment and reliable electric power), in comparison with the cost-effectiveness of other means available. This cost-effectiveness is understood largely in terms of quantitative outputs – the numbers of people who can be lifted out of abject poverty, vaccinated, enabled to become literate and numerate, protected from civil conflict. The key question from the perspective of the MDGs is therefore not about what telecommunications or ICTs can do in ideal circumstances with all necessary resources, or about the level of ICT inputs available, but about where ICTs can add value and enhance delivery of mainstream programmes reliably and cost-effectively within current resource constraints (financial, human, power etc.) at this basic poverty-alleviation output level. Much of the present ICT4D debate does not engage sufficiently or sufficiently objectively with this fundamental and difficult question.

A second element of the Maitland Commission's approach worth noting in this context is its conception of the developmental value of telecommunications. This was primarily seen – certainly expressed – at a societal rather than an individual level. The report refers, for example, to "the economic and social benefits an efficient communication system confers on a community or a nation", and sees assets such as health and education as national rather than individual assets. This way of understanding the potential developmental gains from ICTs is also widespread in today's ICT4D debate, particularly in national ICT strategies;

but it undervalues an important dimension of telephony behaviour for the individual. People value phones because of what they personally gain from them, not for the value they offer to society; and it is personal advantage that therefore drives take-up of telephony and network expansion. Telephones have great empowerment value – they enable people to do things that are important to them quickly and remotely – and that empowerment in itself contributes to development. It is not dependent on applications delivered by the state or donors but on activity generated by individual citizens themselves, including activity which protects them against vulnerability and enables them to take advantage of opportunities that would otherwise pass by. This distinguishes the developmental value of telephony from most other types of ICT – broadcasting, for example, or e-government – whose use is much less determined by the individual citizen.

A further aspect worth noting about the approach to telecoms/ICTs and development by the 1985 Commission and today's ICT4D specialists concerns the relationship between telecommunications/ICTs and information/communications in general. The Maitland Commission's starting point, rightly for its time and purpose, was telecoms, seen largely from a technical point of view. Much of the current ICT4D literature similarly understands ICTs primarily as technologies – the 'T' in 'ICTs' – rather than as media for the transmission of information and communication. As a result, a high degree of discontinuity is often expected between 'pre-ICT' and 'post-ICT' societies, as shown by the widespread use of the term 'Information Society'. Again, however, there are important questions to be asked here. People do not communicate because technology enables them to do so; they communicate because they have a need to share information, experience or social solidarity (for example, in maintaining family relationships). Similarly, people do not seek information for its own sake, but because they can use it to protect themselves against vulnerability or to seize opportunities for advantage. These communication needs and behavioural patterns do not show the same discontinuity as the technology now available to meet them. It is therefore important from an "ICD" point of view – rather than that of "ICT4D"[17], to understand why people want to communicate and with whom, and what information they need in what form – before concluding how a new technology might be most beneficial to them. It is important to recognise the behavioural continuities as well as the technological discontinuities in the development of communications services.

Such understanding is critical, not least because in practice people in all societies rely heavily on information intermediaries rather than seeking information on their own. Such intermediaries include radio programmes, magazines, teachers, basic health workers, parents, agricultural extension officers, astrologers, priests, and politicians – to name but a few. Human behaviour in this respect tends to be conservative: people do not readily replace trusted sources of information with untried alternatives. Much information is therefore best conveyed by development programmes through intermediaries rather than directly to end-users: agricultural extension officers who can interpret soil fertility and rainfall data, for example; or local health workers who understand the nuances required for HIV/AIDS information in particular communities. New modes of communication are likely to be adopted readily where they add substantial value in fulfilling existing needs – the television in providing entertainment, for example, or the telephone in offering immediate access to help from relatives and regular contact with sons or daughters in the diaspora or husbands working as migrant labour – but not where they do not have such value. It is not the availability of technology *per se* that has created high demand for its ownership and use but the extent to which it can meet unmet needs or do so much more cost-effectively or efficiently than alternatives.

A final aspect of the approach of 1985 and 2005 that should be considered concerns the distribution of resources within communities. The concept (and undesirability) of a "digital divide" is central to both the Maitland Commission report and the current ICT4D debate (though in 1985, it would not have been or been called "digital"). That richer countries and individuals should have more of any asset or technology than their poorer peers is, of course, nothing unusual: it applies, pretty much, to all assets and all technologies worldwide. Developing countries and poorer communities within them are at the bottom end of health and education divides, divides in the supply of clean water and electric power, of usable roads and affordable transport, *etc. etc. etc.* If something is worth having, those that can afford it will and those that cannot won't. So there is nothing surprising about the fact that there is a digital divide. The question is whether the potential value of telecommunications/ICTs in enabling people to acquire other assets (better health, quicker remittances etc.) is sufficient to make the "digital divide" more important than other rich:poor differentials in its impact on their lives.

That is currently an open question: there is no clear or convincing evidence either way. The distributional issue, however, works in both directions. If communities and individuals are disadvantaged by the non-availability of telecommunications/ICTs, then providing access to those facilities will not just reduce existing disadvantage for those that gain access; it will also tend to create disparities between these beneficiaries and others who do not. The distributional impacts of changes in information and communication resources are very poorly understood, though there is evidence – not surprisingly – that higher economic and educational status groups, and perhaps (because they tend to be more represented in these groups) also men, are better placed to take advantage of new opportunities. Whether the benefits of this tend to increase differentials or trickle down throughout a community is an important and unanswered developmental question.

One thing that is clear from all of the above is that our substantive knowledge of the impact of telecoms and ICTs on development is still poor.

We can be fairly clear, for example, that IT investment has a measurable impact on overall economic growth in OECD countries, albeit one that is long-term and highly dependent on complementary factors such as human resource capacity and organisational change[18]. The extent to which this conclusion can be automatically extended to developing countries, which have smaller service and larger subsistence sectors and which lack many of the complementary factors identified in OECD studies, is still unclear. The impact of telecommunications, for example, may be very different from that of other forms of ICT[19].

This research deficit is paralleled in other areas. Much of the available research on the impact of ICTs in developing countries collects anecdotes or experiences of individual projects/programmes, assessing this in relation to project users or programme beneficiaries[20]. Very little research has been done to develop understanding of impacts on the whole community, particularly the distribution of benefits between different social groups; to assess the need for complementary resources such as human skills, transport and power; or to compare cost-effectiveness with other delivery mechanisms. Evidence-based understanding of these complex interactions is essential if resources available for the application of ICTs in development are to be effectively targeted.

The Maitland Commission eschewed new research in developing its findings, relying on available evidence to justify its conclusions. That was reasonable given its telecoms-specific mandate and the resources that it had available. It is not sufficient, however, for decision-making processes today which require the effective allocation of scarce development resources to a wide range of new and relatively untried technologies.

Questions for the here and now

So what would or should a new Maitland Commission consider if it were established now?

There have, in fact, been a number of initiatives that come close to repeating the original commission's role in the new ICT context. Perhaps the closest parallel has been the Digital Opportunities Task Force (or DOT Force) established by the G8 at its Okinawa summit in 2000. That task force – made up of government, private sector and civil society representatives from eight G8 and eight developing countries – acted much like an early 1980s international commission, exploring new ideas and developing recommendations, which were published at the G8's Kananaskis summit two years later. Other candidates for the modern Maitland mantle would include the UN ICT Task Force, a more amorphous group the renewal of whose mandate in another form is currently under consideration; the two specialist task forces set up by the UN to consider contentious issues arising from the first session of the World Summit on the Information Society – the Task Force on Financing Mechanisms (TFFM) and the Working Group on Internet Governance (WGIG); and the World Summit itself, though there are huge differences in style between the formal global summit process that will culminate in Tunis in November 2005 and the much less costly, much less formal commission whose anniversary is commemorated by this book.

In practice, there is a clear distinction in purpose and potential outcomes between commissions like that of 1985 and global bodies such as WSIS and the UN ICT Task Force. The latter, established by the United Nations to represent global opinion and develop global plans, are bound by the conventions of global consensus. Because they must have everyone on board, they find it easier to list desiderata than to establish priorities. Their output documents are stronger on rhetoric than they are on planning, more valued as expressions of common aspirations than as strategies for their achievement. Where disputes do arise – as they did in the first session of WSIS over the future of Internet governance and the desirability of particular mechanisms for funding future ICT development – they are often highly contentious, complicated by unrelated international disputes, and draw attention and resources to them from areas in which consensus on plans for action might more readily be achieved.

Narrower fora, outside the constraints of global consensus, can be more innovative and more radical in their thinking. The internationalist commissions of the early 1980s, including the Maitland Commission, drew together groups of experts, usually balanced by region though not at that time by gender, who could consider issues as individuals rather than representatives and develop a consensus amongst themselves that was based on highest common factors rather than lowest common denominators. Certainly, the absence of need for global consensus enabled them (to use contemporary management terminology) if not to "think the unthinkable" at least "to think outside the box". The Commission for Africa, which reported in 2005, is an example of a similar broad-based development initiative today. In the ICT context, the DOT Force and, within their narrower remits, TFFM and WGIG each had characteristics reminiscent of the 1980s commissions – individual rather than representative status for their members; balanced regional and, in some cases, stakeholder participation; and the ability to reach consensus that is more innovative, substantial and provocative than their global counterparts could reach. Of these, however, only the DOT Force tried to take an overall view of the ICT4D picture comparable to that within the WSIS mandate.

A case for something comparable to the Maitland Commission can be made today, but its remit and its purpose would be rather different from those of 1985. The original Commission was concerned with telecommunications; any commission today would need to look at a wider range of information and communication technologies, though it should recognise the different purposes to which these different technologies are put. The Maitland Commission also sought to raise awareness of an issue that was not already the subject of discussion. There is plenty of discussion of ICT4D/ICD today. The problem is that much of this lacks focus and coherence. It is not yet rooted in any real consensus about the relationship between communications and development or any real shared understanding between those specialising in these areas. Strategic priorities for ICTs are still poorly interlinked with those for poverty reduction and other developmental targets. Little research has been done into the impact of ICTs on development, especially in whole communities, and the quality of much that has been published is poor. Most of the discussion of ICT4D focuses on what today's technology can offer; little on the potential impact of the next wave of telecommunications and other information technology developments. (The potential of future wireless rather than cable technologies to deliver Internet access in rural Africa, for example, is a critical and desperately uncertain issue for future resource allocation.)

A modern Maitland Commission could add value, therefore, if it addressed these kind of questions with the greater openness of thinking which an international commission can bring to bear than that generated by a global consensus body such as WSIS – if it identified key areas for research and consideration by policymakers, businesses and other stakeholders; focused attention on issues of critical long-term importance rather than short-term political priorities; looked forward to the potential and uncertainty of future technology and market developments; and, above all, increased understanding and consensus between ICT specialists and the wider development community on the broad dynamics of information and communications in development and the contribution new technologies could make to these.

The mandate for such a commission could be simple and wide-ranging, perhaps along the following lines:

- *To assess the likely future development of information and communication technologies and their relevance to social and economic development during the next ten years.*

- *To review evidence concerning the real impact that technological change is having on development, particularly the achievement of the Millennium Development Goals.*
- *To improve understanding of the relationship between development, information and communications needs and ICTs, in both mainstream development sectors and amongst ICT professionals.*
- *To make appropriate recommendations that will enhance the quality of national and international decision-making in this area, including the development of an appropriate research agenda.*

There is one final question. If such a commission were appointed today, who should be its members? The 1985 commissioners had a wide range of skills within and beyond the telecommunications sector. Most of today's ICT/ICD debate is conducted by ICT professionals and those that specialise in ICTs within development agencies. (The United Nations, for example, invited the International Telecommunication Union rather than, say, UNESCO or the UN Development Programme to organise the World Summit on the Information Society – a decision that had a significant impact on participation in WSIS because it determined which government ministries led national WSIS delegations.) Knowledge of technology is valuable in determining its developmental potential, but not so valuable as understanding of developmental needs.

It is, rightly, commonplace to observe that the international commissions of the 1980s were relatively representative of regions but never genders, and some care is usually taken to make them more representative today. The value of multistakeholder participation – of the involvement of those with experience in government, the private sector and civil society – is also often raised, particularly within the ICT sector (where it has been a matter of contention in WSIS). Again, it seems evident that a commission whose members have diverse backgrounds is likely to resonate more powerfully among more stakeholder groups than one which is confined to the established "great and good". The 1980s commissions were surely right to appoint their members as individuals rather than as representatives of particular interest groups, so liberating them to think more freely than they otherwise would do.

The most important question, though, is the balance of expertise between the ICT sector and mainstream development specialists. In 1985, the Maitland Commission essentially focused on the development of telecommunications, and how that might impinge on development in general: its focus came, primarily, from the supply side of the equation. The supply side has also dominated much of the current debate on information and communication (technologies) for development. This essay suggests that that emphasis should be reversed: that the starting point for any new commission should be general development objectives; that a majority (though not a large majority) of its members should have development rather than ICT expertise; and that the (perhaps) third or so of its participants that come from the information and communication sectors should include specialists in the human dynamics of information and communications as well as the broadcasting, telecommunications and other technologies involved.

At the least, that would inject a different way of thinking into today's analysis of IC(T4)D issues; and new thinking, surely, is the primary reason for having any global commission in the first place.

References

1. It can be found at www.itu.int/osg/spu/sfo/missinglink/index.html.

2. The report was much less cited during the preparatory sessions for the second WSIS session, perhaps because these focused more on issues such as Internet governance.

3. *The Missing Link*, Executive Summary, para. 5.

4. The term 'ICT4D' is used quite extensively as shorthand for 'information and communications technology for development' by ICT professionals. It is often used interchangeably with, but is not the same as 'ICD' ('information and communications for development'), from which the word 'technology' is notably omitted, and which is preferred within the development community.

5. A useful account of the key 1980s commissions, and their more recent successors, can be found in Ramesh Thakur, Andrew F. Cooper and John English (eds), *International Commissions and the Power of Ideas* (United Nations University Press, 2005).

6. The Millennium Development Goals were agreed by the United Nations General Assembly in 2000 and can be found at www.un.org/millenniumgoals/. The Millennium Project's reports are at www.unmillenniumproject.org/reports/index.htm.

7. In 2002, according to data in the ITU's *World Telecommunication Development Report*, about 64% of some 2.25 billion telephone lines were in nine countries, though the largest number by this time were in a developing country, China. Interestingly, the Maitland Commission's original figures live on in an exhibition held in London during the summer of 2005, which claimed that 90% of the world's people had never used a telephone. The time it takes for long-outdated 'facts' like this to be displaced from public consciousness rather neatly illustrates that the way that information and communications content changes at the speed at human behaviour rather than that of technological capacity.

8. *The Missing Link*, Executive Summary, paras. 7 & 8.

9. Available at www.itu.int/wsis/documents/doc_multi-en-1161|1160.asp.

10. The figure in Uganda in June 2005, for example, was 94%: see Uganda Communications Commission data at www.ucc.co.ug/marketInfo/about.html.

11. Recent DFID-funded research on this issue in India, Mozambique and Tanzania is published in D. Souter et al., *The Economic Impact of Telecommunications on Rural Livelihoods and Poverty Reduction* (CTO for DFID, 2005).

12. *Ibid.*

13. The last of the seven targets of the eighth goal reads "In cooperation with the private sector, [to] make available the benefits of new technologies – especially information and communications technologies."

14. See reports at www.unmillenniumproject.org/reports/index.htm.

15. *International Co-operation at a Crossroads: Aid, Trade and Security in an Unequal World*, available at http://hdr.undp.org/reports/global/2005.

16. See OECD Development Assistance Committee, document CCNM/GF/DCD/KE(2003)4 at www.oecd.org/dataoecd/4/30/15987925.pdf.

17. i.e. 'information and communications for development' and 'information and communication technologies for development' – see footnote 5 above.

18. See OECD, *ICT and Economic Growth: Evidence from OECD Countries, Industries and Firms* (2003).

19. See D. Souter, *ICTs and Economic Growth in Developing Countries*, OECD Development Assistance Committee Journal, Vol. 5 no. 4 (2004).

20. A prime example is the stocktaking exercise undertaken for WSIS 2: www.itu.int/wsis/docs2/pc3/html/off3b/index.html.

David Souter is Managing Director of the research and consultancy business ict Development Associates ltd, which works at the interface between development and the ICT sector. He is also Visiting Professor in Communications Management at the University of Strathclyde. From 1995 to 2003 he was Chief Executive of the Commonwealth Telecommunications Organisation.

Contact details: David Souter, Managing Director, ict Development Associates ltd, 145 Lower Camden, Chislehurst, Kent BR7 5JD.
Tel: +44 20 8467 1148 Email: david.souter@runbox.com.

Dr Tim Kelly

Head, Strategy and Policy Unit
International Telecommunication Union (ITU)

2.

Twenty years of measuring the missing link

Dr Tim Kelly

Head, Strategy and Policy Unit, International Telecommunication Union (ITU)

In 1985, through the Report of the Independent Commission for Worldwide Telecommunications Development: The Missing Link, Sir Donald Maitland and his team reported on the lack of telephones worldwide that was impeding the world's economic and social development.

Some 20 years later, in its 16 September 2005 edition, *The Economist* reported on the "death" of the phone business, supposedly killed by the rise of voice over Internet protocol (VoIP). The capacity of the Internet, which is optimised for data, is so great that telephone calls can be carried at a marginal cost which begins to approach zero.

What happened in the 20 intervening years to convert a global shortage of phones into a glut of over-capacity? How has the world changed in those two decades? How has the science of measuring the "missing link" – or the "digital divide" as we are more likely to call it today – affected our understanding of the problem?

What a difference 20 years makes

The Missing Link is probably best remembered for its aphorisms, some of which do not even appear in the report (see box on page 26). It also contained some memorable charts and graphs, based on data from the ITU, which had been collecting telecommunication indicators since the 19th century. This process was formalised in the 1960s with first publication of the Yearbook of Statistics[1]. More recently, in 1994, on the 10th anniversary of *The Missing Link*, the ITU launched the World Telecommunication Development Report series, and a couple of years later the World Telecommunication Indicators Database. These reports provide a much richer range of statistical data than was available to the Worldwide Commission, but nevertheless, comparisons between the Maitland Report and more recent data make for fascinating reading.

The Maitland Report showed a chart on the breakdown of telephones compared with the breakdown of the world's population, by income group of countries (See Figure 1, overleaf, top chart). The Maitland data was based on around 110 economies for which telecommunication indicators were available at the time. They showed that some 96% of telephones were located in high-income or upper-middle income countries. Twenty years on, ITU tracks data for some 206 economies. Those same two categories still account for the majority of the world's phone subscribers (fixed-line

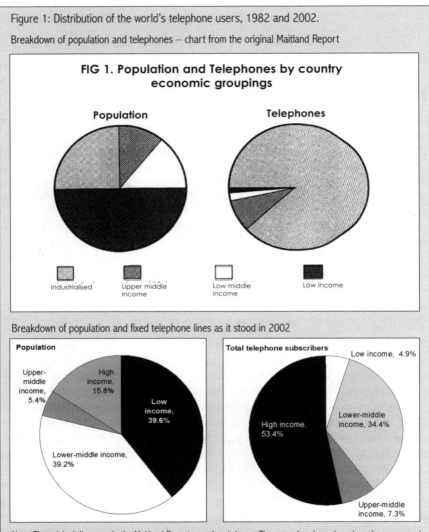

Figure 1: Distribution of the world's telephone users, 1982 and 2002.

Breakdown of population and telephones – chart from the original Maitland Report

FIG 1. Population and Telephones by country economic groupings

Population

Telephones

Industrialised   Upper middle income   Low middle income   Low income

Breakdown of population and fixed telephone lines as it stood in 2002

Population

Upper-middle income, 5.4%
High income, 15.8%
Low income, 39.6%
Lower-middle income, 39.2%

Total telephone subscribers

Low income, 4.9%
High income, 53.4%
Lower-middle income, 34.4%
Upper-middle income, 7.3%

Note: The original diagrams in the Maitland Report were hand-drawn. The examples shown here have been scanned. The countries that fit into the categories "industrialised" (now called "high income"), upper-middle, lower-middle and low income have changed over time as countries have "graduated" from one to another.   Source: The Maitland Report 1985 and the ITU World Telecommunication Indicators Database.

telephones and mobile phones combined), but now their share is down to just 61%. The category of "lower-middle income countries", which today includes India and China, today accounts for around one third of the world's telephone users compared with just 3% in 1982.

Measuring the digital divide

In assessing the extent of the digital divide, it is useful to look at those networks, services and hardware that provide a platform for the development of other information and communication services. The Maitland Report focused on the fixed-line telephone network and, to a lesser extent, telex. Today, as Figure 2 shows, it is worth focusing on the progress in reducing the digital divide among four key information and communication technologies (ICTs):

• For fixed line telephone networks, which still form the main

Figure 2: The digital divide is narrowing, but faster for some than others
The pace of reduction in the digital divide between developed and developing countries 1992-2002, for fixed telephone lines, mobile phones, personal computers and Internet users, per 100 inhabitants.

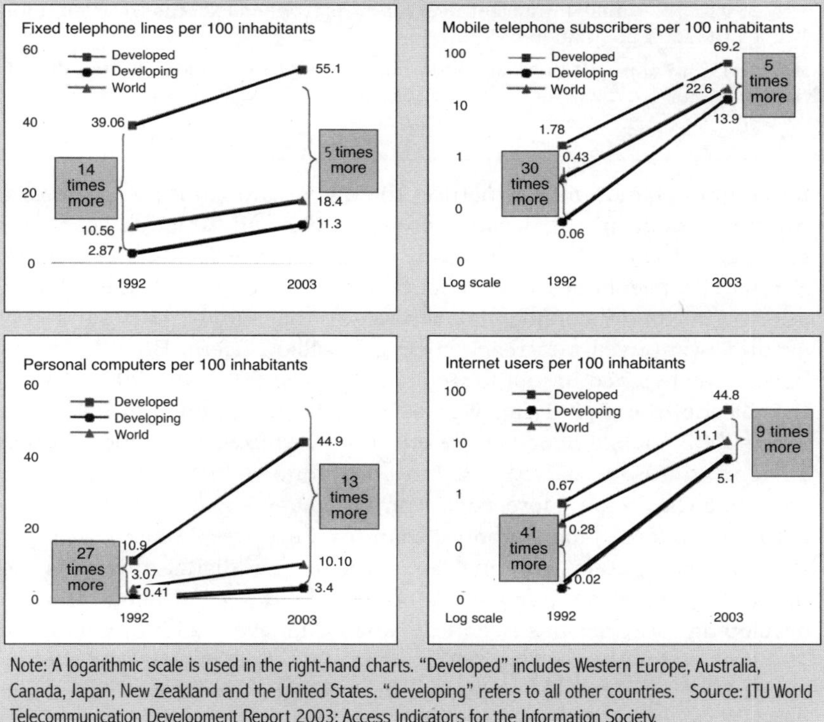

Note: A logarithmic scale is used in the right-hand charts. "Developed" includes Western Europe, Australia, Canada, Japan, New Zeakland and the United States. "developing" refers to all other countries. Source: ITU World Telecommunication Development Report 2003: Access Indicators for the Information Society.

telecommunication infrastructure, the digital gap fell from 14 times to 5 times greater, in the decade between 1992 and 2003, as economies such as China and Vietnam greatly expanded their fixed-line networks.
- For mobile telephones, the reduction is even more dramatic. Mobile phones began in commercial service in the early 1980s, and took around twenty years to reach their first billion users. But the second billion was reached in just four years, between 2002 and 2005. During the decade, the digital gap was reduced from 30 times to five times. Since 2002, mobile phones have outnumbered fixed-lines and will soon be more diffused than them. Indeed several developing countries – including Cambodia, Morocco, South Africa and Uganda – already have many times more mobile phones than fixed line telephones.
- Personal computers are one area where the digital divide is not narrowing quite so quickly. Although the level of penetration in developing countries has risen from one PC for every 243 inhabitants in 1992 to one for every 29 in 2003, this is still a long way behind the rate of one PC for every 2.2 inhabitants in developed economies. The digital divide is wider in PC ownership than any of the other indicators tracked

here. One reason for this is the high cost of acquisition and ownership (e.g. upgrading memory, software etc) of a personal computer. The advent of low-cost computers and laptops, together with the widespread adoption of free and open-source software, may help to reduce the digital divide for PCs[3].

- But the most dramatic reduction of all in narrowing the digital divide has come in Internet use, where, between 1992 and 2003, the gap between developed and developing narrowed from 41 times more to 9 times more. Interestingly, although there are fewer estimated Internet users than PCs in developed countries (44.8 and 44.9 per 100 inhabitants respectively), in developing countries there are more Internet users than PCs (5.1 and 3.4 per 100 inhabitants). This suggests the significance of Internet access from cybercafes, post-offices, schools, universities and other public Internet access centres (PIACs) in the developing world.

As the evidence shows, for the main bearer networks the digital divide is narrowing as diffusion spreads, and in most cases at an accelerating pace. Nevertheless, because technological change is also accelerating, and ICT innovations are being introduced on an almost daily basis, the popular impression is that the digital divide is expanding, because each succeeding ICT innovation starts the diffusion process all over again. Innovations tend to start in the richer countries and spread to the poorer ones.

Visualising the digital divide

One way of visualising this process of diffusion is to use a Lorenz curve, which is a measure of how closely a distribution of a particular innovation or service resembles an idealised one. The Lorenz curve is typically used alongside a Gini coefficient, which is a statistical measure of the gap between the ideal curve (total equality) and the actual Lorenz curve for a particular distribution. By measuring the transition in the Gini coefficient over time, it is possible to gauge the extent to which the digital divide is being reduced.

For instance, as Figure 3 shows (overleaf), the Gini coefficient for the global divide in Internet users has been reduced from 0.728 in 1999 to 0.618 in 2003[4]. However, other evidence suggests that the progress in reducing the digital divide has occurred mainly as a result of middle-income countries catching up, whereas some of the least developed countries (LDCs) have actually been falling behind[5]. This can be seen, for instance, in the lower chart in Figure 3 where the progress at the high and middle end of the scale is much greater than at the bottom end of the scale in those countries ranked at 150 and below.

Because of this problem of the long "tail" of the teledensity curve (in other words, countries with the lowest teledensity exhibiting the slowest growth),

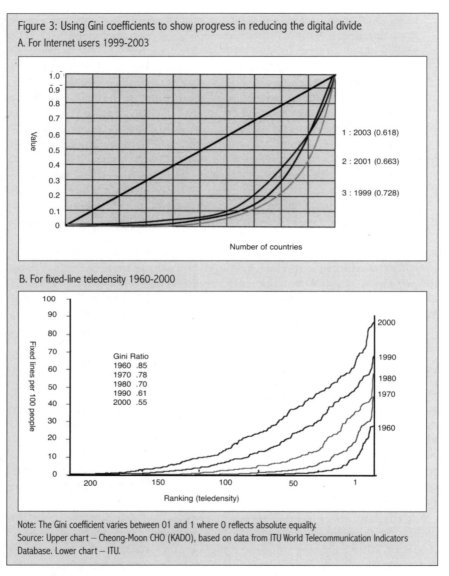

Figure 3: Using Gini coefficients to show progress in reducing the digital divide
A. For Internet users 1999-2003

1 : 2003 (0.618)

2 : 2001 (0.663)

3 : 1999 (0.728)

B. For fixed-line teledensity 1960-2000

Gini Ratio
1960 .85
1970 .78
1980 .70
1990 .61
2000 .55

Note: The Gini coefficient varies between 01 and 1 where 0 reflects absolute equality.
Source: Upper chart – Cheong-Moon CHO (KADO), based on data from ITU World Telecommunication Indicators Database. Lower chart – ITU.

it can sometimes be more meaningful to look at progress in crossing particular thresholds. Consider the following:

- At the time of publication of the Maitland Report, in 1985, some three billion people, or around half of the world's population, lived in economies with a teledensity (telephone lines per 100 inhabitants) of less than one. Global average teledensity was around seven. There were fewer than one million mobile phones worldwide and only a few tens of thousands of Internet users (the World Wide Web did not yet exist).

- Now, in mid-2005, only eight economies*, with a population of less than 160 million, or around 2.5% of the world's population, have a total teledensity (fixed and mobile combined) of less than one. The global average total teledensity is around 50. There are some two billion mobile phones worldwide and around 750 million Internet users.

The examples of the two most populous economies, China and India, illustrate the progress that has been made since 1985:

- In China, where, in 1985, the fixed-line teledensity was just 0.3%, it reached 20.9% in 2003, while mobile density had reached 21.5%.
- In India too, fixed-line teledensity increased significantly, from 0.4% in 1990 to 4.6% in 2003, while mobile teledensity reached 2.5%.

In reality, it is often more politically correct and convenient to stress the downside of the digital divide rather than reflect the reality of rapid growth and diffusion of ICTs that is currently going on in the developing world. Furthermore, to focus on the extent of the digital gap downplays the excellent efforts that are going on across the globe to bridge the digital divide, efforts that are the focus of this report.

Different experiences in different regions

One of the features evident in comparing the average level of Internet penetration and mobile phone penetration in the developing world, as shown in Figure 2, is that the level of development is broadly equivalent to that reached in the developed countries around five years earlier. By contrast, the average level of fixed-line penetration in developing countries at the end of 2003 (just over one for every ten inhabitants), was reached in the developed world as long ago as the 1960s.

This suggests that the process of "catch-up" is occurring much more rapidly among newer services than for older ones. But it also suggests that the developing world's strongly expressed preference for mobile phones over fixed-line systems is likely to put the brakes on Internet development in the near future. That is because the vast majority of the world's Internet users still use copper-based fixed-line technologies (e.g. dial-up, ISDN, DSL, cable modems) to access the Internet. Internet access from wireless devices is certainly possible (e.g. through so-called "third generation" mobile or through wireless LANs), but it is still quite expensive and, in the case of wireless LANs, has only limited range. These constraints are solvable, but there may well be a period of years during which the further development of the Internet in some developing regions of the world is slowed by the absence of a dense copper-based network.

The converging trends in ICTs worldwide have come about in large part

---

* The eight economies with a total teledensity of less than one at the start of 2005 were: Central African Republic, Chad, Eritrea, Ethiopia, Guinea-Bissau, Liberia, Myanmar and Niger.

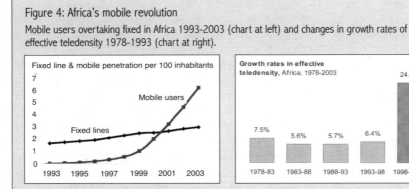

Figure 4: Africa's mobile revolution

Mobile users overtaking fixed in Africa 1993-2003 (chart at left) and changes in growth rates of effective teledensity 1978-1993 (chart at right).

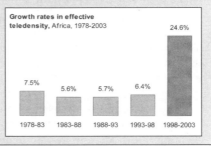

due to changes within the last few years. 2002 was the first year in which the number of mobile phones overtook fixed-lines worldwide. Africa was the first region where this took place and the impact has been most profound in Sub-Saharan Africa. Several countries of the region, including Cameroun, Congo, DR Congo, Mauritania and Uganda have levels of mobile phone penetration that are more than eight times higher than fixed-line penetration. As Figure 4 (above) shows, 2000 was a turning point in Africa's telecommunications history as it crossed the psychological threshold of one user per 100 inhabitants. In the first few years of the new century, more Africans have become telecommunication users than in the hundred years of the previous century.

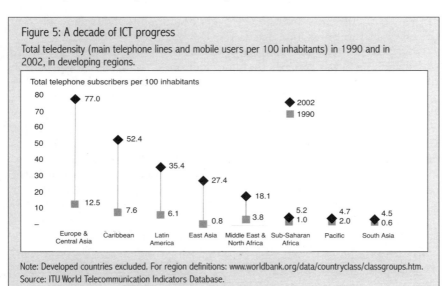

Figure 5: A decade of ICT progress

Total teledensity (main telephone lines and mobile users per 100 inhabitants) in 1990 and in 2002, in developing regions.

Note: Developed countries excluded. For region definitions: www.worldbank.org/data/countryclass/classgroups.htm.
Source: ITU World Telecommunication Indicators Database.

The right chart in Figure 4 demonstrates the extent to which this marks a step change in Africa's telecommunications history. Africa's recent growth rates have been more than four times higher than anything achieved in the recent past. The period of the Maitland Report actually marked the nadir of slowest growth.

As shown in Figure 5 (left), all of the developing sub-regions of the world have grown their fixed and mobile telephone networks at a faster rate since 1990 than before that date. In the exceptional case of East Asia (which includes China), the total number of fixed and mobile subscribers per 100 inhabitants (i.e. total teledensity) in 2002 was more than 35 times higher than in 1990. In all cases except in the developing Pacific, total teledensity was at least five times higher in 2002 than it was in 1990.

In the 1990s, Africa was the main focus of UN system-wide attempts to eradicate poverty and to raise living standards. The problems of that region continue to dominate the development agenda. But there is a danger that other parts of the world may be overlooked. As Figure 5 shows, the problems of the digital divide are also evident in South Asia and especially among the small island developing states of the Pacific, which have so far failed to benefit from the information age. The Pacific has slipped from fifth place to seventh place in terms of total teledensity. Part of the problem is that, with small domestic markets, the introduction of competing mobile operators has not always been viable. These countries have also suffered from the decrease in settlement payments from international voice traffic that helped them overcome the problems of isolation and lack of economies of scale.

Using composite indices to measure the digital divide

As shown above, there is not a single digital divide, but rather a plurality of divides, related to factors like wealth, development, age, gender, education, etc. Furthermore, for each of the different bearer ICTs, which are at different stages of their product life-cycle, there are different degrees of digital divide. For these reasons, it is appropriate to use a composite index, or "basket" approach, to measure the extent of the digital divide. This is specifically called for in the WSIS Plan of Action (para 28a):

> "In cooperation with each country concerned, develop and launch a composite ICT Development (Digital Opportunity) Index. It could be published annually, or every two years, in an ICT Development Report. The index could show the statistics while the report would present analytical work on policies and their implementation, depending on national circumstances, including gender analysis."

In order to initiate this work, consultations were launched at the WSIS Thematic Meeting on Measuring ICT for Development, held in Geneva from

7-9 February 2005. Although several composite indices already exist, notably those from Orbicom, ITU, UNCTAD, GITR and others, it was felt necessary to take a fresh approach, based on the core list of indicators adopted at the WSIS Thematic Meeting. Accordingly, a "straw-man" document on a possible methodology was developed (see background paper at www.itu.int/osg/spu/statistics/DOI/index.phtml) and applied to 40 leading economies. It was presented at the WSIS Thematic Meeting on multi-stakeholder partnerships for bridging the digital divide in Seoul on 23-24 June 2005, and subsequently revised.

The initial results from the "straw-man" document are encouraging, in that the new digital opportunity index appears to be:

- relatively robust: for instance, adding in new factors likely to affect the digital divide, such as variations in knowledge, does not appear to change the rankings greatly;
- flexible and modular: because of the design principles used, new indicators, or groups of indicators can be added relatively easily, meaning, for instance, that it could be combined with existing composite indices (like the UNDP Human Development Index), or extended or adapted for specific purposes;
- easily disaggregated into its component parts, for instance to distinguish between mobile and fixed-line networks and services;
- easily adapted for use within countries (e.g. between regions or between urban and rural areas), as well as between countries;
- strongly-correlated with the main factor underlying the digital divide, namely wealth. This means that further policy analysis can be carried out to exclude wealth as a predictive variable, and to focus on other variables more amenable to policy change.

It is hoped that the digital opportunity index will be one of the lasting legacies of the WSIS process, and will provide a useful tool in measuring national and international progress towards bridging the digital divide.

The digital divide is shifting, and the focus of development efforts must change with it. The successful conclusion to the first phase of the World Summit on the Information Society, held in Geneva 10-12 December 2003, provided a fresh impetus for international efforts to address the digital divide. Those efforts must concentrate on those areas of the world that are not yet benefiting from growth (such as the Pacific) and on those technologies where the catch-up process is proving slow (principally the fixed-line network). In those areas where the digital divide is already narrowing (such as in East Asia) and where developing countries are already leapfrogging ahead (for instance, in mobile communications) successful policies can be studied and copied. As the Maitland Report correctly identified, the digital divide is primarily a problem of geography, not of economics or technology.

References

1. The most recent edition is entitled *Yearbook of Statistics: Chronological time-series 1993-2002*, available at: www.itu.int/ITU-D/ict/publications/yb/index.html.

2. This particular factoid was effectively debunked by Clay Shirky in his 2002 article "Sorry, wrong number" which appeared in *Wired* magazine, see: www.wired.com/wired/archive/10.10/view.html?pg=2.

3. A number of efforts have been launched to bridge the digital divide by developing low-cost, "thin-client" equipment to substitute for personal computers. These include the Nivo and the Simputer. One recent project is the "US$100 laptop" announced by the MIT Media Lab and United Nations University during the WSIS Thematic Meeting on Ubiquitous Network Societies (see: www.unu.edu/hq/rector_office/press2005/mre12-05.doc).
   The partnership aims to have working prototypes available for demonstration at the Tunis Phase of the World Summit on the Information Society (WSIS), from 16-18 November 2005. Initial specifications for the laptops are 500 MHz processor, 1Gb hard drive, wi-fi enabled, and running LINUX. Over time, it is planned that the laptops would become more powerful, but not more expensive.

4. See Cheong-Moon CHO (2004) "How to measure the digital divide?" Paper presented at ITU/MIC/KADO "Digital Bridges Symposium", 10-11 September 2004, Busan, Republic of Korea, available at: www.itu.int/digitalbridges/docs/presentations/02-Cho-Background.pdf.

5. See, for instance, Sciadas, George (ed. 2003) "Monitoring the digital divide ...and beyond", available at: www.orbicom.uqam.ca/projects/ddi2002/2003_dd_pdf_en.pdf. See also the analysis presented in ITU (2002) "World Telecommunication Development Report: Reinventing Telecoms".

6. This is an important methodological step, because the alternative approach (beginning with the index and then deciding upon the component indicators) lays itself open to the criticism that the indicators are chosen to achieve certain results.

7. For more details on the proposed Digital Opportunity Index, see: www.itu.int/osg/spu/statistics/DOI/index.phtml.

Dr Tim Kelly is Head of the Strategy and Policy Unit of the International Telecommunication Union (ITU), where he has worked since 1993. Before joining ITU he spent five years as a Communications Policy Analyst with the Organisation for Economic Co-operation and Development (OECD) and three years with Logica Consultancy Ltd. He has an MA (Hons) degree in Geography and a Ph.D in industrial economics from Cambridge University.

Over the last twenty years, Dr Kelly has specialised in the economics of the telecommunications industry. He has written or co-authored more than 20 books on the subject including the ITU's World Telecommunication Development Report, Direction of Traffic and ITU Internet Reports. He is currently in charge of the "content team" for the World Summit on the Information Society (WSIS).

Contact details: Dr Tim Kelly, Head Strategy and Policy Unit, International Telecommunication Union (ITU), Place des Nations, CH-1211 Geneva 20, Switzerland.
Tel: +41 22 730 5202 Fax: +41 22 730 6453 Email: tim.kelly@itu.int.

Heather E. Hudson, Ph.D., J.D.

Director, Telecommunications Management and Policy Program
School of Business and Management, University of San Francisco

3.

From missing links to digital divides: progress and change since the Maitland Report

Heather E. Hudson, Ph.D., J.D.

Director, Telecommunications Management and Policy Program
School of Business and Management, University of San Francisco

"L'information est la clé de toutes les portes." (Information is the key to all doors.)
~ woman using a telecentre in Timbuktu.

Much has changed in the field of development communications since *The Missing Link* was published two decades ago. Then, mobile phones were brick-sized carphones, and the Internet was a closed network linking a few American research universities and institutes. Telephones in the developing world were primarily in government and business offices and the homes of the elite. Now, technology has effectively erased many distance barriers, as members of rural co-operatives in Latin America use the Internet to check futures prices and exchange rates, African teachers and health workers use community telecentres to find information on the Internet, and Asian villagers use cellphones to stay in touch and arrange transport for their produce.

Telecommunications in the form of plain old telephone service (POTS) has given way to information and communication technologies (ICTs) that can transmit not only voice, but data, graphics, sound and images. Yet this phenomenal change masks both old and new disparities. More than half the world's population has still never used a telephone, let alone accessed the Internet. And of those with telephone access, many find it difficult or impossible to use the Internet's World Wide Web because of limited bandwidth or poor service quality.

What has not changed is the importance of information and the means to share it in the development process, so eloquently stated in the quotation above from a log entry by a woman using a telecentre in Timbuktu. Access to information is now considered vital to development, so that the classifications "information rich" and "information poor" may mean more than distinctions based on GNP or other traditional development indicators. The connection between information and development that was central to the Maitland Report is now widely accepted by leaders in the developing world as well as in industrialised countries. In 1994, the ITU's first World Telecommunication Development Conference in Buenos Aires took up the call for a Global Information Infrastructure (GII) that would link everyone into a worldwide network, or more likely, network of networks. By the turn of the century, world leaders were committing themselves to bridge "digital divides" between the industrialised and developing worlds. In 2000, the G8 countries adopted the Okinawa Charter on Global Information Society and established a Digital Opportunities Task Force (DOTForce) to examine how ICTs could be made more widely available in the developing world. Since then, the global significance of ICTs has been highlighted by the World Summit on the Information Society (WSIS), the final session of which in Tunis in November 2005 can trace its origins to the Arusha conference following the release of *The Missing Link* in 1985.

Information: the development link

As *The Missing Link* pointed out, information is critical to the social and economic activities that comprise the development process. Information is obviously central to education, but also to health services, where providers need training as well as advice on diagnosis and treatment of cases beyond their level of expertise or the capacity of local facilities. But information is also critical to economic activities, ranging from agriculture to manufacturing and services.

Distance represents time, in an increasingly time-conscious world. In countries with economies that depend heavily upon agriculture or the extraction of resources (lumber and minerals), distance from urban markets has traditionally been alleviated only with the installation of improved transportation facilities, typically roads. Yet transportation links leave industries without the access to information which is becoming increasingly important for production and marketing of their commodities. Another disadvantage faced by many developing countries is economic specialisation. As they strive to diversify their economies, timely access to information becomes even more critical. In the provision of physical goods and services, rural areas could only compete across barriers of distance and geography if they had a natural resource advantage. Now they may need some other characteristic (such as low wages) to compensate for distance from markets, or they may need to specialize (growing exotic fruits, "designer vegetables", shade-grown coffee) and use the power of telecommunications to reach global markets.

Historically, rural development took place in regions where there was geographic advantage in the form of arable land or natural resources. Increasingly, new economic development depends on human resources, and on economic diversification. Thus, basic education of children and adults, as well as specific training, are increasingly important. Yet rural regions worldwide continue to face a shortage of teachers and educational facilities. Typically, rural residents also have much more limited access to health care than their urban counterparts because of a lack of health workers, medical supplies and clinics. The results are lower literacy levels, lower life expectancy, and higher infant mortality rates in rural than in urban areas. Again, information and communication technologies can help to improve both the availability and quality of education and social services.

Telecommunications is also vital to the emerging information sectors in developing regions. In the provision of information goods and services, reliable telecommunications infrastructure can make geography and distance irrelevant, as we have seen with the emergence of India as a global outsourcing power, and electronic "back offices" appearing in the Caribbean, the Philippines, Vietnam, and Senegal.

Changing contexts

However, development does not occur in isolation; the analysis of the role of communications in development must be considered in context. Thus it is important to understand the recent changes in many developing economies as well as in telecommunications and information technologies, and the trends that are driving these transitions.

The growth in the service sector is one of the features of the new global economy. Information-based activities account for the largest part of the growth in services, and other sectors are becoming increasingly information intensive. While services tend to be a more visible component of urban economies, this structural shift is mirrored in rural economies of industrialised countries, where public and private services now generally dwarf agriculture and manufacturing. Although this shift may not yet be evident in rural economies of many developing countries, throughout the world, urban and rural activities are being drawn more and more into the global economy. Manufacturers must now be able to respond to changes in demand; suppliers must be able to produce small orders for quick delivery; merchants must be able to update inventory and accounts records instantly. To stay internationally competitive, farmers also must resort to increased specialisation, and react to shifts in consumer demand.

The technological context consists of a whirlwind of technological change that tosses up tantalizing but confusing arrays of equipment and services, resulting from breakthroughs in speed of transmission and processing of data and in storage capacity. The transformation from analogue to digital communication has made possible convergence of services that were once considered completely separate, including transmission of data, but also voice, music, graphics and video; the rise of the Internet as a global web of connectivity enables content to be transmitted between individuals or groups or to be "broadcast", i.e. disseminated to any and all connected to the network. Terrestrial wireless and satellite technologies make possible communication anywhere, anytime. Key technological trends driving the proliferation of new information and telecommunications services include:

- **Capacity**: new technologies such as optical fibre have enormous capacity to carry information, and can be used for services ranging from entertainment and distance education to transmission of highly detailed images for remote medical diagnosis. Satellites and some terrestrial wireless technologies also offer a tremendous increase in availability of bandwidth.

- **Digitisation**: telecommunications networks are becoming totally digital, so that any type of information, including voice and video, may be sent as a stream of bits. Digital compression allows more efficient use of bandwidth so that customers may have more choices (such as compressed satellite television channels) and/or lower costs, such as use of compressed video for distance education and compressed voice for Internet telephony.

- **Ubiquity**: Advances in wireless technology such as cellular networks and rural radio subscriber systems offer affordable means of reaching rural customers and urban areas without infrastructure in developing countries. Low-cost wireless services may also replace wireline in industrialised countries as the primary means of personal access. Wireless Internet access can cover not only buildings and campuses but neighbourhoods and villages.

- **Convergence**: The convergence of telecommunications, data processing, and imaging technologies is ushering in the era of multimedia, in which voice, data, and images may be combined according to the needs of users, and distinctions between the traditional sectors of telecommunications, information processing, and broadcasting are increasingly arbitrary and perhaps irrelevant.

In addition, the telecommunications sector is being restructured through privatisation of formerly government-owned networks and liberalisation to allow competition among services and across technologies. The telecommunications industry itself is also being transformed, with new entrants as well as mergers and acquisitions creating vertically and horizontally integrated providers of both content and conduit, hardware and software. All of these changes are taking place within a context of globalisation, as international trade in goods and services expands and national economies become increasingly interdependent.

Only glimmers of these trends were visible to the Maitland Commission (which took place during the era of the breakup of AT&T and privatisation of British Telecom). They could not foresee the implications, particularly for rural and developing regions:

- *Distance is no longer a barrier* to accessing information. Technologies are available that can provide interactive voice, data and multimedia services virtually anywhere.
- *Costs of providing services are declining.* Satellite transmission costs are independent of distance; transmission costs using other technologies have also declined dramatically. Thus communications services can be priced not according to distance, which penalises rural and remote users, but per unit of information (message, bit) or unit of time.
- *The potential for competition is increasing.* Lower costs make rural/ remote areas more attractive. New competitors can offer multiple technological solutions, including wireless, satellite, optical fibre, copper, and cable.

The explosive growth of wireless

Of course, these new technologies and services are not available everywhere, and in developing regions where they do exist, many people cannot afford to use them. Telecommunications is still a "missing link" in much of the developing world. However, wireless technologies are beginning to bridge that gap. In fact, there are now more mobile phones than fixed lines in the developing world! For most subscribers, their cellphone is their first and only phone. (See Table 1.) How did this happen?

Table 1: Wireless access indicators		
Region	Wireless subscribers /100 population	Wireless subscribers /all subscribers
Africa	4.6	62.4%
Asia	12.4	50.9
Americas	29.9	46.3
Europe	51.3	55.1
Oceania	48.9	54.7
World	19.1	51.5
Derived from: ITU, World Telecommunication Development Report, 2004.		

This dramatic growth in connectivity is due partly to the advantages of wireless technologies in fast deployment of new networks, but perhaps

41

more to the innovations in regulation and policy that have fostered innovation. Where countries have introduced competition in wireless/ mobile services, rates have come down, and innovative wireless carriers have introduced features such as "pay as you go" using rechargeable cards, and inexpensive text messaging. The result has been dramatic growth in access to basic communications.

It should be noted that wireless can also be used for public access. For example, cellular operators in South Africa were required to install 30,000 wireless payphones within five years as a condition of their licence. This policy, plus rollout requirements placed on Telkom, the monopoly fixed operator, contributed to a significant improvement in access to telephone service. By 1998, 85% of South Africans, including 75% of those living in rural areas, said that they had access to a telephone. In townships and rural areas, access typically meant an available payphone within a short walk, as advocated in *The Missing Link*.

Access to the Internet: the digital divide

In developing regions, the need for services besides basic voice is now spreading beyond urban areas, businesses and organisations, to small entrepreneurs, NGOs (nongovernmental organisations) and students, driven by demand for access to email and the Internet. Email is growing in popularity because it is much faster than the postal service and cheaper than facsimile transmission or telephone calls. Such services can be valuable even for illiterates. A Member of Parliament from Uganda stated that his father sent many telegrams during his lifetime, but could neither read nor write. Local scribes wrote down his messages and read them to him. Similarly, "information brokers" ranging from librarians to staff of telecentres can help people with limited education to send and access electronic information[1]. Telecentres equipped with personal computers linked to the Internet enable artisans, farmers and other small entrepreneurs to set up shop in the global marketplace.

As noted above, the good news is that access to voice services has improved dramatically, thanks largely to newly available and more affordable wireless (mobile) services in many developing countries. The bad news is that Internet access is still very limited, and that broadband, a key requirement for productive use of many Internet resources, is still unavailable and/or unaffordable in most of the developing world.

Table 2 (opposite) shows the gap between the industrialised and developing worlds in three indicators that together suggest the limited access to the Internet. The first is estimated Internet users: more than 85% of the world's Internet users are in developed countries, which account for only about 22% of the world's population. The other two indicators selected are personal computers and telephone lines because Internet access requires both communications links and information technologies, typically personal computers or networked computer terminals. High income countries had 22 times as many telephone lines per 100 population as low income countries, but 96 times as many computers. Despite the falling cost of computers, they are still out of reach of much of the world's population. A computer costs the equivalent of eight years' income for the average person in Bangladesh, but less than a month's wages for the average North American.

Table 2: Internet access indicators			
Region	Internet users /10,000	Tel. lines /100	PCs /100
Africa	156.2	3.0	1.4
Asia	690.7	13.4	4.6
Americas	2644.2	34.2	29.0
Europe	2416.5	41.2	22.4
Oceania	4301.9	40.7	44.9
World	1133.8	18.7	10.1
Derived from: ITU data for 2003.			

Internet access in Africa is particularly limited and expensive. Broadband is virtually nonexistent even for business and institutional customers in most African nations. This lack of local and domestic high speed connectivity prevents Africans from connecting to the SAT-3 submarine cable that now lands at most African countries bordering the Atlantic and Indian Oceans. This US$ 650 million cable is estimated to be operating at only 3% of its capacity[2]. And despite the fact that the price of international bandwidth has dropped with the increase in capacity, the price of Internet access was higher in Africa than anywhere else in the world, and completely out of reach of most Africans.

The impact of competition

Several lessons can be learned from the dramatic expansion of wireless and growth of wireless users in the developing world. Wireless technology has the advantage of being faster and cheaper to deploy in many instances than wireline technologies. However, cellular services have been around for two decades, and growth did not take off until prices were lowered. Competition is the key driver of the wireless explosion. Where competition in wireless has been introduced, in general, the growth rates are much higher than where there is one monopoly wireless operator. Wireless competition has resulted in innovative pricing and service offerings. Rechargeable smart cards make phone service accessible to people without bank accounts or credit histories. Cheap messaging can substitute for many email functions. For example, the Philippines is now the world's largest user of SMS (short message service).

Strategies to extend access often focus too much on technology. For example, a VSAT (very small aperture satellite terminal) may be an ideal solution to bring high speed Internet access to a rural school or telecentre, but is it legal in the country in question to install the VSAT, which bypasses the public switched network? Wi-Fi (Wireless Fidelity, an IEEE 802.11 standard using commonly unlicensed bands) can provide broadband access for villages and neighborhoods. Yet in many developing countries it is necessary to have a licence or to register to use these bands, even if they are not being used for other purposes. Such restrictions inhibit investments to extend access.

Many monopoly operators claim that bypassing their networks effectively siphons off revenues that they need to expand their networks, which would also probably create more jobs. This argument was common during the era of the Maitland Commission. However, the relationship is not so simple. Without competition, there is likely to be little incentive to roll out new facilities, to choose the most cost-effective technologies, and to price services affordably.

Protecting dominant carriers may actually hinder economic growth. For example, a West African Internet service provider pointed out that he needed relatively inexpensive international connection to the Internet in order to provide affordable Internet access for his customers. By bypassing the local network, he was creating new jobs in value-added services as an Internet provider, as well as providing an important information resource for economic development of the country.

Extending access through resale

Authorisation of resale of local as well as long distance and other services can create incentives to meet pent-up demand even if network competition has not yet been introduced. Franchised payphones can be introduced in developing countries in order to involve entrepreneurs where the operator has not yet been privatised and/or liberalised. Franchised telephone booths operate in several African countries; in Senegal, private phone shops average four times the revenue of those operated by the national carrier. Indonesia's franchised call offices known as Wartels (Warung Telekomunikasi), operated by small entrepreneurs, generate more than US$ 9,000 per line, about 10 times more than Telkom's average revenue per line[3]. Commercial cyber cafes in many Third World cities resell Internet access and many often sell phone cards as resellers of telephone services.

Individual entrepreneurs, primarily women, now make a living selling prepaid phone cards in Uganda, Mozambique, and many other poor countries. In Bangladesh, village women operate "portable payphones", selling individual calls on cellular phones that they carry with them. In the Philippines, entrepreneurs may even resell small increments of talk time by transferring units from one cellphone to another, to provide service to people to make a single call if they cannot afford to buy a whole prepaid card. A Filipina maid in Hong Kong may transfer funds directly to a relative in the Philippines by visiting a Hong Kong vendor with an international cellphone. She pays the vendor, who can immediately transfer the "electronic cash" to the recipient's cellphone. The recipient can then exchange the electronic cash for a stored value cash card or for Philippine pesos at a local shop.

Demand is greater than assumed

In designing networks and projecting revenues, planners often assume that there is little demand for telecommunications in developing regions, particularly in rural areas. Similarly, telecommunications service providers may be reluctant to extend services to poorer populations who are assumed to have insufficient demand to cover the cost of providing the facilities and services. Their forecasts are typically based solely on the lower population densities than are found in urban areas, coupled with a "one size fits all" fallacy that assumes all rural residents are likely to have lower incomes and therefore lower demand for telecommunications than urban residents. However, a study for the World Bank estimates that rural users in developing countries are able collectively to pay 1.0%–1.5% of their gross community income for telecommunications services[4]. The ITU uses an estimate of 5% of household income as an affordability threshold[5].

The take-up of wireless services in many developing countries has also demonstrated significant pent-up demand for telecommunications services, even among relatively low income users if pricing is affordable. Prepaid phone service has been the primary mechanism for enabling customers to "pay as you go" and to eliminate risk for service providers. This is just one example of how telecommunications services can be made available to poor people at the bottom of the economic pyramid.

Old distinctions are no longer relevant

Classifications and distinctions that once were useful may no longer be relevant. Regulators typically issue separate licences and approve separate tariff structures for fixed and mobile services, yet these distinctions have become blurred. Mobile telephone service was designed for communication from vehicles; however, modern cellular systems are used for personal communications, and can often be considered a substitute for fixed network connections. As noted above, in many developing countries, wireless has become the first and only service for many customers who never before had access to a telephone. The distinction between voice and data no longer makes sense; bits are bits, and can be used to transmit anything. Yet in many developing countries, voice communication is still considered a monopoly service. Eliminating licensing distinctions between fixed and mobile and between voice and data may accelerate access.

Toward universal access

The concept of universal access – that was central to the Maitland Report's recommendation to have a telephone within easy reach of all – continues to evolve, both in terms of services that should be universally included and in our understanding of access, which includes availability, affordability and reliability. Universal access should therefore be considered a dynamic concept with a set of moving targets. Thus, for example a multi-tiered definition of access could be proposed, identifying requirements within households, within communities and for education and social service providers.

Community access was advocated by the Maitland Commission; publicly available payphones were to be available in each village or neighbourhood of towns and cities. Community access remains a commonly applied benchmark for voice services in developing countries. This approach is now being extended to the Internet, as many countries are extending public access through telecentres, libraries, post offices, and kiosks.

From cross-subsidies to targeted subsidies

Although competition and judicious deregulation should serve to extend access by removing barriers and creating incentives to enable facilities and services providers to reach potential customers, there may still be locations where projected revenues would not alone justify the costs. In the era of the Maitland Commission, the traditional means of ensuring provision of service to unprofitable areas or customers was through cross subsidies, such as from international or interexchange to local services. However, in a competitive environment, new entrants cannot survive if their competitors are subsidised. Therefore, if subsidies are required, they must be made explicit and targeted at specific classes of customers or locations such as:

• High cost areas: carriers may be subsidised to serve locations that are isolated and/or have very low population density, so that they are significantly more expensive to serve than other locations. This approach is used in the US and Canada.

- Specific user groups: subsidies may target important development sectors such as education and health through access to schools and health centres, and/or to publicly accessible facilities such as libraries and post offices. For example, South Africa is providing Internet access to government information and electronic commerce services through post offices. The US provides discounted Internet access to schools, libraries, and rural health centres.

Beyond access

Measures of availability such as teledensity (lines per 100 population), familiar since the era of the Maitland Commission, do not adequately reflect access to ICTs. The ITU has proposed a Digital Access Index (DAI) to measure "overall ability of individuals in a country to access and use ICTs." It identifies four fundamental factors that impact a country's ability to access and use ICTs: availability of infrastructure, affordability, knowledge and quality. "If the infrastructure is not available, there can be no access. If the population cannot afford to pay for ICT products and services, there can be no access. If citizens do not have a certain level of education, they will not be able to use newer ICTs such as computers or the Internet. If the ICT experience is poor, people will either cease using them or be incapable of using them effectively or creatively"[6].

While access is necessary, it is insufficient to ensure that disadvantaged populations benefit from ICTs. In its Statement on Universal Access to Basic Communication and Information Services, the United Nations noted:

> ... "The information and technology gap and related inequities between industrialised and developing nations are widening: a new type of poverty – information poverty – looms. Most developing countries, especially the Least Developed Countries (LDCs) are not sharing in the communications revolution, since they lack:
> • affordable access to core information resources, cutting-edge technology and to sophisticated telecommunications systems and infrastructure;
> • the capacity to build, operate, manage, and service the technologies involved;
> • policies that promote equitable public participation in the information society as both producers and consumers of information and knowledge; and a work force trained to develop, maintain and provide the value-added products and services required by the information economy"[7].

These goals of affordable access to ICTs, capacity to use and manage them, and policies that promote these goals were very much the focus of *The Missing Link*.

Forging new links

Information gaps still exist, but there is cause for optimism. New technologies offer the possibility of technological leapfrogging, for example, to reach end users through wireless local loops or small satellite terminals rather than stringing wire and cable. Digital transmission and switching are increasing reliability and lowering cost, as well as making it possible for subscribers in developing countries to use electronic mail and voice messaging, and to access the Internet.

The experience since the Maitland Report has shown how innovative technologies, strategies, and policies can help to increase access to communication services. The operative word here is can. Whether they will depends on the continued commitment of the many stakeholders, and an unwavering focus on the needs of the people in the developing world.

References

1. See Hudson, Heather E. *From Rural Village to Global Village: Telecommunications and Development in the Information Age.* Mahwah, NJ: Erlbaum, 2005.

2. Goldstein, Harry. *Surf Africa.* IEEE Spectrum Online, January 30, 2004.

3. ITU, World Telecommunication Development Report, 1998.

4. Kayani, Rogati and Andrew Dymond. *Options for Rural Telecommunications Development,* Washington, DC: World Bank, 1999.

5. ITU, World Telecommunication Development Report, 1998.

6. World Telecommunication Development Report 2003: Access Indicators for the Information Society. Geneva: International Telecommunication Union, December 2003.

7. United Nations Administrative Committee on Coordination (ACC), "Statement on Universal Access to Basic Communication and Information Services," April 1997. Quoted in ITU: World Telecommunication Development Report, 1998.

Professor Heather E. Hudson is Director of the Telecommunications Management and Policy Program in the School of Business and Management at the University of San Francisco. She received an Honours BA from the University of British Columbia, MA and PhD from Stanford University, and JD from the University of Texas at Austin. Her work focuses on both domestic and international topics concerning applications of telecommunications for socio-economic development and policies to extend affordable access to new technologies and services in rural and developing regions.

Dr. Hudson has planned and evaluated communication projects in northern Canada, Alaska, and more than 50 developing countries and emerging economies in Africa, Asia, the South Pacific, the Caribbean, the Middle East, Eastern Europe, and Latin America. She has also consulted for government agencies, consumer and indigenous organizations, telecommunications companies, and international organizations including the World Bank, the ITU, UNDP, UNESCO, USAID, CIDA, IDRC, and the Commonwealth of Learning.

Dr. Hudson has been a Sloan Foundation Industry Fellow at Columbia University, a Fulbright Distinguished Lecturer for the Asia/Pacific, and held Fellowships at the University of Hong Kong, CIRCIT (the Centre for International Research on Communication and Information Technologies) in Australia, and the East-West Center in Hawaii. She is the author of numerous articles as well as several books including: *From Rural Village to Global Village: Telecommunications for Development in the Information Age*; *Global Connections: International Telecommunications Infrastructure and Policy*; *Electronic Byways: State Policies for Rural Development through Telecommunications*; *Rural America in the Information Age*; *Communication Satellites: Their Development and Impact*; and *When Telephones Reach the Village*.

Contact details: Professor Heather E. Hudson, Director Telecommunications Management and Policy Program, University of San Francisco, 2130 Fulton Street, San Francisco, CA 94117, United States.
Tel: +1 415-422-6642 Fax: +1 415-422-2502 Email: hudson@usfca.edu.

James Deane

Managing Director, Communication for Social Change Consortium

4.

Not a telecoms, nor a digital, but an information divide

James Deane

Managing Director, Communication for Social Change Consortium

O ther chapters in this anthology examine some of the changes in the telecommunication landscape in the 20 years since the publication of the Maitland Commission. This chapter takes a different and rather broader view. It seeks, from a development perspective, to place some of the changes in telecommunication within a wider context of changes to the overall communication environment over this time; and it seeks to make a provocative argument that, so far as those living in poverty on the planet are concerned, changes in the broadcast and media sector have arguably had a greater impact than those of telecommunication – at least until now.

On one level such an argument would contradict one of the introductory remarks of the Maitland Commission Report:

> *"While acknowledging the important role of broadcasting, mass media and private networks, we have concentrated on public telephone systems since it is by improving and expanding these that the greatest benefit can be brought to the greatest number of people throughout the world."*

At the outset, however, it should be stated that the purpose of this chapter is not to suggest that any one type of technology (such as broadcasting) is innately superior in development terms to any other (such as telephony). Rather, its central point is to argue that the choice of technology should be made according to an analysis of the problem that exists and that old, pervasive communication technologies sometimes offer a more appropriate solution than new, more exclusive ones.

Information and communication technologies have become the subject of intensive interest from the development community over recent years. Such interest has not necessarily led to more effective development programming. A key reason for that is this focus is marked by starting with what the technology can do, rather than with what people actually need.

In this chapter, I look at four issues:

• First, how the development context has changed in ways that have made all forms of communication an increasingly central concern for development organisations (a concern not yet fully realised);

- Second, to highlight how changes in the media environment have been every bit as transformative as those in the telecommunication sector, at least so far as the almost 3 billion people on the planet who live on less than US$ 2 a day is concerned.
- Third, how development policy has tended to evolve from a fascination with new technology instead of a realistic assessment of a development problem. This has led to supply rather than demand driven policies that are rooted in determining which technologies are most appropriate to meeting that problem. This has wasted a lot of money.
- Finally, how a future analysis of this arena could be framed, particularly in the light of the fact that the relevance and usefulness of new technologies is likely to play a far greater role in the lives of those living in poverty in the next twenty years than it has in the last.

The shifting development context: today's information and communication challenges

The Maitland Commission ushered in a global debate on the role of telecommunication in development, and is widely seen as being highly prescient in highlighting and forecasting how important telecommunication would become in development thinking. The reasons why telecommunication became more of a priority following the Commission's report are many. Some of them, particularly given that the report was published in the years before the fall of the Berlin Wall, were almost impossible to predict.

From a development perspective, communication in general has become an increasingly central preoccupation, a preoccupation that can be expected to intensify much further in coming months and years. This paper starts by sketching out the main development challenges as generally articulated today, and then goes on to examine what, in communication terms, the most appropriate strategies are in confronting them.

In outlining such development challenges, it is difficult not at least to nod in the direction of the most obvious and largest contextual factor, globalisation. This is a concept that only came into common currency after 1989 and the end of the Cold War. This is not the place for a detailed discussion of the effects of globalisation – other than to remark that in the 1990s much development discourse was preoccupied with adjusting to its realities. The recognition that telecommunication was the essential oil that lubricated globalisation and that securing economic inclusion depended fundamentally on building telecommunication capacity of developing countries was an important factor in many development debates of the

1990s and indeed of today. We will come back to these later in this paper.

However, the pre-eminent current reference point for development policy are the Millennium Development Goals. The eight Goals established at the UN Millennium Summit in 2000 now form a fundamental framework for action by almost all bilateral and multilateral development institutions (a major exception being the United States).

The goals (below) are designed to provide a set of internationally agreed targets aimed at halving the number of people living on less than a dollar

UN Millennium Development Goals By 2015:	
1. Eradicate extreme poverty and hunger.	Reduce by one half the proportion of people living on less than a dollar a day.
	Reduce by half the proportion of people who suffer from hunger.
2. Achieve universal primary education.	Ensure that all boys and girls complete a full course of primary schooling.
3. Promote gender equality and empower women.	Eliminate gender disparity in primary and secondary education preferably by 2005, and at all levels by 2015.
4. Reduce child mortality.	Reduce by two thirds the mortality rates for infants and children under five.
5. Improve maternal health.	Reduce by three quarters the maternal mortality ratio.
6. Combat HIV/AIDS, malaria and other diseases.	Halt and begin to reverse the spread of HIV/AIDS.
	Halt and begin to reverse the incidence of malaria and other major diseases.
7. Ensure environmental sustainability	Integrate the principles of sustainable development into country policies and programmes, reverse the loss of environmental resources.
	Reduce by half the proportion of people without sustainable access to safe drinking water.
	Achieve significant improvement in lives of at least 100 million slum dwellers, by 2020.
8. Develop a global partnership for development.	Open trading system, special needs of least developed countries (LDCs), debt, employment, access to medicines, ICTs.

a day by 2015, together with a series of other important goals in the field of health, education, gender, environment and so on.

The adoption of the goals marked a major shift in development assistance towards a much more structured, coherent and uniform approach to development assistance. It has been described by some as the globalisation of development assistance. This increasing coherence is characterised not only by the adoption of a common set of goals, but also by a common series of strategies and methodologies to meet those goals. Donors, led principally by the World Bank, have committed themselves to work much more closely together, according to a set of frameworks shaped by developing countries themselves. Originally conceived as a series of Comprehensive Development Frameworks by former President of the World Bank, Jim Wolfensohn in the late 1990s, they evolved into what are now known as the Poverty Reduction Strategy Paper (PRSP) process (this jargon is, in turn, now evolving into a more varied, country specific set of descriptions of poverty reduction strategies).

What has all this got to do with a paper on communication? PRSPs are designed to provide a strategic framework for all development action in a country, and donors and other actors are in theory meant to work only in support of the objectives and strategy. Priorities are shaped at a national level through a country driven process. This is a very different development scenario than the one that existed at the time of the Maitland Commission. According to this structure, telecommunication development (alongside all other development interventions) can only be expected to be prioritised in development strategies if an effective case is made for it at the national level. Donor decision making is increasingly being decentralised to national missions, and donor funding is increasingly taking the form of budget support to developing country governments.

More importantly, there are two critical implications as a result of this major shift of development assistance. The first is that these processes are designed to be "owned" by a country. They are designed to be subject to public consultation and public debate, and be the fruit of a process where a representative government forms poverty reduction strategies according to the expressed needs of its citizens, particularly those living in poverty.

Such a process of ownership clearly requires people living in poverty to have access to information on the issues and decision making process that affect their lives; and it requires people to have the capacity to voice their perspectives and concerns in the public arena in ways that can be heard and noticed in a policy process.

Second, current development strategy rests as never before on the capacity of people to hold their governments to account. One central conclusion of the report of the Commission for Africa, commissioned by UK Prime Minister Tony Blair and published in 2005, was that a major increase in development assistance and other resources was required if Africa was to escape poverty. Another was that development assistance policies in the past had too often failed because African governments had come to feel more accountable to western donors than to their own citizens. Unless this changed, development policies would fail, argues the report.

The reports of the Commission for Africa and the UN Millennium Project, together with the G8 Summit in Gleneagles in June 2005 and even the less successful UN Millennium Summit in September all point to one central conclusion: far more money is likely to be available to developing countries, and this money is likely to be subject to less conditionality. The overwhelming implication is that for this development strategy to be successful, citizens of developing countries will need to hold their governments to account more effectively than at any other time in history.

The role of communication in securing economic inclusion in an age of globalisation is one major development concern. The second is equally important – enabling people who have most to win or lose from development decision making to access information on issues that affect their lives; and enabling them to have a voice in those issues. Only if this happens can countries root their policies in a genuine process of ownership; and only if this happens can citizens of developing countries, particularly the poorest, hold their governments to account.

In other words, development policy cannot any longer principally be preoccupied with the economic value of information and communication; it will increasingly be preoccupied with its fundamental political role. These are the key communication concerns of current development debate and they reflect an increasingly heavy focus not only on the critical economic role of access to information, but the political role too.

How do they square up to the analysis of the Maitland Commission and to what extent is it telecommunication that enables people in this way?

The other information revolution

The Maitland Report outlined a series of "random examples" to highlight why telecommunication in a development context was important. A farmer needing advice on how to battle a fungus which is destroying his crop; a rural co-operative wanting to know the price it will get for its beans in the capital; a health worker on an island devastated by a typhoon wants to know whether urgently needed medicine will arrive in time to stem an outbreak of cholera – these are just three examples. Said the Commission Report:

> "All these people need information. Without rapid and effective communications they will have to wait for days or travel themselves to get an answer."

Exactly the same kind of technical information and communication challenges exist today but these challenges are accentuated by the kind of urgent information and voice needs as those laid out in the preceding section of this paper. The question is how cost effectively and appropriately they can be and have been provided.

Telecommunication has been transformed over the last decade and we have witnessed, in the common parlance, an information revolution (particularly with the Internet, mobile telephony and satellite) the like of which could not have been predicted in the Maitland Report. We have also, however, witnessed another far less recognised information revolution, one that has arguably had as much if not a greater impact on the 3 billion people on the planet surviving on less than US$ 2 a day. This "other information revolution" is one that has transformed the media[1].

In 1985, at the time of the Maitland Commission Report, most people on the planet received information beyond their communities from one main source – their governments. They did so through state run and controlled media, mostly in the form of radio. Some of this information was useful, particularly that provided for agricultural advice and extension, or health advice. Most of it was designed to exercise government control of their citizens.

Since then, and in the last decade in particular, we have witnessed a transformation in the media landscape in most developing countries. The fall of the Berlin Wall ushered in a wind of democratic change throughout many parts of the developing world. Consequent and widespread liberalisation of media (linked also to processes of globalisation) has led to a much more democratic, dynamic, crowded and complex media landscape. This is a complex, contradictory revolution marking an extraordinary transformation over little more than a decade. New freedoms, a blossoming of public debate, a resurgent community media movement, a proliferation of channels and titles across all media, a dynamic interplay between old and new technologies and the sometimes rapid, sometimes agonizingly slow but still remorseless loosening of government control over information have all characterised this revolution.

Radio in particular has undergone both a reinvention and a renaissance. In 1926, the Germany playwright and author, Bertolt Brecht, wrote *The Radio as an Apparatus of Communication.* In it he argued that:

> *"Radio is one sided when it should be two. It is purely an apparatus for distribution, for mere sharing out. So here is a positive suggestion: change this apparatus over from distribution to communication. The radio would be the finest possible communication apparatus in public life, a vast network of pipes. That is to say, it would be if it knew how to receive as well as transmit, how to let the listener speak as well as hear, how to bring him into a relationship instead of isolating him. On*

this principle the radio should step out of the supply business and organise its listeners as suppliers."

The problem of radio has, despite its reach in the poorest countries, been its central character as an information delivery tool and not this Brechtian vision of an interactive medium. At least until now. In Uganda little more than a decade ago, there were two radio stations. Today there are more than 100. In Niger there are more than 1,000. Throughout the developing world, new mostly commercial FM radio stations, as well as many community radio stations are mushrooming. While much of the content is often music based, this radio revolution is also characterised by interactivity, by the rise of the talk show, the discussion programme and the phone in. In Uganda, radio stations record the Ekimeeza, a public discussion forum held in a community hall or village, and then use this as the basis of a radio based public debate. Radio has become an interactive medium not, perhaps to the same extent as telephony, but certainly one that makes it a far more significant communication – and voice – provider than was envisaged 20 years ago.

It is impossible here to capture all the elements of the revolution that has characterised the changes in the media over the last decade, but these changes are signalled here simply to suggest that it is not just telecommunication that can provide the solutions to many of the information and communication challenges that the developing world faces today. Far older technologies also have a role to play and this role is particularly relevant to the twin development challenges of securing both ownership and accountability of development policy.

However, this does not only apply to questions of voice and debate and the capacity of citizens to express their view. It applies to many of the challenges outlined in the Maitland Report. A farmer needing advice on how to battle a fungus which is destroying his crop – such advice can be provided through radio; a rural cooperative wanting to know the price it will get for its beans in the capital – such information is a mainstay of radio, and especially of community radio; a health worker on an island devastated by a typhoon wants to know whether urgently needed medicine will arrive in time to stem an outbreak of cholera – again the information can come through radio.

On one level, it is ridiculous to highlight such issues in this bifurcated way. Telephony is a far more flexible medium than radio, and indeed much of the new interactivity of radio is because it is so successfully exploiting the new technologies of telephony and the Internet.

Nevertheless radio ownership in developing countries has far outstripped telephone ownership by multiple factors throughout the last 20 years and continues to do so. Telephony remains for now principally the preserve of an expanding middle class. Although radio too is becoming a more consumer oriented and advertising driven medium, it remains the means through which most people living in poverty access information and increasingly it is the way in which they exercise their voice. Telephony has simply not reached a level of access for those living on less than US$ 2 a day for it to have the kind of marked impact on their lives as radio.

This is going to change of course. Demand for telephony even from the poorest is proven and growing. Cost barriers are rapidly reducing and technology adapted to reaching rural areas is improving extremely rapidly. It is not difficult to envisage telephony being as ubiquitous among poor communities in the next 20 or even 10 years as radio is now. The two information revolutions of telecommunication and broadcasting technologies will increasingly converge into one in ways that do finally reach all levels of society with dynamic and potentially exciting consequences.

Enough of the digital divide

As mentioned earlier, the point being made is not to argue that any one medium is superior to any other. It is that development policy has too often been fascinated by the new technologies without basing policy on a solid analysis of the problem the communication is designed to solve. This has led to failures in ICT spending, and consequently damaged the overall case for new technologies.

Very few of the debates of the last decade on the role of communication in development have rooted themselves in a serious analysis and identification of the problem they are trying to solve. They have almost been a response to a fascination with what new technology can do, not a serious analysis of the information, communication and voice needs of the poor.

The dawn of the information age was transmuted in most development debates into a debate over the role of knowledge in development. In 1997, a group of donors and other development institutions organised a major Global Knowledge Conference in Toronto, Canada, and followed it up with another in 2000 in Kuala Lumpur, Malaysia. In 1998, the World Bank chose to focus its flagship report, the World Development Report on the issue of Knowledge for Development. Many bilateral donors and multilateral organisations developed new strategies and policies on information and communication technologies in development. The 2000 G8 Summit in Okinawa led to the establishment of a Digital Opportunities Task Force, and the UN established a UN ICT Task Force. All of these had as their central preoccupation examining what development organisations could do to overcome the so called digital divide.

The development industry is notorious for going through fads and fashions, and to many this preoccupation with new technologies was a classic of its kind. For many, the fashion is fading. The World Summit on the Information Society, which might be expected to command substantial interest from donor and development agencies increasingly preoccupied with issues of communication technologies, is a subject of ever more lukewarm interest from them. There are concerns that the impact of ICT projects that they have supported have been mixed and that the kinds of resources at their disposal are not, in any case, at the scale to make the kind of difference that is needed. Many donors, having originally set up new policies or departments on ICTs, are now mainstreaming them. More fundamentally, there is a reappraisal perhaps of just what it is they are seeking to achieve through support to the telecommunication sector, particularly in terms of what formal development institutions are best placed to contribute in comparison with the private sector. There is, in short, a confusion over strategy.

Nearly all these initiatives have tended to start with a preoccupation with what technology can do and, later, develop a broader analysis of what the information problem actually is. This, more than the lack of an innate development value of communication technologies, is what underpins much of the current strategic confusion around it. The digital divide is, in this author's view, a red herring. There are a series of huge, and arguably growing information divides, between rich and poor countries, rich and poor people within poor countries, urban and rural, literate and illiterate, young and old and so on. Digital technologies are one extremely important option for bridging this divide but they are not the only one. Old technologies, such as radio, are also reinventing themselves and a series of often repeated development mistakes originating in a fascination with technology should not be allowed to keep repeating themselves. These are though information divides, not simply technological ones.

There are signs that these lessons have been learned. The report of the Commission for Africa is perhaps the best example of this. The Commission went out of its way not to start with a series of assumptions about what Africa needed, or with a series of potential solutions that it could apply. It started with a detailed series of consultations with Africans at all levels of society focused on discovering what they actually wanted and needed to develop.

Given this level of consultation, it is unsurprising that throughout the report a strong emphasis is placed on the role of communication in development. It insists that any development policy should be rooted in a cultural analysis and context. It highlights how important issues of information and voice are to people. It emphasises the critical role of the media in the future of Africa's development. And, within an economic and social analysis of Africa's problems, it places a major emphasis on the role of communication in general, and telecommunication in particular.

"Growth will also require a massive investment in infrastructure to break down the internal barriers that hold Africa back. Donors should fund a doubling of spending on infrastructure – from rural roads and small-scale irrigation to regional highways, railways, larger power projects and Information & Communications Technology (ICT). [p13] Africa needs an additional US$ 20 billion a year investment in infrastructure. To support this, developed countries should provide an extra US$ 10 billion a year up to 2010 and, subject to review, a further increase to US$ 20 billion a year in the following five years. This should support African regional, national, urban and rural infrastructure priorities - ranging from rural roads and slum upgrading to ICT and the infrastructure needed to support greater integration of Africa's regions and to enable Africa to break into world markets." [p226]².

The Maitland Report was a critical and influential one for its day. The need now is for a more comprehensive analysis of the information and voice needs of the poor. Donor and development policies are finding great difficulty in prioritising such an analysis and because of this prioritisation of communication in its entirety is faltering. The report of the Commission for Africa was a major contribution and highlighted many reasons why a stronger focus on communication is desperately needed in the development discourse. There is currently little evidence that donor or development organisations are taking sufficient note of the Commission for Africa, not fully recognising, let alone adapting, to the enormous potential and critical contribution the entire field of communication for development has to make to meeting the Millennium Development Goals.

To this, Sir Donald Maitland may be forgiven for saying, *"Plus ça change"*.

References

1. These arguments have been substantially expanded by this author and others in the *Global Civil Society Yearbook 2002* published by the London School of Economics (www.lse.ac.uk/Depts/global/Yearbook) and updated more recently in *The other information revolution: media and empowerment in developing countries*, by James Deane with Fackson Banda, Kunda Dixit, Njonjo Mue, and Silvio Waisbord in *Communicating in the Information Society*, Ed. Bruce Girard and Sean O'Siochru, UNRISD, 2003 (full text available at www.unrisd.org). Some of this section is drawn directly from previous articles published by the author.

2. *Our Common Interest: Report of the Commission for Africa*, 2005 – available in full from www.commissionforafrica.org.

James Deane is managing director of the Communication for Social Change Consortium, which develops media and communication strategies which amplify the voices of those living in poverty. He is a founder and former director of the Panos Institute, London which works globally with the media to generate public debate on development issues.

Mr Deane has written numerous papers and publications on media, communication technology and other communication issues as well as on HIV/AIDS, PRSPs and other development issues. He speaks regularly to international audiences and has organised many international and national seminars, conferences and training events related to media and communication for development.

James Deane was the organiser of the Global Forum for Media and Development at the Global Knowledge conference in Malaysia in 2000, the convenor of the Bellagio Symposium on Media, Freedom and Poverty, and the Bellagio Symposium on Communication and the Millennium Development Goals (both in 2004) as well as numerous other similar events. He has provided formal strategic advice and consultancies to Dfid, Danida, Sida, the World Bank, WHO, Unicef, Unesco, UNFPA, FAO among other agencies on media and communication for development. Mr Deane has been a visiting fellow at the London School of Economics and has a Masters degree in international communication and development.

Contact details: James Deane, Managing Director Strategy,
Communication for Social Change Consortium,
56 Southbrook Road, London SE12 8LL.
Tel: +44 20 8852 3290 Email: jdeane@communicationforsocialchange.org.

Prof Victor O. Ayeni

Director, Governance and Institutional Development Division,
Commonwealth Secretariat

Chair Co-ordinating Committee, Commonwealth Action Programme
on the Digital Divide (CAPDD)

and

Devindra Ramnarine

Adviser, Governance and Institutional Development Division,
Commonwealth Secretariat; Programme Manager CAPDD

5.

Sharing expertise between countries and across differing ICT environments – the experience of the Commonwealth reflected through the CAPDD

Prof Victor O. Ayeni[1]

Director, Governance and Institutional Development Division, Commonwealth Secretariat;
Chair Co-ordinating Committee, Commonwealth Action Programme on the Digital Divide (CAPDD)

and

Devindra Ramnarine

Adviser, Governance and Institutional Development Division, Commonwealth Secretariat;
Programme Manager CAPDD

"Virtually all economic activity...is carried out not by individuals but by organisations that require a high degree of social cooperation".
~ Francis Fukuyama, Trust, the Social Virtues and the Creation of Prosperity

Information and communication technologies (ICTs) have transformed government, business and education, and have enabled significant social and economic growth. ICTs have become essential to the competitiveness of small and medium sized enterprises (SMEs), large organisations and even nations. This technology has a significant impact on poverty reduction and the creation of wealth. Within this context, the differential between those who have access to ICTs and to those who do not – the 'digital divide' – is threatening to intensify existing social and economic inequalities. Recent evidence confirms that the digital divide exists within the fifty-three countries of the Commonwealth. The disparity in the levels of economic development between these countries exacerbates the situation, with a consequential impact on all indicators of human development.

The digital divide poses a real Commonwealth challenge in four areas:

The authors wish to acknolwedge the assistance provided by Ms Tania Gessi, Research Assistant, Governance and Institutional Development Division, Commonwealth Secretariat, London, in the preparation of this paper.

- between countries, particularly industrial and developing countries, and between many countries and less developed countries (LDCs);
- between different countries within the same geographic region;
- within countries, between different geographic areas such as urban and rural areas;
- within countries, between different income or social groups, between men and women, and between literate and non-literate groups.

The digital divide means there is a huge risk that people without the infrastructure to access ICTs or the capacity to use it effectively, will continue to be marginalised. As the problem continued to grow in the less developed countries and small island states of the Commonwealth, the mandate for action to bridge the divide became self-evident. Heads of Government therefore created the Commonwealth Action Programme for the Digital Divide (CAPDD) in 2002 in response to this real immediate challenge.

While ICTs are not the answer to all development problems, they are a valuable contributor to and enabler of broader development strategies. Major advances in ICTs combined with the rapid growth of global networks such as the Internet, offer enormous opportunities to reduce social and economic inequalities and to enable local wealth creation and entrepreneurship. Consequently, the Commonwealth Heads of Government and the various Commonwealth agencies were convinced that a CAPDD could be created that would significantly influence the uneven spread of ICTs.

It is imperative to note, in the context of the development of an action programme, that all Commonwealth agencies have been actively engaged over the past years in the use of ICTs to further development, including achieving the Millennium Development Goals (MDGs). Commonwealth efforts have been particularly prominent in such areas as advancing education and human resource development, strengthening democratic values and promoting gender equality. This has included advocating effective and transparent public administration and good governance, promoting public health and health information diffusion, building appropriate policy-making capacity and fostering cooperation in technology. The obvious questions therefore arose: "Is there a need for an integrated CAPDD?", "Are the autonomous efforts of the individual Commonwealth agencies not meeting the needs of their stakeholders?", and "How would a CAPDD benefit member countries and its citizens?" This paper reviews the efforts taken to develop the CAPDD in the context of the evolution of a climate of trust between delivery agencies themselves and between delivery agencies and recipient countries, thereby facilitating the sharing of experience and expertise across the Commonwealth.

The CAPDD was created (and is being executed) through an

organisational partnership. The Programme was developed and approved by the Commonwealth Heads of Government Meeting (CHOGM) in 2002, and revalidated in the 2003 CHOGM. The Programme was designed to be executed under the co-ordination of the Commonwealth Secretariat with identified lead agencies, namely the Commonwealth Network of Information Technology for Development (COMNET-IT), Commonwealth Telecommunications Organisation (CTO), Commonwealth Business Council (CBC), Commonwealth Secretariat (ComSec) and the Commonwealth of Learning (COL). One of the key recommendations of the 2002 CAPDD Report was the requirement to report on progress at the 2005 CHOGM to be held in Valletta, Malta, in November 2005. That report also mandated the establishment of a Co-ordinating Committee under the Chairmanship of ComSec to monitor progress on the CAPDD, and to report to CHOGM 2005. The results of this review are integrated into this paper.

Built on trust and a sense of purpose

The CAPDD can be viewed as a product of the Commonwealth's experience and its way of working. This way of working has been built on trust and a common sense of purpose, that is, social capital – which for the purpose of this paper is defined as *"an instantiated informal norm that promotes co-operation between two or more individuals"* (see ref. 4). There is a sense in which it was anticipated that the CAPDD would be implemented with little or no co-ordination challenges and at the same time deliver well on its mandate established in 2002. In this context, the review of the work done under the CAPDD umbrella during the period 2002 to 2004 revealed that a great deal of work was done by the various lead agencies. But it was equally apparent that much more could have been possible still under the CAPDD.

The analysis indicated that implementation modalities that would build on teamwork and trust were not clearly defined in the 2002 CAPDD. This situation makes the management role of the Governance and Institutional Development Division of the Commonwealth Secretariat all the more critical and challenging. For a programme of this nature, effective management and programme support from the centre driven by a dedicated and technically sound leadership are vital ingredients for success. Equally, it was felt by the Co-ordinating Committee that it was necessary for the CAPDD to be refocused and put into a tight implementation mode, if it was to deliver maximum benefit and value for money to member countries. This meant that strategies had to be created to realign the approaches taken by the lead agencies on the CAPDD such that greater synergies would emerge and duplication of effort minimised. It is noteworthy that each of the lead agencies have their own charter, objectives, deliverables and management processes. It was clear that the agencies were delivering to the satisfaction of their various stakeholders. A new approach had to be developed which would confirm that a revitalised CAPDD was possible and indeed relevant. The process for "moving forward" had to be acceptable to all partners, but more importantly acceptable to member countries and their citizens.

In retrospect, the updating of the CAPDD can be considered as illustrative of an innovative evolving multi-stakeholder process, which is fundamentally based on building social capital. As Smith claims:

> "Social capital promotes greater co-ordination among individuals and between departments. Teamwork can enhance efficiency and quality in small companies as well as multinational corporations. Social capital within and beyond the firm improve morale and enhance productivity" (see ref. 15).

In this context, social capital can be measured by the degree to which organisations or bodies collaborate and co-operate through mechanisms such as common networks, norms, values and shared trust to achieve mutual benefits. From this perspective, Commonwealth countries have the advantage of sharing a common set of values, which include gender equality, cultural diversity, and freedom of expression, community security and stability, good governance and the peaceful resolution of disputes. ICTs provide powerful instruments to widen economic and social opportunities for women, to permit the free expression of ideas and opinion, and to enhance the sharing and diversity of cultural experience. Given the extensive existing social capital between Commonwealth countries and their publics, it was felt that the Commonwealth would have a comparative advantage in being more receptive and better positioned to use ICTs to pursue and reinforce these values.

It follows that the advantages of the CAPDD stem from the core set of values that binds the various Commonwealth member countries together and from its existing social capital. Furthermore, its constituents have had the opportunity to foster strategic trust, based on shared information and prior experience. Offer illustrates the latter point by claiming in his *Economy of Regard* that experienced partners can create an environment of credibility (see ref. 11). The Commonwealth brings together a wealth of expertise from different economic, cultural, and social backgrounds, and the consequential strategic trust should enable all partners to work collaboratively to create outcomes in a cost-effective and efficient manner. The Commonwealth's significant social wealth would facilitate cooperation and co-ordination thereby diminishing transaction costs arising from negotiation and enforcement, imperfect information and layers of unnecessary bureaucracy. As rightly noted by The World Bank Group: "reciprocal, interdependent relationships – models of social capital –

embody enforcement" (see ref.18). In other words, the overhead costs associated with the delivery of the CAPDD are expected to be significantly lower than similar programmes, which do not enjoy the Commonwealth's common language, history, heritage and core values.

In review, it is now considered important that the various actors who participated in the CAPDD process recognised and had high regard for each other's expertise in their domains of competence, as "regard is a powerful incentive for trust" (see ref. 11) and therefore co-operation. In this context, the CAPDD development process involved extensive discussions within the Co-ordinating Committee in order to develop an approach that was acceptable to all parties. The debate produced five new areas of focus and priority, which represented the few areas that the Commonwealth had clear comparative advantage on the international stage. By focusing on these well-defined areas, it was felt that the Commonwealth would enhance and support the global effort of the World Summit on the Information Society (WSIS) and the MDGs, rather than simply duplicating work. These five focus areas are as follows:

- Building policy and regulatory capacity;
- Modernising education and skills development;
- Entrepreneurship for poverty reduction;
- Promoting local access and connectivity;
- Regional networks, local content and knowledge.

A review of the mandate and experience of the various lead agencies would indicate that the areas of priority and focus represent areas of strength of the Co-ordinating Committee, and were therefore acceptable to all parties. The focus areas also represented areas of known demand from member countries as determined by the independent experience and work of the agencies themselves. Notwithstanding the high level of confidence that the focus areas were most appropriate to meet the needs of Commonwealth citizens, it was considered mandatory to extend the consultation process to the member countries and its citizens in order to confirm the extent of the demand. Several regional consultations were therefore completed and many programmes and projects received from participants. This indicative demand, expressed through the programme and projects, clearly confirmed the demand from member countries and fully validated the expert and experienced judgement of the lead agencies. The indicative demand is summarised in an Annex in the CAPDD Report.

Widening the range of stakeholders

With hindsight, the CAPDD can be considered an exemplar approach to building a multi-stakeholder partnership for delivery in an environment of competing initiatives. Strategic trust and regard play a crucial role in the process. Crafting a successful multi-stakeholder partnership, besides being built on trust, is also about reaching a common objective amongst numerous actors, through understanding various interests, identifying mutual benefits, accommodating organisational, cultural, and social differences, and most importantly collectively gauging their individual competencies and resources for the implementation phase.

At this stage of the development of the CAPDD, it became necessary to engage a wider range of stakeholders and therefore consultation was organised with key country representatives, the private sector, NGOs and civil society. In addition to regular consultation with selected member governments, the Commonwealth Partnership for Technology Management (CPTM), selected Commonwealth civil society organisations, and the Commonwealth Foundation were invited to join the membership of the CAPDD Co-ordinating Committee.

This engagement revealed issues of gender, local content and knowledge. These areas were then reworked and emphasised within the Report. In particular, it was felt that the issue of local content and knowledge was critical to less developed countries and small island states as it would encourage the development of new ICT-based industries and create sustainable employment.

The need for strategic leadership was considered key to the continued development and success of the CAPDD, and for its effective co-ordination. This need led to the development of a well-structured Steering Committee. The need to support core co-ordination functions was identified and a dedicated Secretariat was proposed to support this requirement. A small amount of dedicated funding was also identified to support core co-ordination activities vital to sustaining the Programme.

Identifiyng areas of common wealth

In the final analysis, the CAPDD has a renewed focus based on a federated approach that is transparent, open and inclusive, involving all Commonwealth agencies, member countries and organisations. Its Steering Committee would report to the Board of Governors (COMSEC), would advise on strategic direction and priorities, and would promote policy coherence. The Steering Committee would operationalise and execute the CAPDD strategy. It would build on the implementation experience that it gained in the execution of the CAPDD itself.

Another critical and unique facet of the CAPDD is the identification and utilisation of common ICT wealth. It was felt that because of the Commonwealth's common language (English), similar legislative frameworks, and governance structures, much of the codified ICT knowledge and experience of the Commonwealth can be shared and adopted. This would accelerate learning and progress by reducing the time taken to create such knowledge locally. For example, the similarity of legal and political institutions across the Commonwealth greatly facilitates the sharing of technology model laws and best practices on the application of ICTs to government and public administration. The Commonwealth common ICT wealth includes:

- best practice guidelines, policies, legislation, white papers, technical specifications & standards, national ICT strategies, and regulatory frameworks & tool kits;
- business application software;
- specialists in the various disciplines, including capacity for local digital content development.

It was felt that Internet technology should be used to facilitate the dissemination of policy and other resources – the Commonwealth's intellectual capital. This Internet-based capability could embrace a collection of thematic and regional nodes or centres of excellence. It would entail commitment to content development and maintenance by multiple stakeholders and significant on-going co-ordination for consistency, currency and effectiveness. The extent to which countries and their agencies would contribute to this pool of knowledge is heavily dependent on the climate of trust and sharing that would be engendered by the acceleration of the CAPDD implementation.

> *"The fact of the matter is that co-ordination based on informal norms remains an important part of modern economies, and arguably becomes more important as the nature of economic activity becomes more complex and technologically sophisticated..... A number of empirical studies suggest that high-tech R&D is often dependent on the informal exchange of intellectual property rights, simply because formal exchange would entail excessive transaction costs and slow down the speed of interchange"* (see ref. 4).

In this context therefore, the CAPDD portal is a 'free-for-all' platform that combines the informal element for exchanging intellectual property. This reduces transaction costs and improves the speed of knowledge sharing amongst Commonwealth member countries. It would also encourage south-south knowledge exchange.

The final key aspect of the refocused CAPDD is the proposed special voluntary Digital Divide Fund. This fund would be open to member countries, the private sector, funding agencies and individuals who would wish to make monetary or non-monetary contributions. In this context, it is clear that the success of this fund would be heavily dependant on the trust that potential contributors would need to have, in that the fund would effectively meet its objectives through a credible CAPDD, and the extent to which they would support such objectives. Such contributors would need to be convinced that the Commonwealth environment is able to facilitate achievement of the defined benefits for citizens of the Commonwealth at a lower cost than other agencies.

This means that it is imperative that the on-going implementation of the CAPDD be managed to strengthen trust between executing agencies themselves and executing agencies and beneficiaries, so that transaction costs are reduced, goodwill generated and an environment of credibility created. This would clearly give the CAPDD a comparative advantage in an environment of ICT competing initiatives.

The Maitland Report revisited

At this point, it is useful to examine the Maitland Report, as there are some striking similarities with the CAPDD, although both initiatives are of different scales and in different eras.

The Maitland Report introduced the notion of a necessary link between information flow through telecommunications and new commercial opportunities. It envisaged that widespread and effective communications systems would result in a safer and better world to live in, and emphasised that developing countries could learn lessons from the experience of others.

The Report identified the great disparity between the availability of telecommunications (the number of telephones to the population) between developing countries, where the number of people far outnumbered the number of telephones, and industrialised countries, where telecommunications networks were widely accessible. It further revealed that, in developing countries especially, there is greater telephone density (and hence a more developed network) in urban centres than in remote areas. The Report further acknowledged, well before the Human Development Index (a composite indicator that measures human welfare) was developed by the UN, that "conventional analysis fails to consider the indirect economic and social benefits of telecommunications development" (see ref. 10). These facts greatly resemble the digital divide challenge, as telecommunications networks and computer systems evolved to ICTs and began to make knowledge available to all.

In fact, the Maitland Report made a case for the necessary expansion of telecommunications, as a lack of it would undermine the process of development. Telecommunications therefore should complement development for they would ultimately foster new economic opportunities and enhance the quality of life in the developing world. "The telecommunications system in a developing country can be used not only to disseminate information of immediate importance on a national scale, but also as a channel for education, for strengthening the social fabric for enriching the national culture" (see ref. 10).

The Report represented an important watershed for the year 1984, which was proclaimed as "World Communication Year: Development of Communications Infrastructure", and after the 1982 Plenipotentiary Conference of the ITU, as it recognised the importance of establishing communications infrastructure. In this context, the ITU played a fundamental role, as one of its purposes was to "maintain and extend international cooperation between all members of the Union and promote and offer technical assistance in the field of telecommunications" (see ref. 10) in addition to initiating projects that involved inter-regional co-operation. The reason behind the desire to expand international co-operation was that the communications networks in the industrialised nations were better equipped to provide "advanced data communications facilities", hence the developing nations were losing out on the acquiring of data on trade and global market conditions. The Report therefore emphasised the need for a "closer co-operation between industrialised and developing countries in the data communications field" (see ref. 10). It is clear that the issues of collaboration and co-operation in order to develop synergies, to establish trust, to reduce transaction costs and to share the common ICT wealth of the Commonwealth as detailed in the CAPDD, have continued to challenge the world over the last twenty years. The proposed Steering Committee, the support Secretariat to manage core functions of co-ordination and regional/pan-Commonwealth programmes and projects have clear commonality with the strategies of the Maitland Commission.

The way ITU supported the development of an effective telecommunications system in developing countries was through the provision of assistance and advice, more specifically, the Report recommended that a "Centre for Telecommunications Development" be established with the main purpose of collecting information about telecommunications policies and experience to make them freely available to the countries concerned. Again, the similarity with the proposed CAPDD portal to share common ICT wealth is clear.

The Report made a point in highlighting the fact that investing in telecommunications would be beneficial for both industrialised and developing countries. Providing the basic conditions of an enabling infrastructure were met, investment in telecommunications would have occurred mainly through commercial means, and the Report also recommended making available a small proportion of revenues from the members of the ITU that would be specifically aimed at developing the telecommunications sector in the countries concerned. The proposed voluntary digital divide fund would find much support from the Maitland Report, as the issue of funding continues to challenge countries and international agencies to this day.

Besides supporting financial investment for the development of a more extensive telecommunications system in a "cost-effective and efficient manner", the Maitland Report also emphasised the need for governments to "prescribe policy and set specific objectives". One of the recommendations in the Report was to expand telecommunications to remote areas mainly for socio-economic reasons. The Report also emphasised that development aid should be aimed most importantly at training workers. It was suggested that in order to create self-reliance, local R&D institutes should be established with the aim of transferring knowledge between developing countries and the industrialised world, to ultimately tailor programmes and projects to suit local needs. The CAPDD is built on utilising execution agencies that through their core mandates, attempt to build national and public sector capacity to develop and implement policy. Many of the programmes and projects requested by member countries under the CAPDD are in the area of capacity building.

The Maitland Report was ahead of its time in acknowledging the fundamental role that information and communication would play in the social and economic spheres of society. The "informatisation of production", phraseology used by M. Hardt and A. Negri in their book *Empire* (see ref. 7), is now at the essence of post-industrial economy, or "informational economy", wherein information and communication technologies are progressively redefining the manufacturing processes of traditional industry. This shift from modernisation, which had industrial production at its base, to what is now known as post-modernism, or informatisation, is the result of a gradual redefinition of all the elements of the social plane. People went from being part of an agricultural society, with agriculture being the main source of livelihood, to an industrial society, which was brought about by the Industrial Revolution, to what is now widely known as an information society, whose economy is based on productive information flows and networks.

Conclusion

Finally, the CAPDD, besides befitting the current world order of the "information society" and helping bridge the digital divide in the Commonwealth in a pragmatic way, embodies an innovative approach through its implementation. It recognises the importance of cross-sectoral partnerships for sustainable development, and as it is noted on the World Bank Group's website: "...the Prince of Wales formed his Business Leaders Forum to promote synergy, interdependence and social capital across the public, private and civil society sectors" (see ref. 18).

As was acknowledged in the Maitland Report, the CAPDD (twenty years later) recognises the potential that multi-stakeholder partnerships hold in implementing the programme. The CAPDD represents an innovative, highly visible, results-based approach that focuses on the specialised five areas of the Commonwealth, therefore building on its strengths and acknowledging the implementation challenges of the Maitland experience.

Additionally, through the CAPDD portal, there is room to freely exchange intellectual property, which would ultimately reduce transaction costs and speed up the process of interchange. The CAPDD also symbolises a new trend in economic development theory that results from building an organisational network based on trust.

As Fukuyama emphasises, human and societal behaviour cannot be satisfactorily explained within neoclassical economic models, as there is an underlying theme of Trust, which constitutes a major contributing source and explanatory variable of varying prosperity around the world (see ref. 4). The CAPDD contains within it the necessary features for successful implementation and can therefore harness its full development potential, while integrating closely with the global agenda.

References

1. *The Commonwealth, ICTs and Development*, A Report to CHOGM 2005, prepared by the Coordinating Committee, Commonwealth Action Programme for the Digital Divide for the Commonwealth Secretary-General, London, UK.

2. Commonwealth Partnership for Technology Management, Annual Report 2001-2002, Networking People and Ideas, CPTM, www.cptm.org (October 2005).

3. Francis Fukuyama, *Trust, the Social Virtues and the Creation of Prosperity*, Free Backs Paperbacks, New York, USA, 1996.

4. Francis Fukuyama, *Social Capital and Civil Society*, The Institute of Public Policy, George Mason University, October 1, 1999, IMF. www.imf.org/external/pubs/ft/seminar/1999/reforms/fukuyama.htm (October 2005).

5. William A. Galston, *Trust: The Social Virtues and the Creation of Prosperity* – Book Review, Public Interest, Winter 1996. www.findarticles.com/p/articles/mi_m0377/is_n122/ai_17884723 (October 2005).

6. Global Knowledge Partnership Secretariat (GKP), Multi-Stakeholder Partnerships, Issue Paper. www.globalknowledge.org (October 2005).

7. Michael Hardt & Antonio Negri, *Empire*, first Harvard University Press Paperback Edition, 2001.

8. Robert D. Hof, *Power of Us*, BusinessWeek OnLine, June 20, 2005 www.businessweek.com/magazine/content/05_25/b3938601.htm (October 2005).

9. Shumbana Karume, *Conceptual Understanding of Political Coalitions in South Africa: an Integration of Concepts and Practices*, The Electoral Institute of Southern Africa (EISA), Cape Town, 19 June 2003, www.eisa.org.za (October 2005).

10. *The Missing Link*, Report of the Independent Commission for World Wide Telecommunications Development, Chairman Sir Donald Maitland, December 1984.

11. Avner Offer, *Between the Gift and the Market: The Economy of Regard*, Economic History Review, L, 3(1997), Oxford, UK.

12. Quddus, Munir, Goldsby, Michael, Farooque, Mahmud – *Trust: The Social Virtues and the Creation of Prosperity*, a Review Article, Eastern Economic Journal, Winter 2000 www.findarticles.com/p/articles/mi_qa3620/is_200001/ai_n8890278 (October 2005).

13. William Sheridan, *The Limits of Criticism*, InSite Reviews www3.sympatico.ca/cypher/mistrust.htm (October 2005).

14. Ramakrishna Sithanen, *Coalition Politcs under the Tropics: Office Seekers, Power Makers, Nation Building, A Case Study of Mauritius*, The Electoral Institute of Southern Africa (EISA), Cape Town, 19 June 2003, www.eisa.org.za (October 2005).

15. Smith Adam, *An Inquiry into the Nature and Causes of the Wealth of Nations*, Methuen and Co. Ltd., ed. Edwin Cannan, 1904. Fifth edition www.econlib.org/library/Smith/smWN.html (October 2005).

16. UNDP, *Human Development Report 2005, International Cooperation at a Crossroads, Aid, Trade and Security in an Unequal World*, published for the United Nations Development Programme (UNDP), New York, USA, 2005.

17. Eric M. Uslaner, *Varieties of Trust*, KTHC-Knowledge, Technology, Human Capital, Department of Government and Politics, University of Maryland. Downloadable from the Fondazione Eni Enrico Mattei www.feem.it/feem/pub/publications/wpapers/default/htm (October 2005).

18. The World Bank Group, *Social Capital and Firms*, http://www1.worldbank.org/prem/poverty/scapital/sources/firm1.htm (October 2005).

Professor Victor Ayeni is Director, Governance and Institutional Development Division of the Commonwealth Secretariat, London and chair of the Co-ordinating Committee of the Commonwealth Action Programme on the Digital Divide (CAPDD). Prior to his current appointment, he was Deputy Director and lead adviser with responsibility for Governance and Public Management programmes. Before joining the Commonwealth Secretariat, Dr Ayeni was Professor and Head of Public Administration at the University of the North in South Africa. He has lectured in universities in Nigeria (his home country) as well as Botswana, Australia and Canada. In the 1980s he worked briefly in one of the state civil services in Nigeria. He has been consultant to several Commonwealth and non-Commonwealth governments as well as a range of international and bi-lateral agencies. He is widely published with some 12 books and over 100 papers on various aspects of Governance and Public and Development Management to his credit. He is the current editor of the African Journal of Public Administration and Management (Africa's only journal for scholars and practitioners in the field). Prof Ayeni holds a PhD in Public Administration from Ife University in Nigeria.

Devindra Ramnarine is Adviser (Public Sector Informatics) in the Governance and Institutional Development Division at the Commonwealth Secretariat based in London. He is responsible for the Public Sector Informatics Programme of COMSEC and is the Programme Manager for the CAPDD. He was the Head of the National ICT Planning Secretariat in the Government of Trinidad and Tobago prior to joining the Secretariat.
Mr Ramnarine has extensive experience in information technology and telecommunications in both the public and private sectors. He is an experienced

project manager with a special interest in telecommunications liberalisation, managing large high-risk integrated ICT projects and on the linkages between ICT and public sector reform. He is a telecommunications engineer by training with an MPhil in electrical engineering science, an MSc in telecommunications systems and a BSc in electrical engineering. He has been a lecturer on several ICT courses on the University of London external BSc programme and the Heriot Watt external MBA programme.

Contact details: Professor Victor Ayeni, Director Governance and Institutional Development Division, Commonwealth Secretariat, Marlborough House, Pall Mall, London SW1Y 5HX, England. Tel: +44 20 7747 6349 Email: v.ayeni@commonwealth.int.

Professor Robin Mansell

Department of Media and Communications,
London School of Economics and Political Science

6.

The fragility of knowledge societies: ambiguity, cost reduction and access in developing countries

Professor Robin Mansell

Department of Media and Communications,
London School of Economics and Political Science

The Missing Link authors sought to achieve an important goal – "All mankind could be brought within easy reach of the telephone by the early part of next century" (Maitland 1984: 69). The main challenge was to improve the reach of the telecommunication infrastructure and to do so by emphasising not only technology, but the strategies, market and regulatory mechanisms, technical and management capabilities, training and financing that would be required to achieve this goal.

Twenty years on, much has been achieved in terms of new opportunities to enable the poor, and especially those in rural areas, to be connected to the telecommunication infrastructure and the services on offer today. Whereas in the mid-1980s three-quarters of the world's telephones were concentrated in nine industrialised countries, by the mid-2000s the World Bank (2005: 10) was claiming that more than half the world's households have access to a fixed line telephone and that the footprints of mobile operators are accessible to 77% of the world's population. However, the gaps in access to this infrastructure remain 'considerable' in rural areas.

The deployment of fixed and mobile networks, together with the arrival of the Internet protocol, means that the potential for achieving some form of connectivity is improving. These figures unfortunately do not tell us anything about the quality or cost of the services provided, much less their affordability.

The problems of achieving access and benefiting from the potential benefits of such access have not diminished. In this chapter I emphasise issues that arise when connectivity is a realistic prospect. Apart from the huge investment required to put the necessary infrastructure in place[1], the challenges of addressing additional issues associated with ensuring that connectivity brings advantage, rather than new forms of disadvantage, are also considerable.

One way of interpreting *The Missing Link* is to suggest that its authors believed that it was imperative to get people connected to networks in whatever way, whether by using older or newer telecommunication technologies. I argue that achieving connectivity is very important, but that since the Report's publication we have learned a great deal about the ways in which these technologies are related to development aspirations and poverty reduction. Although the 'promise' of new technology is substantial, it is clear that, once connected, ambiguous consequences often follow. If the visions of knowledge societies that are in play today are to have any chance of being fulfilled, then these consequences need to be examined from a variety of vantage points. This is essential to ensuring choices are made that give people a chance of using telecommunication connectivity to escape from poverty or to make other improvements in their lives.

All forms of connection to electronic networks bring new ambiguities into people's lives whether they are citizens or the employees of firms in various information and communication technology (ICT)-using sectors of the economy. On the basis of empirical evidence, there is not necessarily a relationship between achieving connectivity – even affordable connectivity – and enabling people to make improvements in their lives, *as they choose*. Therefore, it cannot be argued that achieving access to global networks should be the imperative in every instance. Local circumstances must be taken into account.

Whether by virtue of their presence or their absence – or indeed the specific nature of their presence – ICTs have a 'politics' and these politics affect everyone. It is necessary to consider the entitlements and responsibilities of individuals and firms because decisions about whether to invest in new networks and content involve assessments of whether to allocate scarce resources when there are many other priorities requiring a response in the development context.

In this chapter, I use two illustrations to reinforce this observation. The first comes from the supply side in the form of industry efforts to reduce the costs of accessing the Internet for the poor. One of the recommendations of *The Missing Link* (8j) was to encourage manufacturers and operators to develop systems that would enable people living in remote areas of developing countries to access networks at lower cost. I assess some of the ambiguities associated with recent initiatives aimed at achieving this.

The second comes from the demand side through an examination of the way e-commerce applications are perceived by potential users in developing countries and the ambiguous outcomes for firms that have achieved connectivity. In both instances, we encounter evidence of the fragility of knowledge societies, which arises from a failure to foster developments in technologies and services that are fully responsive to the needs of their intended users.

Technologies of power

In *The Missing Link* it was observed that "...from the beginning we all recognised the *political character* of our task ... neither in the name of common humanity nor on grounds of common interest is such a disparity acceptable" (emphasis added) (Maitland 1985: 3). It is crucial that we think of ICTs as 'technologies of power' in the broadest sense. This does not mean that events are determined by technology; nor does it mean that these technologies are entirely malleable in the hands of individual political and other actors. Thomas Hughes, an economic historian, studied the history of many different kinds of large technical systems. His work tells us that "we have understood for centuries that technology is an instrument of power" (Allen and Hecht 2001: 1). Whether one is a producer or designer of ICT systems – or one is seeking to use technology to communicate or to exchange information, these artefacts and their contents are 'instruments of power'. Whether and how they are deployed is a reflection of a highly political process, as the authors of *The Missing Link* acknowledged. In the light of Michel Foucault's analysis of institutions, we know that power relations are embedded in technologies and in the social relations around them (Martin et al. 1988: 1). The outcomes are not predetermined, but they are often ambiguous depending upon whose point of view is taken into consideration. These perspectives make it clear that it cannot be assumed that connectivity is always advantageous. There may be negative consequences, including new forms of exclusion from emerging knowledge societies (Castells 2001).

At about the same time that *The Missing Link* was issued, another analyst of technological change was asking whether 'artefacts have politics'. Langdon Winner's (1980) answer was that they do. Just as the telecommunication infrastructure can be said to have a 'politics', so the immaterial flows of data and information and complex patterns of communication that are pervasive today can be seen in this way. As Winner (1986: 20) put it, "what matters is not technology itself, but the social or economic system in which it is embedded". The challenge is to understand the politics of today's ICTs. The stakes are high because of the opportunity presented by the second phase of the World Summit on the Information Society (WSIS). It is important to answer Winner's question because of the necessity to become more aware, not only of the economics of change, but also of the politics of change.

In the run up to the WSIS in November 2005, the International Telecommunication Union (ITU) launched a new initiative to 'bridge the digital divide'. *Connect the World* is an initiative in which partnerships are seen as central to connecting communities (ITU 2004). It is estimated that about 800,000 villages – or 30% of all villages worldwide – are still without any kind of connection. ITU Secretary-General, Mr Yoshio Utsumi, said at the launch, "ICTs now underpin just about every aspect of modern life. They are basic infrastructure, as necessary to economic and social development as postal services, banks, medical centres and schools" (ITU 2004: 1). *Connect the World* emphasises the importance of partnerships between the public and private sectors, UN agencies and civil society. Alcatel, Huawei, Intel, Microsoft, KDDI, Telefónica, Infosys and WorldSpace, and others have joined. This initiative is "about harnessing the power of people working together to connect the unconnected" (ITU 2004: 1).

How do we ensure that lessons about the political character of technology are considered in this case? Our track record of doing so is not very good. For instance, in 1980 UNESCO published its *Many Voices, One World* Report. Its authors emphasised content and communication rather than telecommunication, but they argued that, "... the basic decisions in order to forge a better future for men and women in communities everywhere ... do *not* lie principally in the field of technological development: they lie essentially in the answers each society gives to the conceptual *and political foundations of development*" (emphasis added) (MacBride et al. 1980/2004: 12-13). Many studies have been undertaken to measure the impacts of investment in ICTs on economic and social development, especially in developing countries. Such studies embrace both older and newer technologies from the radio to telecommunication networks, personal computers, community telecentres, entrepreneurs' kiosks and prepaid mobile phones (Kenny 2001; Spence 2003, UNDP 2005). Unfortunately, few of these studies are designed to throw light on the politics of technology or on the ambiguities that connectivity can create. Such studies rarely examine the political, social or cultural contexts of the production and consumption of technology or services. They cannot, therefore, shed light on the ambiguities that may arise – that is the possibility that investment in technologies and services can be empowering and, at the same time, disempowering. If reasoned judgements are to be made about whether to give a high priority to investment to achieve connectivity for the poor, it is this kind of understanding that is required. This means that we must put the analysis of the politics of technology at the centre of our concern.

Technological choices and digital divides

One instance where choice is being made over connectivity is with respect to the design of Internet access devices that are intended to enable lower income people to connect with the Internet. The WSIS Action Plan (WSIS 2003) set targets for bringing connectivity to those who remain unconnected to global networks; the Millennium Development Goals also include a reference to ICTs[2]. One possibility is to reduce the costs of hardware and software. During the 2004 World Economic Forum in Davos, AMD (Advanced Micro Devices), the microchip manufacturer, launched a campaign called 50x15 (AMD 2005). Through partnerships, the company's goal is to connect 50% of the world's population to the Internet by 2015.

AMD's 'ecosystem' of companies aims to develop usable, affordable technologies and to make them easily accessible for people in global, high growth markets. AMD has released the PIC – a Personal Internet Communicator – that the company initially expected to sell at about US$ 185 (Torres 2005)[3]. Solectron in Mexico is manufacturing prototypes. Launched in India by Videsh Sanchar Nigam (VSNL), the largest telecommunication company, the PIC is being offered to broadband customers as part of a bundled Internet service. A variety of financing options is available to people on limited incomes (Sadagopan 2004; TATA 2004). In this case, the price is US$ 250 and the PIC is being targeted at households with an annual income of between US$ 1,000 and 6,000. India is expected to provide more than 16 million customers and, with China, Mexico, Brazil and the former Soviet Union, the target market rises above 200 million. The PIC allows customers to access an Internet browser, email, word processing and spreadsheet applications, using the Microsoft Windows operating system. The PIC is also being offered by Cable & Wireless as part of a broadband package in the Caribbean (AMD 2004).

In a similar vein, the chairman of the MIT Media Lab, Nicholas Negroponte, wants to launch a US$ 100 portable computer for the developing world. He has reported promises of support from companies such as AMD, Google, Motorola, Samsung and News Corp (Siddle 2005)[4]. However, neither the PIC nor Negroponte's low cost personal computer are the first attempts to market low cost alternatives for very low income people. The development of the Simputer based on Linux by Encore Technologies in Bangalore beginning in 1999 is an attempt to make the Internet accessible to rural Indians, but there have been problems in scaling up this initiative. Launched at a cost of US$ 240 in 2004, it was eventually manufactured by the government-owned Bharat Electronics. Fonseca and Pal (2003: 3) suggest that "bringing the PDA [Personal Data Assistant] interface to low-attainment users without the contextual establishment of their utility then seems like a quantum leap". Similarly, BV Jagadeesh, who founded iNabling Technologies in Bangalore in 2001, has been trying to offer simple, low-cost email access to India's rural population using an 'iStation'. Intel has been considering the idea of low-cost personal computers for some years and Wal-Mart has been selling the Linspire Linux open source operating system bundled with a personal computer for US$ 199 since 2002 (Maguire 2002). Microsoft's CEO Steve Ballmer has also talked of the need for US$ 100 personal computer for developing country markets (Riccuiti 2004). Why have these and other initiatives yet to provide solutions to connect many of the poor? It seems clear that it is not simply a question of cost, nor is it simply a matter of a 'missing link' insofar as, in some cases, the mobile or fixed telecommunication infrastructure is in place.

The question is whether the PIC and similar technological designs are responsive to problems that result in people continuing to be excluded from the potential advantages of connectivity, however it is achieved. To answer this question we have to look both to the economics and politics of these kinds of initiatives.

Discussions about 'digital divides' highlight oppositions which suggest that technological solutions such as the PIC offer a means of alleviating the huge differences that persist (with respect to content, hardware and software) between the poor and the wealthy in terms of their access to ICTs. The last three decades of debate and research on the problems of exclusion from knowledge societies illustrate that a wide range of strategies is needed to address the underlying problems and that, politically, this is very difficult to achieve. Scaling up production of Negroponte's US$ 100 computer will require public investment if it is to succeed even on its own terms. Innovative technologies are often introduced with great optimism in the hope that that they will provide a part of the solution to exclusion; but history shows that optimism needs to be tempered with caution (Howcroft and Fitzgerald 1998; Kling 1996; Mansell and Steinmueller 2000; Mansell and Wehn 1998; Robins and Webster 1999).

Improved access to the Internet using the PIC or a similar slimmed down device is unlikely to address the underlying development problems because the scale of the problems and the reasons for them are substantial and complex. According to the Computer Industry Almanac, the worldwide Internet population of 2004 was 934m and was projected to grow to 1.07bn in 2005[5]. China had the second largest Internet population with 99.8m in 2004 as against 185.5m in the United States, but China had a total population of 1.31bn as compared to the US population of 296m. While China is a rapidly growing economy and may well surpass the US in total output, the figures for smaller poorer countries help to illustrate the observation about the scale of the connectivity problem. Bhutan, with a population of 2.23m, had only 2,500 online users in 2004; the Republic of Congo had 3.04m people with 500 Internet users in the same year. Liberia with a population of 3.48m had 500 Internet users. And compare South Korea, with a population of 48.42m and 31.67m Internet users, with Sudan with a similar sized population of 40.19 million, but only 56,000 Internet users.

In the light of these figures, what is the likely impact of the PIC in alleviating access problems or, indeed, in reducing poverty? One journalist expressed considerable optimism under the by-line 'selling to the poor' –

"Blocked in saturated developed markets, start-ups and major companies are targeting lower-income regions, giving them cheaper—and sometimes better—products than those in the West" (Red Herring 2005). However, 'selling to the poor' in the case of the PIC means marketing to those with incomes of between US$ 1,000 and US$ 6,000 annually; at the lower end, around US$ 2.00 per day. The PIC initiative is designed to promote broadband connectivity and it is being marketed by existing telecommunication operators. For instance, Cable & Wireless in Jamaica is charging US$ 15.00 per month over two years for the PIC but a broadband subscription is also needed, costing US$ 29.95 per month. Thus, the total cost to the user in the first year is US$ 540.00. This is a considerable amount for a potential user if his or her annual income is about US$ 1,000. In addition, there appears to have been little attempt to coordinate this initiative with investment in local digital content or new electronic services, despite the fact that AMD has promoted the PIC, in part, based on its educational value. Finally, although the PIC represents a partnership among a number of corporate players, there is little sign of partnerships with other stakeholders such as representatives of civil society.

In summary, there is little evidence of a reasoned debate involving those who seek to use new technologies in ways that can help to reduce poverty. The corporate players participating in the development and marketing of the PIC are motivated by their forecasts of returns on their investments and they may achieve their targets. But in what sense can it be argued that these initiatives are consistent with optimistic visions of knowledge societies? Even when access is achieved, consideration must also be given to whether services are appropriate and whether they harbour new ambiguities. The absence of a reasoned, inclusive debate about needs and requirements easily gives rise to a mismatch between technological choices and the interests of various users.

Technological opportunities and digital divides

Once connectivity is established, e-commerce applications for businesses are regarded as a major opportunity for firms based in developing countries. Many theoretical analyses of the implications of the development of e-commerce are concerned with how such services affect transaction costs (Wigand 1997; Williamson 1985). By helping to reduce transaction costs, e-commerce and, specifically, e-marketplaces are expected to facilitate trading across national boundaries, especially for firms in developing countries (Malone et al. 1987). Propositions about the impact of e-commerce have appeared in many UN agency reports. These propositions include the notions that e-commerce is likely to work through e-marketplaces; that e-commerce will offer high returns to firms in developing countries (UNCTAD 2001); and that e-commerce will help smaller firms to enter global markets (ITC 2000; UNCTAD 2001).

The expectation underlying these propositions is that the spread of the Internet and the use of the Web will lead to greater market efficiency and transparency. However, as empirical evidence comes to light in the industrialised countries, it seems that the structure and operation of markets are not automatically modified to achieve greater efficiency and transparency as a result of the application of new technologies (see Chircu and Kauffman 2000; Kraut et al. 1998; Steinfield et al ; 2000; and Molla and Licker 2005). The notion that they will be modified in this way is implicit, however, in speculative considerations of the development of e-commerce in developing countries. Empirical research in Europe suggests that the outcomes for firms that adopt e-commerce can be enormously varied and that they are likely to be informed by prevailing commercial practices and the structural features of specific sectors, rather than by any elixir of technology (Hawkins, et al. 2000).

One examination of e-commerce in developing countries focused on two sectors: garments and horticulture (Humphrey et al. 2003). When the research was conducted, e-marketplaces supporting these two sectors were in operation. Seventy-four smaller and larger firms in Bangladesh, Kenya, and South Africa were selected in this interview-based study. If firms in these countries are to make use of e-marketplaces, they need to have a means of accessing networks. Despite the generally acknowledged weakness of the telecommunication infrastructure in Bangladesh, Kenya and South Africa, all the firms in the sample had some means available to them to access the Internet. Despite the availability of e-marketplaces providing a range of services, the majority of the firms had never registered with one of these services (77% of 74). The availability of e-commerce was, nevertheless, influencing the way that the firms were doing business. E-mail was the most important Internet application, but it was being used to facilitate communication with *existing* customers and suppliers, rather than with new ones. In this study, even though more than half of the firms had websites, more than 75% of respondents said they rarely used the Web to obtain general information or information about specific customers or suppliers. Nearly all of them wanted to continue to rely mainly on interpersonal networks and face-to-face meetings to exchange information.

The observations of several respondents are instructive. A South African garment intermediary respondent, owned by a large Hong Kong trading group, observed that although email was used extensively, e-commerce was not supporting transaction activity. In addition, he suggested that "we don't want to work with the other 10 per cent", because these are micro-firms. A South African horticulture company had an Internet site catering to domestic producers. Although it was acknowledged that there were technical problems, the main difficulty was that "the industry is perhaps naive and uniformed. The potential benefits need to be proven". E-commerce was expected to grow, but it was not expected to become seamless because "if you shorten the supply chain you will likely short-change yourself". Face-to-face interactions remained essential so that deals could be negotiated on the basis of trusted relationships. In Kenya's horticulture sector a small company in the sample was exporting fruits and vegetables. It was using the Internet to sell its products and had registered with an e-marketplace. However, the respondent said that "we get constant requests, orders" but there are payment problems and the company was unable to satisfy requests for orders for capacity reasons. In another Kenyan company in the same sector, a respondent highlighted continuing infrastructure problems, saying that "sometimes the line works, sometimes it doesn't – it's a nightmare".

What we find in the empirical evidence is a cluster of problems and issues that come under the rubric of the 'politics of technology'. E-commerce does not seem to offer high returns to firms in developing countries as compared to other ways of conducting trade – and e-commerce on its own is unlikely to help many small firms to enter global markets (Humphrey et al. 2003). In this study there was evidence of growing use of supply chain management software. However, even where innovative e-commerce applications were being developed, the importance of trust, face-to-face interaction, and offline transacting was emphasised. International market conditions were being influenced more by existing market structures and commercial practices than by the introduction of new technologies. This is a reflection of the 'politics of technology' and it is these circumstances and constraints that should be the principle focus of any inquiry into how connectivity influences the commercial positioning of firms in developing countries. Although investment in ICTs is important, choices should be based on what is best for each sector and firm in a given country – not on abstract assessments of technological potential. As in the case of the PIC and other access technologies, there is too little evidence of serious attempts to discover what those with few resources, themselves, wish to prioritise.

Conclusion

I have highlighted the importance of examining the wider politics of technology in order to consider how future initiatives to address digital divides may have a greater chance of reducing poverty. The initiatives in the coming years will need to be a reflection of people's aspirations and their objectives for development. It is imperative that actions aimed at building knowledge societies acknowledge that technologies – whether the

PIC or mobile phones or radios – "must ... avoid giving the impression that information, knowledge and communication are magic wands. They are essential but not sufficient elements to address poverty". Approaches are needed "that represent a process of dialogue, information sharing, mutual understanding and agreement, and collective action". The aim should be to "link private sector interests and expertise into a new generation of investment in which the empowerment and development of people is central"[6]. This is a very tall order. There was little evidence of large-scale efforts to develop this kind of approach following *The Missing Link*. While there is more discussion of the need to take the politics of technology into account today, the illustrations in this chapter suggest that it is still very difficult to design and implement technologies and services that are responsive to people's needs in poor communities.

It is essential to assess ICT initiatives in terms of the incentives guiding the corporate actors into new markets and in terms of whether these initiatives are likely to introduce new ambiguities for those affected by their technological choices. When such initiatives seem likely to introduce new forms of exclusion or disadvantage, complementary action is needed. A starting point for analysis of the ambiguous outcomes of connectivity is to apply Amartya Sen's (1999) concepts of capabilities and entitlements. These concepts provide a departure point from which to debate the relative importance of achieving connectivity for the poor in a way that takes people's expressions of their needs into account. Sen argues that citizens have an entitlement to acquire certain capabilities because they are the underpinnings of the freedom of citizens to construct meaningful lives. In discussions about investment in ICTs, it can be argued that access to online content or the capabilities for sending and receiving emails or text messages amplifies the 'real choices' that people have available to them. This provides a justification for investing in the technologies that enable connectivity. However, even if there is a consensus on this point, this offers no indication of the relative priority that such investment should receive as compared to other courses of action (Garnham 2000).

Sen suggests that decisions about priorities must be established through an evaluation process involving a public and highly political discussion among the relevant stakeholders. Heeks (2002a,b) points out that much can be accomplished by extending existing technology initiatives to citizens through creative organisational and investment strategies. However, it is important to decompose what is meant by ICT and to ensure that choices about technologies are responsive to people's needs, as they understand them. Without evaluation, potential users are simply responding to the latest package of technology – such as the PIC or a prepaid mobile phone – without regard to the specific needs that they might have expressed if such an evaluation had been conducted. All forms of connectivity have a politics.

If investment in connectivity leads to further divides in the populations of poor areas from the wealthy areas, thereby reinforcing pre-existing inequalities associated with gender, social status or earning capacity, then the consequences of such investment will be highly ambiguous and will further heighten the fragility of emerging knowledge societies.

The WSIS civil society declaration (Civil Society 2003: 2) put people and poverty reduction at the centre of its concerns: "at the heart of our vision of information and communications societies is the human being. The dignity and rights of all peoples and each person must be promoted, respected, protected and affirmed. Redressing the inexcusable gulf between levels of development and between opulence and extreme poverty must therefore be our prime concern". By coupling a consideration of individuals' entitlements to connectivity with a consideration of the politics of technology and their ambiguous consequences for the poor, there will be a better opportunity to evaluate when a high priority should be given to investment in connectivity and content creation and when other development concerns should take the lead. The responsibility of decision makers is to conduct an evaluation of the kind that seeks to understand people's needs and development aspirations as well as their entitlements.

Research on e-commerce in developing countries is beginning to highlight how different the needs of those who are intended to benefit from connectivity are as compared to the perceptions of those needs by many technology designers. For example, the ambiguity of connectivity is visible in research documenting the threat of e-commerce to the livelihoods of micro-business entrepreneurs in the mueblista (furniture) industry in Chile[7]. New e-commerce services are bypassing micro-entrepreneurs in villages in rural Chile who have been earning a livelihood in this industrial sector. The implementation of e-commerce has meant that larger suppliers that are better prepared to trade using their access to the Internet have captured the micro-entrepreneurs' markets. The micro-entrepreneurs have few resources to enable them to retrain to enter other types of industrial activity. While the urban, larger firms are benefiting from connectivity, despite its availability to the rural micro-entrepreneurs and ICT skills training initiatives, they are not capturing the potential advantages.

This illustrates the profound importance of the politics of technology, the ambiguity of connectivity, and the fragility of knowledge societies. People's livelihoods do not change because of technology; they change in the light of the way technology becomes embedded in the overall context of the local and the global. Where that context is consistent with poverty reduction, then it is possible for the newer and older technologies to make positive contributions. Discussion in support of reasoned decision-making about entitlements and responsibilities with respect to connectivity must start from a detailed appreciation of those contexts.

References

1. Estimated by the World Bank as being in excess of US$ 100 bn between 2005 and 2010.

2. Millennium Goal 8. Develop a global partnership for development – Target 18. In cooperation with the private sector, make available the benefits of new technologies, especially information and communications.

3. Before taxes and without a video monitor. AMD is using its Geod chip, typically used for making computer kiosks and set-top boxes for broadband connections. The PIC uses one watt of electricity and runs without a fan, provides 128 MB of memory and a 10-GB hard drive.

4. In this case, the low cost computer would have a 14-inch/35.5cm colour screen, AMD chips, and run open source Linux software.

5. www.clickz.com/stats/web_worldwide/ accessed 21 Sept 2005.

6. Quotations here are from an online moderated discussion, "Measuring the Impact of Communication in Development Projects and Programs", January-February 2005. Extracts from comments by participants are anonymous and permission to use the texts was sought from the World Bank moderators.

7. Unpublished research undertaken by Dorothea Kleine, PhD candidate, London School of Economics.

- Allen, M. T., and Hecht, G. (eds) (2001) *Technologies of Power: Essays in Honor of Thomas Parke Hughes and Agatha Chipley Hughes*, Cambridge MA: MIT Press.

- AMD (2004) *AMD and Cable & Wireless Enable Internet Connectivity and Computing Power throughout the Caribbean with the Personal Internet Communicator*, see www.amdboard.com/pic_120104.html accessed 21 Sept 2005.

- AMD (2005) Personal Internet Communicator, at www.amd.com/us en/ConnectivitySolutions/ProductInformation/0,,50_2330_12264,00.html?redir=PCPC01 accessed 22 Sept. 2005.

- Castells, M. (2001) *The Internet Galaxy: Reflections on Internet, Business and Society*, Oxford University Press.

- Chircu, A. M. and Kauffman, R. J. (2000) *Reintermediation Strategies in Business-to-Business Electronic Commerce*, International Journal of Electronic Commerce, Vol. 4, No. 4, pp. 7-42.

- Civil Society (WSIS) (2003) *Shaping Information Societies for Human Needs*, Declaration to the World Summit on the Information Society, 8 December, www.worldsummit2003.de/download_en/WSIS-CS-Decl-08Dec2003-eng.rtf accessed 21 Sept 2005.

- Fonseca, R. and Pal, J. (2003) *Bringing Devices to the Masses: A Comparative Study of the Brazilian Computador Popular and the Indian Simputer*, University of California, Berkeley, Final Report, ICT4B, December, at www.sims.berkeley.edu/~joyojeet/Simputer-CP.doc accessed 22 Sept. 2005.

- Hawkins, R. W., Mansell, R. and Steinmueller, W. E. (2000) *Controlling Electronic Commerce Transactions* in R. Mansell and W. E. Steinmueller, *Mobilizing the Information Society, Strategies for Growth and Opportunity*, Oxford University Press, pp. 289-337.

- Heeks, R. (2002a) *i-Development Not e-Development: Special Issue on ICTs and Development*, Journal of International Development, Vol. 14: pp. 1-11.

- Heeks, R. (2002b) *Information Systems and Developing Countries: Failure, Success, and Local Improvisations*, The Information Society, Vol. 18, pp. 101-112.

- Howcroft, D. and Fitzgerald, B. (1998) *From Utopia to Dystopia: The Twin Faces of the Internet*, Information Management Proceedings at, http://infomgt.bi.no/wg82-86/proceedings/howcroft.pdf accessed 22 Sept. 2005.

- Humphrey, J., Mansell, R., Paré, D., and Schmitz, H. (2003) *The Reality of E-commerce with Developing Countries*, report prepared by Media@lse and IDS for the DFID Globalisation and Poverty Programme, March at www.gapresearch.org/production/Report.pdf accessed 22 Sept. 2005.

- ITC (International Trade Centre) (2000) *Export Development in the Digital Economy*, Geneva, 2000, at www.intracen.org/execforum/ef2000/publication2000.htm accessed 22 Sept. 2005.

- ITU (2004) *ITU Launches New Development Initiative to Bridge Digital Divide*, 16 June, www.unis.unvienna.org/unis/pressrels/2005/pi1664.html accessed 22 Sept. 2005.

- Kenny, C. (2001) *Information and Communication Technologies and Poverty*, TechKnowLogia, July/August, at www.digitaldividend.org/pdf/kenny.pdf accessed 22 Sept. 2005.

- Kling, R. (1996) *Computerization and Controversy: Value Conflicts and Social Choices*, 2nd Ed., San Diego CA: Academic Press.

- Kraut, R., Steinfield, C., Chan, A. P., Butler, B., and Hoag, M. (1998) *Coordination and Virtualization: The Role of Electronic Networks and Personal Relationships*, Journal of Computer Mediated Communication, Vol. 3, No, 4, at http://jcmc.indiana.edu/vol3/issue4/kraut.html accessed 22 Sept. 2005.

- MacBride, S. et al. (1980/2004) *Many Voices, One World – Towards a New, More Just, and More Efficient World Information and Communication Order* – The MacBride Commission, Report of the International Commission for the Study of Communication Problems first published by UNESCO, Lanham NJ: Rowman & Littlefield Publishers.

- Maguire, J. (2002) *New Lindows Release Stands Alone*, Newsfactor Magazine Online, at www.newsfactor.com/perl/story/20039.html accessed 22 Sept. 2005.

- Maitland, D. (1984) *The Missing Link* Report of the Independent Commission for World Wide Telecommunications Development, December, Geneva: ITU at www.itu.int/osg/spu/sfo/missinglink/index.html accessed 21 Sept. 2005.

- Malone, T. W., Yates, J. and Benjamin, R. (1987) *Electronic Markets and Electronic Hierarchies*, Communications of the ACM, Vol. 30, No. 6, pp 484-497.

- Mansell, R. and Steinmueller, W. E. (2000) *Mobilizing the Information Society: Strategies for Growth and Opportunity*, Oxford University Press.

- Mansell, R. and Wehn, U. (eds) (1998) *Knowledge Societies: Information Technology for Sustainable Development*, published for the United Nations Commission on Science and Technology for Development by Oxford University Press at www.sussex.ac.uk/spru/1-4-9-1-1-2.html accessed 21 Sept 2005.

- Martin, L., Gutman, H. and Hutton, P. (eds) (1988) *Technologies of the Self: A Seminar with Michel Foucault*, Amherst: The University of Massachusetts Press, pp. 16-49, and see www.thefoucauldian.co.uk/tself.htm accessed 22 Sept. 2005.

- Molla, A. and Licker, P. S. (2005) *eCommerce Adoption in Developing Countries: A Model and Instrument*, Information & Management, Vol. 42, pp. 877-899.

- Red Herring (2005) *Selling to the Poor*, 11 April, accessed 22 Sept. 2005 at www.redherring.com/Article.aspx?a=11848&hed=Selling%20to%20the%20Poor.

- Riccuiti, M. (2004) *The $100 PC: How Do We Get There?*, CNET News.com, 12 November, at http://news.com.com/The+100+PC+How+do+we+get+there/2010-1016_3-5448784.html accessed 22 Sept. 2005.

- Robins, K. and Webster, F. (1999) *Times of the Technoculture: Information, Communication and the Technological Order*, London: Routledge.

- Sadagopan, S. (2004) *AMD's Personal Internet Communicator: A Great Product Backed by a Powerful Idea*, 12 November, at www.financialexpress.com/fe_full_story.php?content_id=73946 accessed 21 Sept 2005.

- Sen, A. (1999) *Development as Freedom*, Oxford University Press.

- Siddle, J. (2005) *Digital Guru Floats Sub-$100 PC*, BBC News, February, http://news.bbc.co.uk/2/hi/technology/4243733.stm accessed 1 Oct. 2005.

- Spence, R. (2003) ICTs, *the Internet, Development and Poverty Reduction*, Background Paper: Discussion, Research, Collaboration, April, IDRC at http://old.developmentgateway.org/node/133831/sdm/blob?pid=4351 accessed 22 Sept. 2005.

- Steinfield, C., Chan, A. and Kraut, R. (2000) *Computer Mediated Markets: An Introduction and Preliminary Test of Market Structure Impacts*, Journal of Computer Mediated Communication, Vol. 5, No. 3, at http://jcmc.indiana.edu/vol5/issue3/steinfield.html accessed 22 Sept. 2005.

- TATA (2004) *VSNL and AMD Launch the Personal Internet Communicator*, 28 October, at www.tata.com/vsnl/releases/20041028.htm accessed 21 Sept 2005.

- Torres, G. (2005) *PIC: AMD's Popular Computer*, Hardware Secrets, 22 April, at www.hardwaresecrets.com/article/125 accessed 21 Sept. 2005.

- UNCTAD (2001) *E-Commerce and Development Report, 2001*, Geneva: UNCTAD, 2001, at www.unctad.org/ecommerce/docs/edr01_en.htm accessed 22 Sept 2005.

- UNDP (2005) *Regional Human Development Report: Promoting ICT for Human Development in Asia: Realizing the Millennium Development Goals*, Amsterdam: UNDP/Elsevier.

- Wigand, R. T. (1997) *Electronic Commerce: Definition, Theory, and Context*, The Information Society, Vol. 13, No. 1, pp. 1-16.

- Williamson, O. E. (1985) *The Economic Institutions of Capitalism: Firms, Markets, Relational Contracting*, New York: Free Press.

- Winner, L. (1980) *Do Artifacts Have Politics?* Daedalus 109 in D. MacKenzie and J. Wajcman (eds) (1999), The Social Shaping of Technology [2nd ed] Buckingham: Open University Press, pp. 28-40.

- Winner, L. (1986) *The Whale and the Reactor: A search for limits in an Age of High Technology*. Chicago, IL: The University of Chicago Press.

- World Bank (2005) F*inancing Information and Communication Infrastructure Needs in the Developing World: Public and Private Roles*, Draft for Discussion, Global Information and Communication Technologies Department Washington DC, February 2005.

- World Economic Forum (2002) *The Global Information Technology Report: Readiness for the Networked World 2001-2002*, Oxford University Press.

- WSIS (World Summit on the Information Society) (2003), *Plan of Action* 12 December, www.itu.int/dms_pub/itu-s/md/03/wsis/doc/S03-WSIS-DOC-0005!!PDF-E.pdf accessed 22 Sept. 2005.

Professor Robin Mansell holds the Dixons Chair in New Media and the Internet in the Department of Media and Communications, London School of Economics and Political Science. She is President of IAMCR (International Association for Media and Communications Research) 2004-2008. Her research is concerned with the social, economic and policy issues arising from innovations in information and communication technologies. Professor Mansell's most recent book is *Trust and Crime in Information Societies*, Edward Elgar, 2005 (ed/cont with B. S. Collins).

Contact details: Professor Robin Mansell, Department of Media and Communications, London School of Economics and Political Science, Houghton Street, London WC2A 2AE, England.
Tel: +44 20 7955 6380 Email: r.e.mansell@lse.ac.uk.

Yasuhiko Kawasumi

Rapporteur for ITU SG2 Q10-1/2 on Communications
for Rural and Remote Areas;
Executive Staff, Japan Telecom Co. Ltd.

7.

Focus on rural connectivity

Yasuhiko Kawasumi

Rapporteur for ITU SG2 Q10-1/2 on Communications for Rural and Remote Areas,
Executive Staff, Japan Telecom Co. Ltd.

The year 2005 commemorates the 25th anniversary of the MacBride Report *Many Voices, One World* and the 20th anniversary of the Maitland Report *The Missing Link*. Both Reports identified the imbalance of information or information infrastructure between North and South at that time. They recommended various remedies for building the sound future Information Society. The ITU, a leading UN agency for information and communication technologies, has been promoting various initiatives over the past 25 years to follow up the recommendations in the Reports, aiming to build on the information society and to enhance the quality of life in the 21st century. The ITU's conferences, meetings, seminars, forums and TELECOM events, electronic media, among others have concentrated on the promotion of telecommunications development for more than twenty years through activities that were related to standardisation of technologies, radio communications, regulatory frameworks, human resource development, knowledge sharing, etc. for developing countries. After the activities of CTD (Centre for Telecommunications Development) of the ITU (1985-1990), telecom development activities of the ITU were succeeded by BDT (Bureau for Development of Telecommunications) and ITU-D meetings since the first World Telecommunication Development Conference in Buenos Aires (WTDC'94) to best meet the needs of developing countries. Activities have included assistance to developing countries for mobilisation of technical, human and financial resources in the field of information and communication technologies, and for related project development and implementation. This article will look specifically at the initiatives by the ITU and its Focus Group on rural communications that were inspired by the 1985 Maitland Report.

ITU activities relating to rural communications development

At the second WTDC'98 in Valleta, Malta, Sir Donald Maitland was invited to deliver the speech on the future of telecommunications. It was 13 years after the submission of the *Missing Link* to Richard Butler, Secretary General of the ITU at that time when the digital information and communications technologies and services were emerging. During the same conference, the Japanese delegation proposed launching a programme to study the new technologies, to be applied to rural communications development in order to bridge the communications gap, or "digital divide" (later on so-called), which was raised by *The Missing Link*. The conference approved the programme as one of seven questions to be studied by the focus group scheme in the Valleta Action Plan (VAP). The question was defined as topic 7 in the VAP i.e: "Study various mechanisms by which to promote the development of new telecommunication technologies for rural application". At the following Telecommunication Development Advisory Group meeting of the ITU in April 1999, it was agreed that the study of this question should be handled by the Focus Group on topic 7 and the task completed in one year. The Japanese government contributed to the fund to support the activities of Focus Group 7. The study was conducted mainly via the Internet with short meetings in conjunction with ITU-D SG2 meetings. FG7 collected 60 case studies contributed to its newly created website by members for analysis.

The following basic recommendations of *The Missing Link* were paid special attention during the work of FG7:

- Governments, development agencies and financing institutions are to give a higher priority to investment in the telecommunication sector.
- Developing countries should review their development plans to ensure that sufficient priority is given to investments in telecommunication.
- Existing networks (specifically rural ones) should be made more effective and commercially viable and should gradually become self-reliant.
- All projects or development activities with economic or social components should have a telecommunication element built in.

FG7 also paid particular attention to the recommendations of *The Missing Link* regarding technology development and selection:

- We recommended that manufacturers and operators be encouraged to develop systems that would enable the needs of the more remote areas of developing countries to be met at lower cost.
- Selection of product can be as important as choice of technology. Buyers must know what is available on the market. We recommended that the ITU, in conjunction with manufacturers of telecommunication equipment and components, consider compiling a comprehensive catalogue of telecommunication suppliers and systems currently in use.

As the world enters the 21st century, many of the conclusions and recommendations of *The Missing Link* remain valid. Focus Group 7 cited these conclusions as important and useful guidelines for the information age, even as it concluded its own study and recommendations to promote the development of new telecommunication technologies for rural applications.

The final report was completed in 2000 and published in 2001 from the ITU with six recommendations to BDT Director of the ITU such as;

- Promote development of low-cost information appliances for rural use.
- Create a renewable energy handbook on small-scale power systems for rural information and communication technologies.
- Increase collaboration with micro-finance organisations to help develop communication-based rural businesses and applications.
- Conduct pilot projects of packet-based wireless access infrastructure for multimedia applications.
- Maintain and expand the ITU website related to the work on new technologies for rural applications.
- Hold a symposium on new technologies for rural applications.

The study was succeeded in 2002 by the ITU-D SG2 Rapporteur's Group on Question 10-1/2 on "Communications for rural and remote areas". Based on its work plan set out by the Istanbul Action Plan (IsAP) of WTDC'02 (March 02, Istanbul), RGQ10-1/2 conducted the global survey (2003-04) followed by the analysis of case studies collected from the countries/territories (2004-05), which responded to the global survey questionnaires with positive development policies.

Reports on the global survey on rural communication and analysis of case studies on successful practices were approved by the ITU-D SG2 in September of 2005 and will be published accordingly.

The reality of rural and remote areas

The study on rural communications identified the following key issues, as may be easily understood:

- Low per capita income;
- Difficult topographical conditions (lakes, rivers, hills, mountains, or deserts, etc.);
- Scarcity and absence of reliable electricity supply, water, access roads and regular transport;
- Severe climatic conditions that make critical demands on equipment;
- Low level of economic activity mainly based on agriculture, fishing, handicrafts, etc.;
- Low population density (age group of low mobility left in rural areas);
- Low literacy rate.

In particular, key issues for the provision of telecommunications services for rural and remote areas were also identified:

- Disparity of information and communication services between urban and rural areas;
- The availability of public communication is limited in the rural areas but the needs are high and the affordability of the services is key factor for the provision of services;
- Unavailability of technical personnel;
- Needs of e-health, tele-education, e-administration are high and the lack of basic infrastructure is the barrier;
- Universal Service Obligation and Universal Service Funds schemes are the new methodology subsidising the cost for rural communication services;
- New technologies to reduce the cost for rural communications development should be investigated and wireless technologies (Wi-Fi, WiMax etc.) with IP platform are deserved to be paid attention.

The global survey report of ITU-D Study Group 2 Doc.2/111 demonstrated that the largest age group in rural and remote areas is the group younger than 16 years old and women. They have less mobility than those in towns, resulting in less economic activity and productivity and the consequent separation of rural communities. The other reasons for rural/urban separation leading to a communications gap was accessibility by road to rural areas, which was a significant challenge in most developing countries. Island countries such as the Maldives use other means of transportation.

The study of low cost technologies for rural applications

The following are basic requirements for deployment of communications systems in rural areas of developing countries:

- Implementation and operation is possible at a low cost in areas where population density is low;
- The system can be easily installed, even in remote/inaccessible areas;
- System operation and maintenance can be carried out even where qualified technical personnel are scarce;
- Implementation is possible even when basic infrastructure such as mains electricity, running water, paved road networks, etc., are absent.

An increasing number of technologies are available that can meet the above requirements at a reasonable cost to rural network operators. The Focus Group concentrated on packet-based wireless technology combined with Internet Protocol (IP) routers as most suitable for implementation in rural and remote areas for the following reasons:

- Advantages over circuit-switched networks becoming the platform: alternative for new telecommunication network;

- Data-path (channel) to be shared simultaneously among users in the network (low cost services);
- Multi-media platform including voice services (VoIP), facsimile etc;
- Automatic rerouting capability (protection for facility failure);
- Wireless provides fast roll-out time;
- Wireless provides lower maintenance cost and greater network flexibilities.

Wireless access system

Wireless communication technologies, such as fixed wireless access (FWA) and very small aperture terminals (VSATs), are effective means of establishing telecommunication networks in rural areas due to their advantages over wired communications in terms of cost and ease of installation. For example, when installing telephones in sparsely populated rural areas, wireless communication technologies such as PHS, GSM, and other cellular technologies can be used in conjunction with satellite stations and point-to-multipoint radio systems to achieve coverage of isolated settlements over long distances.

IP-related technologies

With the Internet becoming internationally widespread, the focus of new network construction around the world is shifting rapidly from conventional PSTN to IP-based technologies. Emerging packet-based wireless access technologies, such as IMT-2000 and wireless routers, are being designed to deliver a wide range of traffic types more efficiently and inexpensively than traditional wired and cellular telephony networks.

Existing satellite operators and planned satellite systems are retrenching in order to serve the global market for Internet access and broadband communications. These technologies have much potential for use in rural areas, but they are just beginning to enter the marketplace. In order to lower the risks faced by network operators in developing countries, new systems offering transitions to packet- and IP-based network architectures need to be tested and, in all probability, developed further in order to meet the requirements of rural areas. Furthermore, the integration of wireless, IP-based routers with voice-over-IP software offers developing countries the additional technology option of constructing wide area networks to solve the last mile problem in rural areas. Wide area networks can be configured to share bandwidth between telephony and Internet efficiently, while taking advantage of the low cost of network servers and the easy installation of wireless systems.

Multimedia terminals

The installation of inexpensive multimedia user terminals can be an effective way of providing access to Internet and multimedia services without resorting to costly and complex personal computers. Email, voice, facsimile, data and video communications are becoming available through non-traditional devices. These systems can be installed at multipurpose community telecentrse and shared by many users.

The proliferation of multimedia devices, and the ability to custom design and modify them, offers tremendous flexibility in the design of applications for rural areas. The price of this flexibility, however, is that service providers must understand the unique needs of their rural customers in order to determine the criteria by which to select technologies and applications.

Deployment of remotely managed networks of multimedia terminals should be explored in order to make it easier for rural inhabitants to learn how to use the Internet by doing away with the need for many PC management skills. Another expected advantage would be lower lifetime maintenance costs and slightly lower power requirements per unit. Social benefits could be increased by providing a mechanism for service providers to direct relevant content to rural inhabitants who might be unable to navigate the Internet on their own. Internet appliance solutions may be able to provide some or all of these benefits at a lifetime cost no higher than that of a comparable PC-based solution.

The following is a summary of the advantages of Internet use over wireless for rural applications, based on case studies;

- Low cost/channel – it provides TCP/IP packet based channels that are shared by users (advantage over circuit-switched network);
- Multi-user terminal interface (voice, fax, Internet, Web browsing, teleconference, healthcare equipment, etc.);
- Low power requirements;
- Standard compliance products available in the market;
- Simple configuration and operation;
- Modularity and scalability;
- Shared use of equipment and facilities at multi-purpose community tele-centres, university or school extension centres, hospitals, post offices, etc;
- Possible in-kind contribution from recipient local communities or participatory groups for installation, operation and maintenance of the facilities of telecentres, etc;
- Possible government/operator/private partnership;
- Possible subsidy of start-up cost by aid funds.

Applications for quality of life

Global survey analysis (Ref. 6) showed that the needs of e-health, e-education, e-administration are high in rural areas of developing countries in developing countries. ICT training, e-business and e-banking, awareness programmes follow the preceding applications. There are other applications such as e-agriculture, e-shopping mall, Internet-café, etc. as may be planned by the entrepreneurs of rural communities. E-education, e-health, e-administration in particular are believed to contribute to the improvement of the quality of life or poverty alleviation of rural people. The provision of e-healthcare services is considered as priority government policy in most developing countries, in order to contribute to control over government healthcare costs and to reduce the mortality of rural people. Services of local government will be improved by the provision of e-administration applications for the rural communities, and rural dwellers will benefit through the various information services relating to quality of life issues.

Funding rural projects, and their sustainability

In *The Missing Link*, mechanisms to set aside portion of international telephone charges were taken into consideration, but these were not implemented adequately by the international community of telecommunication industries nor by the ITU. Instead, the scheme of universal service obligation (USO) and the universal service fund (OSF) are being introduced in developed and developing countries.

Global survey analysis showed that twelve countries/territories have established USF for subsidising rural communications services. There are some countries/territories that have USO schemes and USF planned but not implemented. The recipient governments/financing agencies/private sector partnership for funding rural communications projects are observed in the collected case studies. The size of the rural communications projects is in general rather smaller compared with the most of the national communications development projects in developing countries, which is sometimes the barrier for funding opportunity, and would not attract the interests of financing agencies, project planners, developers and suppliers etc. In this respect, as was recommended in *The Missing Link*, higher priority should be given to rural communications projects by the political leaders of developing countries, and communications projects should be incorporated in all national development projects. This may facilitate the subject problems.

Global challenges for rural connectivity

The ITU-D SG2 Rapporteur's Group collected 19 case studies for rural communications projects from five regions of the world i.e. Africa, Americas, Arab Region, Asia and Europe & CIS. Countries were selected from among the respondent countries/territories to the questionnaire for the preceding global survey by the Rapporteur's Group. The following case studies are examples of successful practices extracted from analysis reports of the Group, providing guidelines for the development of rural communications in developing countries. There are a variety of technologies implemented in the rural and remote areas of the selected countries depending on the geographical and terrestrial conditions of the areas in consideration. As for the last mile solutions, as are observed in the given case studies, not only the wireless systems but also optic fiber cables, copper wires and the combined fibre cable and copper wire solutions are deployed to reach the customer in rural and remote areas.

Africa: Burkina Faso

The project allowed the establishment of telecommunication infrastructures in the zones of Koudougou and Tenkodogo in the country's rural area. This supported the accessibility of 160,000 inhabitants in 25 villages to a minimum of telecommunications services, which contribute to the improvement of their standard of living through growth noticed in agropastorales, artisanal and small trade activities. This telephone service project appears to have been a powerful tool in the fight against poverty. It deploys a microwave point-multi-point system linking between and to hub stations in rural areas with two wire copper extensions to the user.

Americas: Brazil

Brazil has three programmes related to universal service access. The first is the universal service provided by the Fixed Telephone Service Connection – STFC. This type of universal service is the exclusive responsibility of the four incumbent operators of the STFC, which made it possible to install at least one public telephone in all localities with more than 100 inhabitants. Nearly 30,000 localities have already been taken care of in this programme. Users pay the total cost of its use. It is managed by Anatel. The second programme, called Digital Communications Service, is being developed through the partial use of resources from the Globalization Fund by means of a telecommunication service created by Anatel, the telecommunications regulating agency in Brazil. Though still in the implementation stage, it will have to primarily take care of state schools and health and community centres in rural areas. The users pay for part of its use. Joint management is provided by Anatel and the Ministry of Communications. The third programme is the GSAC (Gobierno Electronico-Servicio de Atencion al Ciudadano: Electronic Government) and is intended to take care of communities in rural areas. Implementation, operation and maintenance needs are subsidized by government budgetary resources. It is totally free of charge to the user and managed by the Ministry of Communications.

Arab Region: Egypt

The biggest challenges for serving rural areas and villages are to overcome different topologies. From an economic point of view, the operator has to choose the most suitable communication system for the areas to be served. Efficient deployment of appropriate communication system according to the terrestrial and terrain topography (topology), enhances the services, provides higher rate, and increases revenue. The systems that may be used in providing telephony services to rural areas and villages are outdoor optical fibre unit system, wireless system, and point-to-point wireless system. The wired line access method, utilising copper wire cables, is the conventional system. It is normally used for local networks at a maximum range of 5Km. With ordinary topology, using optical fibre cable as one of the network access methods is considered a great privilege. The fibre cable is connected to a remote unit; this remote optical unit provides service to subscribers through copper wire. This system is used when communities are located apart from each other and far from the host exchange. Another network access is the fixed wireless access (FWA) method. The application of FWA for telephone service is generally called 'Wireless Local Lop (WLL)', which applies radio systems in the distribution zone instead of wire lines. This system is used when low to medium subscriber density areas are located apart from each other, and deployment of primary or secondary local networks is difficult.

Asia: India

India has over 700 million people living in over 600,000 villages with an average per capita income of around US $200 per annum. The key issue that needed to be addressed is whether technology can bring about a difference in the lives of people who can earn less than a dollar a day. Can health and education be made available to them? Can they afford the Internet? And ultimately, can it significantly enhance their livelihoods and income. The TeNet (Tenet Indian Institute of Technology, Chennai) group's primary objective was to create a rural services organisation that would work towards delivering relevant and cost-effective technologies to rural areas, which can be used to improve the living standards of Indian villages. TeNet believed that any solution which is confined to either a few hundreds or a few thousands of villages and which could not scale up to meet the needs of most of the 600,000 villages in India, would remain an experiment and would not be instrumental in enhancing the lives of people. With the objective of building a scalable, sustainable model to provide commercial ICT services to rural India, the charter of n-Logue (n-Logue Communication Private Ltd.) is dedicated to providing services only to rural areas and the organisation is barred from servicing the urban populace. Through n-Logue, TeNet intends to deliver ICT applications for essential services such as education, healthcare and e-governance, through setting up a network of village Internet centres called Village Kiosks. The dream, however, is to significantly impact rural livelihood and income.

Indonesia

This project has been developed from Desa Maju services, i.e. a system that provides information based on voice, where the content of the information is related to economic activity, education, health etc. in rural communities. As Desa Maju evolves, voice Internet will be introduced, an alternative solution to access Internet and email without using personal computers.

Europe & CIS: Bulgaria

The strategic objective of this pilot project is to develop packet-based wireless access infrastructure in the Septemvri rural area – and to test its application, not only for telecommunications and information services but for telemedicine care with a special emphasis on tele-cardiology. This project will be the first in the country and can be replicated at other sites in Bulgaria and other countries with similar conditions.

Conclusion

The target set in *The Missing Link* was that by the early part of the 21st century virtually the whole of humankind should be brought within easy reach of a telephone. Pekka Tarjanne, who served as ITU Secretary-General from November 1989 to January 1999, took this goal to heart and appealed to the United Nations "to recognise the right to communicate as a basic human right". Since then, higher investment in telecommunication development, coupled with the implementation of new technologies and innovative strategies, as well as the general understanding of the socio-economic effect of communications infrastructure, have led to a remarkable degree of telecommunication development observed in most of the developing countries throughout the 1990s.

Whereas the goal set in the Maitland Report is deemed to be a realistic and achievable target, the progress of digital technologies and the proliferation of Internet style services and applications have brought us new challenges. At ITU TELECOM 99, ITU Secretary-General Yoshio Utsumi set a new goal in his opening speech, namely: to bring Internet-style services to all humankind within the first decade of the new millennium, and apply all the new technologies and impulses so that the gap in connectivity to the Internet can be reduced. He is leading the ITU, the private sector and NGO actors to meet this challenge since he assumed his post, by leading the World Summit on the Information Society and related Preparatory Conferences. National political leaders and decision makers, the heads of international agencies, industry leaders among others concerned with the building of future information society are now getting together under these common goals. The interests of most developing countries and concerned organisations may be the digital solidarity funds to be agreed upon by the WSIS for the development of information and communications for the developing world.

Through the activities of the ITU-D Study Group to date, it has been recognised that the needs and requirements of rural communities in developing countries should be paid particular attention. Rural inhabitants are still left behind in isolated areas of developing countries, where 40% of the world population lives and is digitally divided from the modern information society. It is in these regions where the lion's share of poverty, illness and human violence is felt – reiterating the urgency for the call to action. It is now time for project development and more focused implementation in every corner of the world towards these goals.

References

1. The MacBride Report: *Many Voices, One World*, Paris: Unesco, 1980

2. Maitland Report: *The Missing Link*, Report of the Independent Commission for World Wide Telecommunication Development, 1985, ITU Publication Dept.

3. The Final Report of the Focus Group on Topic 7: New Technology for Rural Applications, 2001, ITU-D SG2

4. ITU News No.7, 2001, *Connecting rural communities*, Yasuhiko Kawasumi, General Manager of Japan Telecom Co., Ltd.

5. ITU News No.2, 2002, *Challenges for rural communications development*, Yasuhiko Kawasumi, General Manager of Japan Telecom Co., Ltd.

6. Report of the Rapporteur's Group on Q10-1/2: Analysis of the Global Survey on Rural Communications, 2004, ITU-D SG2

7. Report of the Rapporteur's Group on Q10-1/2: Analysis of case studies on successful practices in telecommunications for rural and remote areas.

Acknowledgements

The words of Sir Donald Maitland, Mr. Yoshio Utsumi, Secretary General of the ITU, Mr. Hamadoun Toure, BDT Director of the ITU, given to the FG7 final report encouraged us to continue the subject study by the concerned group of people in the ITU-D Study Groups and BDT of the ITU. Ms Rebecca Mayer, Ms. Carole Chaplier, Dr. Paula Murphy, Mr. Phillip Trotter, who have contributed to the collection of case studies and information of emerging technologies, their analysis, meeting arrangements, correspondence over the Internet as the focal point of FG7 in the BDT.

Thanks to the co-operation of Member States of the ITU, private sector members, institutes, etc. which have contributed to the case library, their responses to the global survey questionnaires, and the request of successful case reports, we could accomplish tasks charged to FG7 and ITU-D SG2 Rapporteur's Group on the question of "Communication for rural and remote areas". The financial support of the Japanese government, with their understanding of the work of rural communication development has made the work associated with these reports feasible. And last but not least, we would like to appreciate the continued support of BDT staff, in particular, Mr. Alexander Ntoko and Ms Fidelia Akpo and the Chairman of SG2, Mr. Nabil Kisrawi.

Yasuhiko Kawasumi is Rapporteur for ITU-D SG2 Q10-1/2 on "Communications for rural and remote areas" and is on the Executive Staff in the External Affairs Division of Japan Telecom Co., Ltd.
Mr. Yasuhiko Kawasumi started his business carrier at the Japanese overseas telecommunication operator KDD (Kokusai Denshin Denwa Co.Ltd.) in 1961 after graduating from the Electrical Engineering Faculty of KEIO University. His experiences cover the works for the construction of Transpacific Submarine Cable No.1, the maintenance and operation of submarine cable systems and Intelsat satellite systems at the international gateway station of the company, engineering of network management systems, telephone traffic management. He was stationed in Geneva 1972-1976 as the company's representative and attended CCITT, CCIR Plenary Assembly Meetings, World Administrative Radio Conferences (WARC), Administrative Council Meetings and Plenipotentiary Conferences (Nice, Minneapolis and Marrakesh) as a member of Japanese delegation. He contributed to the standardization of G3 facsimile machine in CCITT in late 1970s, 32KbpsADPCM Speech Codec etc.
Mr Kawasumi participated in Maitland Commission meetings as advisor to Dr. Koji Kobayashi in Arusha (Tanzania) and Bali (Indonesia) in 1984 and the Advisory Board meetings of the Centre for Telecommunication Development of ITU as an expert. After taking up the position of director of the international affairs department of KDD, he took the posts of secretary general of ITU Association of Japan, Executive Vice President of Kokusai Telecommunication Installation Co. and Secretary General of International Communication Foundation (ICF). He moved to Japan Telecom Co., Ltd. in 1997 taking his present position.
Yasuhiko Kawasumi was appointed as rapporteur of the Focus Group on topic 7 "New Technologies for Rural Communications" of the ITU-D Study Group 2 in 1999 and submitted the final report on "New Technologies for Rural Applications" to the Study Group 2 of ITU-D and Telecommunication Development Advisory Group (TDAG) of ITU-D. He was one of the Vice-Chairmen of TDAG (2000-2001) in charge of Rural Communications Development. He is now the rapporteur for Q10-1/2 of ITU SG2 "Communications for Rural and Remote Areas" for the study period 2002-2006. He is Professor for Department of Emergency and Critical Care Medicine in Nakajima Laboratory of Tokai University, Isehara, Kanagawa Prefecture Japan.

Contact details: Mr Yasuhiko Kawasumi, External Affairs Department, Japan Telecom Co Ltd, 9-1 Higashi-Shimbashi 1-Chome, Minato-ku, Tokyo, 105-7316 Japan
Tel: +813 5540 8012   Fax + 813 5543 1969
Email: yasuhiko.kawasumi@japan-telecom.co.jp

Dr. Gillian M. Marcelle

Principal Consultant, Technology for Development (TfDev)

8.

Making the link between ICT and development: lessons from the Caribbean

Dr. Gillian M. Marcelle

Principal Consultant, Technology for Development (TfDev)

Although information and communication technologies (ICT) have the potential to contribute to the achievement of human development objectives, we have not yet understood how to manifest benefits for the majority of the world's population. In the twenty years since the publication of the Maitland report, the ICT sector has increased exponentially in scale and scope but its impact on improving the lives of the world's poor has not been realised.

There is a commitment to increase access to ICT and to spread its benefits more widely across and within countries. This is reflected in a number of international agreements, including the Declaration and Action Plan of the Geneva Phase of the World Summit on the Information Society (WSIS) and the work of the Millennium Project. But despite the rhetorical commitment, international efforts, are not working. The international community has provided financial resources and development agencies have exhorted countries to 'catch-up'. There has been a great deal of both intellectual effort and spin aimed at providing examples of the benefits to be derived from increasing access to these technologies. However, even after nearly two decades, the concrete evidence of ICT producing developmental impacts is still fairly thin and the results achieved by many interventions are not clear cut. If the international community cannot produce tangible and measurable development impacts under conditions where there is little extreme poverty, educational enrolment levels and literacy are high, there is little hope for doing so in the least developed countries, where the need is greatest.

It is in this context that the experience from the Caribbean region provides many lessons for the international community as it tries to fashion strategies to improve the developmental impact of investments in ICT. This region demonstrates clearly that ICTs are socially constructed and as a result the inputs, process and outcome of ICT planning efforts are embedded in social, cultural and political structures. These are also disruptive technologies which deliver maximum benefit, only when technology adoption is accompanied by organisational and institutional change. As we will show in this review, which focuses on the Caribbean, there is no possibility of ICT serving as a quick fix or magic bullet and this should provide a salutary lesson for other developing regions. We will argue that in order for ICT investments to deliver benefits for education, health, environmental protection, efficient public administration, and poverty reduction, developing countries must embrace continuous change and develop their local capacities. Without these adaptations, the investments will constitute a waste of resources and ICT projects will be the Information Age equivalents of white elephants.

Towards development focused ICT policy

In order for ICT to yield increased developmental benefit, strategic thinking and creative leadership are required. This section outlines key principles and processes recommended for taking developing countries from current status to ICT policies that are more aligned with broader development goals.

The following are suggested as key principles to guide the processes of ICT sector planning:

- Engage society in defining policies which have a clear and unambiguous focus on development and putting people first
- Emphasise impact evaluation and continuous monitoring
- Build on existing strengths and assets and facilitate continuous learning in planning and implementation
- Focus on sustainability and institution-building
- Effective engagement with the global ICT policy community

Developing countries using these principles should engage in the following processes to improve the developmental impact of ICT.

First, national or regional ICT programmes should be formulated on the basis of clearly defined objectives produced through consultative processes involving all stakeholders, including the intended beneficiaries. It has been conclusively shown that wide participation of stakeholders in planning and coordination is important. ICT programmes that incorporate principles of democratisation and good governance have been a success. In Estonia, Costa Rica and Brazil, national strategy has been formulated and implemented by teams that bring together actors from the state, private sector, and civil society. Without that diverse mix of stakeholders, these countries would not have been able to use ICTs to support development efforts. Opportunities exist everywhere for civil society to be effectively engaged in the process of harnessing ICTs for development. These opportunities should not be frittered away. Caribbean governments are not yet making the best use of a range of stakeholders, including the Caribbean diaspora.

The consultative process of policy development should be supported by a research programme that is geared to providing insights into how, why and under what conditions ICTs may be beneficial and in what ways they may be burdensome, irrelevant, meaningless, costly and harmful.

Second, ICT programmes should consider ICT infrastructures, facilities and capabilities to be classical public goods, for which the social and overall benefits for the system as a whole exceed specific benefits to any single actor. Planning should take market failure in the supply and distribution of public goods into account. It has been shown in theory and daily life that the market alone can neither ensure optimal provision of nor equitable distribution of public goods. Developing countries therefore should not rely only on market mechanisms to accelerate deployment and application of ICT. The market can play a role in delivering ICT to consumers, but creation of an Information Society in which ICTs are applied to development problems of all citizens cannot be achieved through reliance on the market.

Governments must play a leadership role; the state is the guardian of the public interest and should manage markets to achieve public policy objectives. Publicly funded ICT programmes, particularly those financed through loans and grants should focus on disenfranchised and underserved customers. The market is able to serve the needs of well-off consumers in middle-income countries. The rapid acceleration in demand for mobile phones in the Caribbean demonstrates that no special effort, apart from market liberalisation, is required to satisfy the needs of customers who fit the typical profile of a third generation mobile phone user. No public policies are necessary to increase utilization rates by elites and the middle-class. However, pubic policy is needed to ensure that ICTs are affordable and meet the needs of the majority. This shift in focus will require a fresh approach to ICT policy and regulation, capability building, research and innovation – and cannot be accomplished without genuine partnership among governments, private sector and civil society.

The brightest and best minds in the developing world should be galvanized to develop ICT applications that serve the developmental needs of the majority. Firms, universities and public institutions should undertake more relevant technological learning, and accelerate efforts to share technological knowledge, particularly among Southern partners. India, Brazil, South Africa and Nigeria have been vocal in emphasizing the urgent need to initiate and support local and regional research and technological effort.

Third, the design of ICT programmes must engage the intellect and creative imagination of the intended beneficiaries. As we will show using the Caribbean as an illustration, ICT policy is a job that is too important to be left to external actors, no matter how well intentioned. Countries require

117

homegrown solutions, developed by appropriate institutions that are equipped to use a variety of methods of engagement. Developing countries, particularly those that have small, migrant populations should use their diasporas as a source of knowledge and financial resources. In order for this to be workable, developing countries will have to find ways to build and establish networks of trust and mutual respect between national decision makers and diaspora professionals.

Fourth, there is no cookbook or magic formula that can guarantee success in exploiting ICT for development. International experience suggests that the most responsive and effective national ICT strategies are the ones that address felt needs and provide for differences in emphasis and priority. A common characteristic of effective ICT policies is the presence of a strong effective champion who is willing to invest political capital in achieving the policy objectives. His or her role goes beyond planning, and includes stimulating and supporting action at the national level. The response to each country's problem should be tailored to suit its individual situation. For example, Cuba has focused on the use of ICTs in healthcare, Costa Rica has used ICTs for effective environmental management, Morocco has emphasized ICT applications in public administration, while Tonga and Mauritius have given priority to ICT applications in tourism. The evidence from the Caribbean will confirm that different countries should have different starting points, and ought to be based on processes that are appropriate to their own needs and cultural settings. In the Caribbean, there have also been examples of good practice: Grenada's Chief Information Office in the Office of the Prime Minister reports that critical IT infrastructure fared well during the devastation by hurricane Ivan owing to design of redundancy and backup systems. St Lucia has gone through an impressive planning exercise to design an ambitious programme for ICTs in public sector reform. Jamaica has rolled out telecentres and multimedia centres that are encouraging young people to use ICTs to produce music and videos. Suriname has an extensive e-education programme. Several Eastern Caribbean countries have introduced popularisation campaigns through the Internet Fiestas programme. Barbados and Trinidad and Tobago have embarked on comprehensive national ICT policy processes, which have strengthened institutional capacity.

Fifth, ICT policy needs to move from top-down, external-driven exhortation to a more careful approach. Developing countries need to develop ICT and development strategies that are located centrally within their broader development visions. These strategies should be built-up, through careful research and analysis, and should include convincing explanations of exactly how proactive ICT sector development and application of ICTs in other sectors can produce benefits[1]. Developing countries should move beyond market liberalisation and pro-competition recommendations, that are, on the evidence only partial and often not explanatory. Taking this approach is likely to attract political goodwill and improve understanding from stakeholders, including political decision-makers, who remain unconvinced about the benefits of ICT. ICT strategies should be explicitly designed to make a contribution to day-to-day realities, which for example in the Caribbean include, trade diversification, poverty alleviation, human resource development, heath sector management, disaster preparedness and environmental management.

Finally, developing countries should become more effectively engaged in global ICT policy debates, moving from being 'idea-takers' to contributors. The global ICT policy community includes the ITU, ICANN, WIPO, WTO, UNCTAD, and a range of standards-setting bodies. Many of these organisations are responding to critiques regarding the extent which they have been partners in development and this provides an opportunity.

Caribbean development and ICT

"...the Caribbean" is a socio-historical category, commonly referring to a cultural zone characterised by the legacy of slavery and the plantation system. It embraces the islands and parts of the adjoining mainland—and may be extended to include the Caribbean diaspora overseas. Girvan (2001)

It is difficult to establish a single definition of the Caribbean, since categorisation can be made on the basis of language and identity, geography, history and culture, geopolitics, geoeconomics, or organisation. The islands of the Caribbean are extremely fragmented and heterogeneous, with variations in income, political institutions, language, culture and economic structure. In the rest of this essay, the focus will be on the insular Caribbean (hereinafter the Caribbean) and within that the CARICOM countries primarily because this region is often overlooked in public policy research and analysis on the impact of technologies. The Caribbean consists of small economies that have a relatively decent standard of living, with most countries except Haiti being in the middle to high category of human development. However, the region faces threats in terms of its ability to stimulate growth, reduce poverty and stem the tide of growing inequality across and within countries in the region. Basic data for the Caribbean region can be found in the 2005 UNDP Human Development Report.

Mining in Trinidad and Tobago's petrochemical based economy, tourism and the construction sectors are the main drivers, with economic growth averaging 3.5% in 2004. The threats to the Caribbean include pressures on the agriculture sector as a result of the deterioration of the terms of trade for traditional export products, the negative impacts of natural disasters and low productivity conditions. Manufacturing has continued to stagnate in most cases reflecting long standing structural problems characterized by high costs, low productivity, and inadequate technological levels (UNECLAC 2005).

There is considerable variation and unevenness among the various countries, and the majority of the Caribbean's poor with the exception of Barbados, live in the rural areas. While most countries have managed to make progress on eradication of poverty and extreme hunger, there are still significant pockets of poverty in several countries, notably, Guyana, Haiti and Jamaica. In some countries there are also significant disparities in the distribution of wealth.

In terms of enrolment at primary school level, the Caribbean was doing better than many other middle-income developing countries. There was parity in female rates of enrolment at secondary school and tertiary levels. Caribbean women had high rates of labour force participation in agriculture, but not in any other sectors of the economy and continued to be under-represented in politics and public decision making positions.

The Caribbean has made progress in meeting goals to reduce child and maternal mortality rates, but faces a major challenge with respect to the HIV/AIDS pandemic. The Caribbean (including Cuba and the Dominican Republic) is seriously affected by HIV/AIDS with an overall prevalence rate of between 1.4 and 4.1 percent (at the end of 2003) and between 410,000 and 720,000 adults and more than 20,000 children throughout the region living with the disease (Benn 2004).

Caribbean countries face many challenges in terms of environmental sustainability, including deforestation, watershed degradation, waste disposal and energy conservation with specific problems such as response to climate change and the protection of coral being priorities for the countries of the region. The region has a high level of vulnerability to natural disasters including hurricanes and earthquakes. The economic effects of these disasters are significant – and negative effects are lagged and can be a drain on economic growth and dynamism for many years after the actual event.

Over the last decade, the Caribbean has faced threats of increasing marginalization as heightened tensions and a changed geopolitical climate turn strategic interest and resources away from this part of the world. Benn (2004) estimated that the region would require between US$50-$100 billion in overseas development assistance (ODA) to support implementation of the MDGs. In 2002, total ODA stood at $50.2 billion, which was the lowest quantum recorded in recent years and illustrative of the significant decrease in ODA between 1995 and 2002 as some traditional donors sought to meet new obligations in other parts of the world. In addition to the decline in absolute terms, there is evidence that there is room for significant improvement in the co-ordination of international donor activities in the region (OECS 2002).

The Caribbean's history and structural features has meant that the region has had a long experience of the good, the bad and the ugly effects of globalisation. In the most recent period, this has meant that the the region grapples with a range of thorny problems associated with ensuring that the net effect of increased mobility of capital, goods and information produces benefits for the region. (OECS 2002, UN-ECLAC 2005)

To summarise, the Caribbean region is poised at an important watershed in its history. Vulnerability, differentiation and fragmentation continue to be major issues, while an attractive climate, abundant natural resources, creativity and a young vibrant population provide hope for the future. Globalisation pressures arising out of shifts in the world economy and other developments have led to serious difficulties and has increased uncertainty. Some mini-states and dependent territories have been able to secure relatively high incomes by specialising in tourism and financial services. Poverty and growing inequality are major problems in the larger countries and in several of the smaller societies, notwithstanding their higher per capita incomes. Even those relatively prosperous societies are highly vulnerable to events not of their own making and to forces outside of their control such as natural disasters and trade liberalisation by Europe. Caribbean people continue to move in search of survival and a better life, as they always have and continue to experience the world as global citizens, providing opportunities for wealth creation and improvement in the quality of life. It is in this complicated terrain that ICT interventions seek to make an impact.

Unlike many other developing countries, for the Caribbean the 1990s were a period of relative stagnation as far as ICT and development effort is concerned. In a comprehensive review of Caribbean ICT policy, Stern (2004) suggests that pressure for reform came about as a result of a World Bank (Schware and Hume 1996), which identified one of the main obstacles to developing an information-based industry in the Caribbean as being the high prices that users have to pay for international calling, Internet use, and leased lines. He further suggests that the momentum for reform was assisted by the WTO negotiations and European liberalisation. In the late 1990s, the Organization of Eastern Caribbean States (OECS) and the Dominican Republic began the process of reform and sought financial support from the World Bank. Others including Trinidad & Tobago, Haiti, Barbados, Jamaica, and Guyana received support from other funding institutions including the IADB, ITU, the Canadian International Development Agency (CIDA) and US Aid. With the assistance of these international partners, over the last ten years, the process of sector reform has advanced in the whole region, with the mobile segment being the most liberalised. Nearly all countries have put new legal and regulatory structures into place and have established independent regulators. A few have yet to complete the process. Tellingly, Stern (2004) concludes that ..." in spite of this the benefits of reform still elude most Caribbean (citizens) who continue to pay high prices in most countries and territories and for whom the availability of good affordable telecommunications services continues to be a barrier to the development and growth of the ICT sector."

Although privatisation and deregulation took place slowly and efforts to increased competition and liberalise markets were thwarted by the incumbent, Cable and Wireless; in 2005 there are several competitors in the region including Digicel and AT&T. For example, of the progress made in sector reform, in 1999, according to Golding and George (2003) "Jamaica had about 20 Internet Service providers (ISPs), of which five had direct international connectivity and the rest used the Cable and Wireless (C&W) international gateway. Since 1999 the Government of Jamaica has approved 146 telecommunications licensees, including 49 ISPs in early 2003. Further expansion is expected with the granting of 32 licenced Internet voice service providers, 20 data service providers, 13 domestic voice service providers, 11 domestic carriers and 6 Internet service providers for subscriber television operators". The Jamaican state has generated significant proceeds from this licensing bonanza.

However, the region still relies heavily on bilateral and multilateral financing strategies, using a combination of overseas development assistance credits and loans rather than capital market financing strategies to fund ICT investment. Thomas, M. (2005) provides an interesting analysis of how Jamaica's effort to creatively finance universal service roll-out and particularly to invest in national e-learning projects has been halted as a result of the power wielded by US investors. At the urging of firms such as AT&T, the US Federal Communications Commission has launched an investigation into Jamaica's proposed universal service fund, which would have imposed a universal service levy on local carriers of international voice traffic of (US$ 0.02 -mobile and US$ 0.03 – fixed).

In terms of basic connectivity, access to fixed line and mobile phones, the middle and high human development countries in the Caribbean compare well with other developing country nations where ICT strategy has been a focus of policy such as Estonia, Malta and Mauritius. However, in terms of Internet connectivity, the region trails behind, with the exception of Barbados.

According to Stern (2004) the average fixed telephone penetration for the 23 countries and territories in the Caribbean for which the ITU keeps statistics is about 16% compared with nearly 70% in North America. Between 1991 and 2001, the penetration rate for fixed telephone was just above 10%, and has grown only at 4.2% per annum. Mobile penetration has grown much more rapidly, rising from a negligible 0.2% in 1991 to over 16% at the end of 2003 (CAGR = 56.3 %).

Barbados, the Dominican Republic, Trinidad and Tobago and Jamaica are considered to be doing comparatively well according to international rating schemes such as the e-readiness index. These countries appeared in the top 75 countries in terms of educational levels and the extent to which ICTs are incorporated into the learning systems; extent and quality of network infrastructure and the level of competition in telecommunications.

The Caribbean region has been preoccupied, often at the imposition and insistence of international partners, with market liberalisation as an end in itself. These policies have produced some benefits – such as increases in teledensity levels, price reductions, increased economic activity, proliferation of suppliers and increased customer choice. However, recent analysis has shown that there has been a high opportunity cost associated with this preoccupation and ICT policy efforts have had minimal impact on overall development (see for example, Thomas, C. 2005, Thomas, M. 2005, and Baksh, 2005). All of these authors point to the inherent risks involved in pinning hopes on strategies that are heavily dependent on multinationals, noting that the Caribbean regrettably has centuries of experience with investors that are 'fleet of foot' and demonstrate little evidence of making a sustained contribution to long-term development.

Thomas, C (2005) shows that in the case of Trinidad and Tobago's ICT policy, the costs of reform were underestimated while the benefits were overstated. He includes the cost of establishment and operations of regulatory bodies, and the import costs for ICT related hardware and software equipment and net effect on employment as costs that were not taken into account in Trinidad and Tobago's ICT policy design. Thomas, M (2005) in her evaluation of Jamaica's reform experience identifies dividend transfers to foreign investors as a potential loss of foreign reserves. She recommends that Caribbean countries in their negotiations with development partners focus on improving access, securing favourable terms and conditions, and improving harmonisation of lending policies across institutions. She argues that there should be a demand led approach to lending that channels financing to priority areas of need, as defined by the countries themselves. Baksh (2005) using a case study of Trinidad and Tobago, illustrates many design flaws in current ICT planning practice and suggests that in that country, Canadian led development of ICT policies failed to take sufficient account of structural rigidities, such as low rates of entrepreneurship, high import propensity, and the cyclical nature of government revenues in a petrochemical economy. Both Baksh and Thomas, C (2005) were critical of the process by which e-education policies in Trinidad and Tobago were developed, arguing that the information base on which plans were designed was woefully inadequate – and more importantly that the planned ICT investment was not integrated into clear education policies with well defined expected outcomes. Since the government intends to fund its planned computerisation of schools through loan financing, there were also concerns about sustainability.

Many of these policy reports on ICT and development in the Caribbean, authored by consultants or staff of the region's development partners, do not adopt a critical approach to assessing ICT and development but proceed from a deterministic set of assumptions[2]. The recommendations are often formulaic and appear to be based on models which assume that investments in ICT infrastructure and ICT sector expansion automatically lead to development benefits. These analyses commonly do not specify factors that influence causality or delineate specific transmission vectors through which expected benefits would be realised[3]. As a result of this limited foundation, the recommendations suggest that the Caribbean should invest in telecommunications infrastructure, computerisation, development of informatics as an economic sector, and in specific activities such as e-business facilitation – but do not provide a context that integrates these interventions. These studies often did not take small size into account as a limiting constraint of any ICT-sector expansion efforts. In addition, these externally funded studies, while concerned with development problems, did not include methods that permitted evaluation or measurement of impact of ICT on any specific areas of concern. For the most part, and this is an increasing trend, the studies applied indicators designed elsewhere to the Caribbean and then produced rankings of various countries in the region.

Over the last decade there has been insufficient development of local policy analysis capability. The policy undertaken as part of donor-funded ICT and development programming missions are typically conducted by overseas experts, working with Caribbean researchers and officials as junior partners in study teams. The ICT studies for the most part, made little effort to draw on Caribbean intellectual theorising and/or analysis of development, and appear to have made recommendations in a conceptual vacuum[4]. There has also been considerable overlap and duplication in the terms of reference for these studies and little effort to build on the lessons learned over time or to draw on analysis from previous work, particularly because of limited co-ordination among donors. There has also been a conceptual bias in so far as most of the studies have focused on the effects of market liberalisation and efforts to develop the ICT sector itself rather than on the role of ICT as an enabler. This has meant that the ICT studies and associated projects often have not won political sponsorship from national governments and as a result implementation has been spotty and inconsistent. The funding cycles for ICT programming have also been inconsistent and uneven across the region.

The heavy reliance on external 'expertise' has meant that there is often a disconnect between the judicious analysis of policy choices and implementation. Despite the number of studies completed, there is only a very tenuous link between the analysis and recommendations contained in these studies and the design and execution of actual national or regional ICT programmes. International donor operations in the Caribbean also continue to be plagued by problems of lack of co-ordination, duplication and fragmentation. An IADB study of Jamaica identified thirty-nine initiatives: seven classified under agriculture, eighteen under education, four under governance and ten under livelihood/business opportunities. There was ample evidence of poor coordination among donors and across projects, with little evidence of improvement in design or achievements over time.

Caribbean experience also shows that there is an urgent need to strengthen the analytical foundations of ICT and development strategy. Insufficient time, effort and attention have been invested in interrogating the conditions under which the intended benefits of competitive markets, such as increased supply, lowered costs, increased quality and expanded range of services can be realised. Studies are needed to investigate the conditions under which application of ICT improves efficiency in delivery of social services, and improves the quality of outcomes in social sectors such as education, health and environmental management. More analysis and evidence are needed to explain how ICTs can improve citizen participation and empowerment and facilitate distribution of new goods and services. The Caribbean has a dynamic competitive advantage in areas such as culture and leisure industries and faces a loss of its traditional markets in bananas, sugar and poultry, yet few ICT policy studies have focused on these areas as a priority. There needs to be a basis to establish credible explanations as to how and why ICT may be able to assist with poverty reduction through evidence-based analysis[5].

In summary, as the evidence shows, Caribbean ICT policy and programming have had only relatively limited success in delivering a developmental impact. The mistakes experienced in the Caribbean provide lessons for other developing countries. On the basis of the Caribbean experience, developing countries should avoid undue external influence and institutional sponsorship of policy analysis; reduce preoccupation with changing monopoly market structure; improve articulation with broader development challenges and structural realities and carry out research and analysis to guide policy.

The next section presents recommendations for a new approach that is based on a regional ICT strategy developed for CARICOM (Marcelle 2004).

A Caribbean Agenda for Action

In 2004 CARICOM commissioned the development of regional ICT strategy which made recommendations on how the region could accelerate the alignment of its ICT efforts with broader development goals and create momentum. In October 2004, the Ministers of ICT in the Caribbean Community (CARICOM) considered and recommended the adoption of a pro-development regional ICT strategy (Marcelle 2004).

This author recommended that the Caribbean region use the opportunity of a radical departure in ICT policy and implementation to craft a living experiment that could produce insights that are relevant for broader and deeper development questions. The 2004 CARICOM ICT regional strategy included elements of philosophy and models of organisational architecture that could help the Caribbean deal with age old questions and challenges. It recognised that the region faced many challenges in engaging with the world in a manner that is beneficial and mutually rewarding rather than exploitative. The strategy argued that because technological artifacts and knowledge that constitute ICT are not created in the Caribbean, the region needed to acquire specific capabilities in order to benefit from technologies produced in geographically and psychologically distant contexts. Finally, the proposed regional ICT strategy asserted that it was necessary to explicitly underpin a strategy with Caribbean sensibilities, aesthetics and personality. Without this feature, the region would continue to be a perennial consumer but not an active contributor and producer of thought, ideas, technologies, goods, services and ways of being.

The regional strategy recommends that the Caribbean create new institutions and strengthen existing knowledge-creating institutions in order to build the capacity to articulate its own vision for Caribbean Information Society. It further argued that this vision be informed by a critical intellectual tradition, rigorous research, regular data-collection and careful analysis. The proposed strategy also recommended the increased involvement of civil society, particularly regional academic institutions, in the articulation and implementation.

The basis for the recommendations included in the proposed regional strategy was an analysis that concluded that the Caribbean has not achieved much success in developing ICT policies that articulate well with local conditions, challenges and culture (Marcelle 2004). The proposed strategy found that in the past there have been serious problems with implementation, and limited success in building institutional capacity. It also showed that in the Caribbean, there has been an over reliance on externally shaped and financed ICT programmes which are not well integrated into an overall development strategy.

A central feature of the proposed strategy was the suggestion that the region implement a number of ICT flagship programmes. It was argued that these programmes would serve multiple purposes; they could be used as a platform to promote awareness of the benefits of ICT, to develop ICT research and training capability, to provide links between knowledge and production networks, to develop the Caribbean human resource base, to involve civil society, to demonstrate benefits of active public sector leadership, to encourage private sector participation and to stimulate and promote innovation. It was also noted that flagship programmes take ICT policy to the people and form the basis of a process of capturing the imagination, hearts and minds of people who would otherwise be uninterested and uninvolved. In the political culture of the Caribbean, it was felt that without this step to build a constituency, it was unlikely that ICT projects would be given adequate budget appropriations or legitimacy and as a result implementation would continue to be sluggish. The flagship programmes were in areas that respond to urgent needs, and have the potential to deliver sizeable and visible multiplier effects, both in economic and social terms.

These large-scale living experiments provide an opportunity to engage technology and service providers and to encourage them to look beyond short term profit maximising. By partnering with Caribbean governments in the execution of flagship projects, the private sector can undertake investment in learning and capability development and improve their ability to innovate in rural applications. Firms operating in the region will also be provided with opportunities to investigate and implement technology adaptation and to develop applications that meet the specific needs of Caribbean consumers, including the urban poor and rural communities. Even from the limited perspective of growing a future market, these investments would be prudent. For example, the Caribbean has a unique opportunity to use the hosting of a global mega-event, the ICC Cricket World Cup, as a giant canvas on which to paint a model of how small countries can benefit from technology.

By becoming involved in the design and implementation of flagship programmes, Caribbean civil society, including research and academic institutions, professional bodies, NGOs, trade unions etc. would have a means to provide their collective experience and creativity. Flagship programmes also provide a means for encouraging Caribbean governments to engage in consultative and participatory policy design. The 2004 regional ICT strategy noted that many governments still do not understand the positive contribution that the professional bodies such as library associations, national computer societies and professional engineering associations, can make and prefer to rely on external consultants. By fostering communication between governments and indigenous civil society, these flagship programmes provide a useful vehicle for civic engagement that further public interest objectives.

In line with the recommendations of the proposed regional ICT strategy, Caribbean ICT Ministers agreed to implement ICT projects in the following areas (CARICOM 2004):

- Disaster preparedness and environmental awareness;
- Facilitating regional integration by support for the Caribbean Single Market and Economy (CSME) programme;
- Cultural entrepreneurship skills development;
- Participatory e-governance at community level;
- Wireless access connectivity;
- The ICC Cricket World Cup 2007.

The recommended strategy also included specific recommendations for institutional strengthening including proposals for radical change of the institutional arrangements through which the Caribbean carries out its ICT for development programming, including the assignment of specific Ministerial portfolios for ICT and development, establishment of an executing agency, strengthening of existing institutions including the specialised training and education programmes of the University of the West Indies and improving coordination with international partners. It was further recommended that the region implement a broad-based digital literacy public education programme to engage Caribbean people and win the political commitment of senior decision-makers. The background paper to Ministers that laid out the basis for the regional strategy concluded that these efforts together with the results of the flagship programmes could demonstrate the beneficial impact of ICT on Caribbean development and simultaneously improve the region's capacity to be innovative producers of ICT (Marcelle 2004).

The proposed regional ICT strategy defined leadership as a process by which visions, dreams and aspirations are transformed into manifest realities. Based on an evaluation of past experience, and the characteristics of technology intervention, the proposed strategy identified gaps in the existing leadership styles and recommended improvements. The report (Marcelle 2004) recommended that leaders adopt a transformative leadership style that is non-authoritarian, and is based on solidarity and service. It further argued that leaders who empowered others, served as champions and at a personal level, expressed integrity, commitment and personal responsibility are likely to be more effective because their efforts would be sustained over time and not held hostage to political patronage or intellectual fashions. This author suggested that the ability to collaborate in multi-stakeholder networks and to foster collective engagement is a critical requirement, particularly because ICT strategies require the energy, talent and creativity of a wide variety of groups. In delivering ICT and development programmes, leaders direct tasks of analysis, reflection and problem solving as well as manage implementation. These processes draw on mental, emotional and spiritual faculties and require patience, sustained disciplined effort and resilience. By displaying these characteristics, the leaders of ICT and development programmes can serve as a source of inspiration and confidence building, which encourages Caribbean people to value themselves and psychologically empowers them, thereby increasing their ability to develop novel, inventive and reflective solutions.

Concluding remarks

Using evidence from the Caribbean, this essay has shown that ICT policy in developing countries ought to be directed away from a preoccupation with usage and connectivity statistics towards improving ownership of policy and measurement of impacts and outcomes. The acid test for ICT policy practitioners and scholars is the demonstration that deployment of ICT actually can contribute to building human capacity, income and wealth creation, enjoyment of health and well being, and self expression for the world's majority.

At the time of writing, few of the institutional strengthening mechanisms recommended in 2004 have been put in place, including those relating to improving the decision-making processes within CARICOM and the urgent need to identify and give legitimacy to national champions. There is still no effective executing agency taking the lead on assessment of regulatory and policy alternatives, strategy design, planning, project execution, monitoring and evaluation and there has been no progress on the flagship programmes.

The Caribbean is on the radar screen of the ICT for development community, but unfortunately, there has been little co-ordination of efforts. International partners are yet to improve their funding allocation methods so that they avoid duplication and make interventions that produce synergistic effects across the region.

There has been limited progress in building a strong intellectual foundation that informs the design of ICT programmes in the Caribbean. Much greater intensification of effort is needed to build research and analysis institutions that focus on ICT and development. There has been a significant milestone in the development of regional policy analysis capability in the Caribbean. In December 2003 the University of the West Indies (St Augustine, Trinidad and Tobago) launched an ambitious training programme, the Masters in Telecommunications Regulation and Policy (MRP), which provides specialised courses in telecommunications policy and regulation targeted to executives and senior professionals. The MRP cohort of trainees and faculty have the potential to constitute the core of a regional research and analysis community that is needed to support efforts to develop an ICT strategy that is responsive to Caribbean realities. At secondary and post-secondary level there are many curriculum design initiatives that encourage and expand training opportunities in ICT related disciplines. In addition to formal educational programmes, there are popularisation programmes that aim to increase familiarisation and ease with ICT.

Countries around the world vary in their abilities to benefit from changes in the global economic system. Those nations that have taken action to widen the base of involvement in the ICT revolution have transformed the nature of that revolution. Developing countries need to own their ICT and policies and strategies and execute them with the support of international partners. This requires marshalling intellectual and financial capital. Without an acceleration of effort, transformed leadership and creativity, the ICT and development agenda is unlikely to meet the legitimate expectations of the majority of the world's people. The Caribbean region offers lessons as the international community moves towards crafting an ICT for development agenda for action.

It is these very vexed problems, in a relatively well-off part of the developing world, that should challenge the ICT community. If transformation of the ICT and development paradigm cannot succeed in the Caribbean then the likelihood of having an impact in countries with much more severe levels of poverty, larger populations and land-mass is even more remote. On a positive note, the Caribbean also presents a number of opportunities for applying ICT to development at a manageable scale where effects and impacts are discernable and likely to be immediate.

References

1. Impact evaluation methodologies, such as those suggested by Ravallion 2001 and Rouse et. al 2004, ought to be included in the design of ICT for Development programmes.

2. See Marcelle (2004) for a fuller discussion and references to studies by World Bank, IDB, CIDA, USAID and associated consultants.

2. A selection of critical and cutting-edge analysis that appears not to have been considered in the recommendations for the Caribbean include: DFID (2002), *The significance of ICTs for reducing poverty*; Mansell (2002) *From Digital Divides to Digital Entitlements in Knowledge Societies*, Special issue on: *The Social World in the 21st Century: Ambivalent Legacies and Rising Challenges*, Current Sociology, 2002, Vol. 50, No. 3, pp. 407-426.; IDRC (2003) *Beyond Connectivity*; UNDP (2002) *National and Regional ICT for development strategies*, paper presented to Second Meeting of the United Nations ICT Task Force.

3. In this respect, the work differs markedly from seminal studies on Caribbean science and technology policy which proceeded explicitly from a contextual basis, taking economic, historical and structural realities into account.

4. Tongia et al (2005) provide an excellent example of conceptual analysis and empirical studies of ICT applied to social and economic sectors, drawn mainly from Asian examples. Microeconomics evaluation techniques which draw on epidemiology and other experimental sciences are being used with success in the design of investment projects in the transport, health and rural livelihoods sector. The ICT for development research community should explore collaboration across these fields. There is some evidence that the ICT community is recognizing the need to strengthen and expand its analytical tools, with Gillholly and the UN ICT Task Force calling for evidence of impact.

*   Baksh, S. 2005. RP68G Final Assignment. Trinidad and Tobago: Masters in Regulation and Policy MRP (Telecommunications) Programme, Department of Electrical and Computer Engineering, Faculty of Engineering, University of the West Indies (unpublished).

*   Benn, Denis (2004) *The Millennium Development Goals in the Caribbean: A Situational Analysis*, research report prepared for presentation at the UNDP/CDB workshop, 'Achieving the Millennium Development Goals in the Caribbean' Port-of-Spain, Trinidad and Tobago 21-23 September, 2004.

*   DFID. 2002. *The Significance of Information and Communication Technologies for Reducing Poverty*. London: DFID. www.dfid.gov.uk/pubs/files/ictpoverty.pdf.

*   Gilhooly, D. (undated) *Innovation and Investment: Information and Communication Technologies and the Millennium Development Goals*, Report Prepared for the United Nations ICT Task Force in Support of the Science, Technology & Innovation Task Force of the United Nations Millennium Project., unpublished and undated.

*   Girvan, N. (2001) *Reinterpeting the Caribbean*, in Folke Lindahl and Brian Meeks, eds., New Caribbean Thought, UWI Press, 2001.

*   Golding, Paul A, Waller, George 2003. *Landscape Assessment on ICT-Enabled Development Initiatives and Stakeholders in Jamaica*, IADB, http://www.IADB.org

*   Mansell, R. 2002. *From Digital Divides to Digital Entitlements in Knowledge Societies*, Special issue on: The Social World in the 21st Century: Ambivalent Legacies and Rising Challenges, Current Sociology, Vol. 50, No. 3, pp. 407-426.

*   Marcelle, G. 2004a. *Mobilising ICTs for Caribbean development, a 21st century imperative.* Background report prepared for the Caribbean Community (CARICOM) presented to the ICT Ministerial Meeting, October 12-15, Barbados.

*   OECS (2002) OECS Human Development Report, *Building Competitiveness in the Face of Vulnerability.*

*   Schware, Robert, Susan Hume, *Prospects for Information Service Exports from the English-Speaking Caribbean*, The World Bank, Latin America and Caribbean Region, March 1996.

*   Spence R. 2003. *Information and Communications Technologies (ICTs) for Poverty Reduction: When, Where and How?* Background Paper: Discussion, Research, Collaboration July 15, 2003. Ottawa, Canada: International Development Research Centre web.idrc.ca/uploads/user-S/10740245751106184692 03RS_ICT-Pov_18_July.pdf.

*   Stern, P. 2004. *Action Plan Promoting Investment in Information and Communication Technologies in the Caribbean*, report prepared for the Inter-American Development Bank.

*   Thomas, C. 2005. RP68G Final Assignment. Trinidad and Tobago: Masters in Regulation and Policy (Telecommunications) Programme, Department of Electrical and Computer Engineering, Faculty of Engineering, University of the West Indies (unpublished).

*   Tongia, R. Subrahmanian, E. and Arunachalam, V.S. (2005) *Information and Communications Technology for Sustainable Development: Defining a Global Research Agenda.* Allied Publishers, Bangalore. www.cs.cmu.edu/~rtongia/ict4sd_book.htm.

- UNDP (2005) Human Development Report.

- UNDP. 2003. *National and Regional e-development Strategies, a Blueprint for Action*, Chapter 3 in Haqqani, A. (ed) UN ICT Task Force (2003b), The role of Information and Communication Technologies in global Development, Analyses and Policy Recommendations, a UN ICT Task Force Series 3. pp. 27-70. www.unicttaskforce.org/perl/documents.pl?id=1360.

- UN-ECLAC (2005). Preliminary overview of Caribbean economies 2004-2005, Technical report LC/CAR/L.28 17 January 2005, Port of Spain: United Nations Economic Commission for Latin America, Sub-regional Office for the Caribbean. www.eclac-pos.org/.

- UNICT Task Force (undated) The Millennium Development Goals & Information and Communications Technology (ICT), report prepared by the United Nations ICT Task Force Working Party on ICT Indicators and MDG Mapping. www.unicttaskforce.org.

Dr. Gillian Marcelle is Principal Consultant at Technology for Development (TfDev). An international development specialist with over 15 years experience, she is a citizen of Trinidad and Tobago who currently lives in Southern Africa after spending many years in Europe and the United States.

Recent projects include serving as Special Adviser to the Vice Minister of Science and Technology in the Republic of Angola, Hon. Prof. Pedro Teta, and advising the Caribbean Community (CARICOM). In these roles Dr Marcelle provides strategic advice, policy research, international relations and resource mobilisation services on matters relating to ICT and development. She has been involved in designing creative programmes that seek to accelerate computer literacy in Angola, which is one of the government's top priorities as it seeks to achieve social integration and rehabilitation of former freedom fighters and displaced people.

These assignments build on her expertise and experience in telecommunications and information and communications technology (ICT) policy. She has worked as a full-time academic, and currently holds a position as a Visiting Research Fellow at SPRU, University of Sussex (UK); as a telecoms regulator, with Oftel in the UK; in the private sector with BT and JP Morgan Chase; and as a consultant to NGOs, private sector companies, national governments and international organisations including UN-DESA, UNCTAD, UNDP, UNIFEM, UN-ECA, ITU and UNU-INTECH. She began her career with CANTO, a regional industry association for telecommunication operators in the Caribbean in 1988. Dr Marcelle holds a number of public service appointments: she currently serves on the Board of the UN ICT Task Force, and was previously a member of the High Level Panel, which advised the UN on ICT & Development issues. She has been active in gender equality issues serving in Board level capacity on a number of civil society bodies including the WSIS Gender Caucus and the ITU Working Group on Gender Issues.

Her new book *Technological Learning: A Strategic Imperative for Firms in Developing Countries* was published by Edward Elgar in December 2004. She also serves on the editorial board of the University of Witwatersrand journal, Southern African Journal of Information and Communication and recently completed development of a Masters level course on Telecommunication Sector Planning for University of the West Indies.

Contact details: Dr. Gillian M. Marcelle, PO Box 2032, Parklands 2121, Gauteng, South Africa. Tel/Fax: +27 11 447 7538 Email: gmarcelle@worldonline.co.za.

Astrid Dufborg

Ambassador and ICT Adviser, Government of Sweden, UN Mission Geneva

9.

The missing links in ICTs for global education and community development

Astrid Dufborg

Ambassador and ICT Adviser, Government of Sweden, UN Mission Geneva

The power of harnessing ICTs for development and the improvement of people's lives is clear and its need is urgent. In education it is particularly clear that ICTs, applied inclusively and imaginatively can act as a catalyst to repair failing education systems in the developing world – and to help unlock the creative potential of entire societies. In recent years thousands of diverse, small and medium scale projects and pilot projects – aimed exactly at this harnessing of ICTs for social good – have been implemented and are leaving their mark worldwide. Although their individual results may be small in face of the magnitude of the global education crisis, the difference they are making to individual classrooms and communities is at times astonishing.

Overall, these pilots show that ICTs *are* improving education. Implicitly they also show that up-scaled end-to-end strategies could ensure such improvements are made even more immense and wide-reaching in effect. In this context, in 2003 the UN ICT Task Force, inspired by the NEPAD initiative on e-schools and promoted by Sweden, Ireland, Switzerland and Canada, established the concept of the Global eSchools & Communities Initiative. Taking up the challenge of the Millennium Development Goals, GeSCI's purpose is to support stakeholders in the development of comprehensive strategies for whole-system deployment of ICTs in education. Now an independent NGO with a secretariat in Dublin, GeSCI believes that the missing links can be made visible and joined-up in the ICTs for development chain, by convening comprehensive multistakeholder partnerships at local, regional and national level – anywhere there is a demand – and creating end-to-end, holistic strategies and implementing them in a sustainable, collective manner.

The imperative is to respond to the needs of real people – and real gaps in educational strategies and community development. So we try to bring all stakeholders to the table in a collaborative way, and to complement and coordinate existing efforts already underway. We aim to understand the context and then clearly articulate where we can add value. Typically our value is inherent in our ability to bring stakeholders to the table, build and implement a plan and to mobilise resources to do so.

We are currently working to a varying degree with such stakeholders in Namibia, India, Ghana and Bolivia. All four countries have in common a proven readiness to take on ICT in education strategies in a comprehensive and national way and believe in the importance of ICTs and the potential for greater impact.

Having held wide-scale consultations and surveyed the spectrum in our four partner countries, we co-hosted a Global Forum in Dublin in April 2004 with the UN Task Force to share our findings and plan the next steps. The forum brought together representatives of industry, implementing NGOs, ICT and education specialists from all around the world to discuss the most important challenges in education and ICTs. It was concluded that to get to the core of the challenges, comprehensive strategies in programme countries would have to take the following priority issues into realistic account:

- It is teachers who shape the future through their work. They are multipliers, authority figures and agents of socio-economic change that must be empowered. Therefore, they should have all available tools at their disposal, including the full range of information and communication technologies – not just the Internet, but also standalone computers, radio, TV and telephones. However, in order to provide them with the skills they need to become facilitators of learning, to improve their own effectiveness and to ensure that the ICTs which are finding their ways into schools in the developing world are put to good use, teachers urgently require training in ICT. It was also recognised that educators who had been trained in ICT often abandon their teaching careers for jobs that pay better salaries – a form of teacher brain-drain.

- Many excellent ICT-for-education projects cannot be implemented on a large scale or in a sustainable manner due to a fundamental lack of support. Ways to overcome such challenges were suggested. One of them was to urge the private sector not only to be innovative in addressing hardware, software and connectivity issues, but also to invest in schools and to support teacher training programmes. Universities in the South were also encouraged to act as incubators and supporters of community centres to bring educational opportunities to adult learners.

- ICT needs to be integrated into all national education systems in order to realise the higher quantity and quality of education. But in order to succeed in this effort, it is imperative to have a strong institutional commitment and well-defined political will. The integration of ICT into education systems is of particular value to developing countries because it gives them an opportunity to leapfrog inherent limitations and to acquire new resources and formulate innovative strategies.

- New models of capacity development of teachers and administrators are key to the success and sustainability of education strategies and to a systematic approach in the use of ICT for education.
- It is important to create more knowledge of, and experience with, multistakeholder partnerships (MSPs) in ICT for Education efforts. MSPs have become a popular vehicle for addressing development challenges, and their use in the ICT for education efforts is relatively new.
- ICT for Education efforts should be targeted at all age levels. In particular there was a call to develop a research framework to engage young people further.
- There was also a call to further engage universities in both identifying models for sustainability for ICT4D projects, and to encourage universities in developing countries to participate in ICT4D activities.
- The results of the GeSCI experiment have a bearing on other initiatives aimed at addressing the Millennium Development Goals.

Invigorated by the success and support at the Forum, and with a new international team in place, the GeSCI teams have set to work in programme countries with increased energy and enthusiasm.

GeSCI has been working in **Namibia** and has established a national office to support the Namibian National ICT in Education Initiative. In addition to developing a national and regional educational strategy, GeSCI is creating impactful partnerships to build teacher capacity, knowledge share, scale up successful innovations, create hands on tools and mobilise resources. Most recently GeSCI has agreed targets for a national implementation plan with stakeholders from all sectors across the country.

In **India** GeSCI is working at federal, regional and local levels. We are advising the federal government on ICT in Education policy and working out tailored strategies with a number of different states. Our work is presently centred in Rajasthan, with further activities imminent in Madhya Pradesh, Karnataka, and Andhra Pradesh. For 2006, GeSCI has proposed the launch of an International Centre for Innovation in ICTs for Education to demonstrate Indian innovative solutions to a global audience.

The **Ghanaian** component of GeSCI's work is in the crucial early stages. GeSCI is carrying out research and planning activities aimed at facilitating sustainable solutions that work over the long-term. GeSCI is forging partnerships with government, private sector and local civil society to create a long-term, inclusive strategy for Ghana.

GeSCI is also in the early stages of consultation with relevant stakeholders in **Bolivia**. As an honest broker in the country, GeSCI is cultivating the growth of ICT in education environments.

To complement its national and regional work, GeSCI is developing a Total Cost of Ownership Assessment Tool, to enable practitioners and policy makers articulate their educational needs and to determine ICT solutions with their different costs and benefits.

GeSCI is also partnering in the Return on Investments in ICT in Education Study, which is a multi-year, multi-country research project to understand the long-term, quantifiable benefits a country can anticipate with investments in ICT in education. A preliminary phase of the study has just been completed.

GeSCI supported models are starting to have a large-scale impact on the ground. We have only begun, but working with our partners – in Namibia, in India, with the World Bank, UNESCO, and others – we can close up the gaps in the mission to harness ICTs for education and community development, with an increasing and equalising impact in many of the world's most under-resourced and information-deprived schools and communities.

(More information on any aspect of GeSCI's work and approach to ICTs in education and community development can be found at www.gesci.org.)

Astrid Dufborg is a Swedish national with an educational background in political science. After a short period of teaching, Ms Dufborg has spent 30 years working with the Swedish International Development Co-operation Agency (Sida) where her most recent postion was as Assistant Director General. She was posted in a number of African countries for 10 of those years.

Since 2002, Ms Dufborg has been an Ambassador and ICT Adviser at the Swedish UN Mission in Geneva, leading the Swedish work within WSIS. She has also been a member of the UNICT Task Force since 2001, within which she is convenor of the Working Group on 'Enabling Environment', and vice-chair of the Global e-schools initiative, GeSCI.

Contact details: Ambassador Astrid Dufborg, Permanent Mission of Sweden
Case Postale 190, CH-1211 Geneva 20, Switzerland.
Tel: +41 22 908 0800 Email: astrid.dufborg@foreign.ministry.se.

Shafika Isaacs

Executive Director, SchoolNet Africa

10.

Empowering women in the information society: towards a more concerted global and local effort

Shafika Isaacs

Executive Director, SchoolNet Africa

O ver the past decade, the potential of information and communication technologies (ICTs) to facilitate gender equality and women's empowerment has gained increasing recognition, albeit still uneven and limited. This is evidenced by *inter alia*, the references to gender inclusion in the Information Society in the *Plan of Action* and *Declaration of Principles* of the World Summit on the Information Society (WSIS) and more recently, the Economic and Social Council (ECOSOC) Report (2004) on progress achieved since the Fourth World Conference on Women in 1995, as well as numerous initiatives by gender equality advocates, practitioners and policy makers across the world.

However, the rapid growth, innovation and diffusion of ICTs which underlie the globalisation process together with its concomitant societal impact continues to hold the very real danger of extending and intensifying the social exclusion of women and girls all over the world, particularly in least developed economies. For as long as the majority of the women of the world are excluded, there cannot be a global information society. Therein lies the challenge.

The cumulative effect of all existing pioneering and path-breaking initiatives which specifically promote gender equality and women's empowerment in the information society, appears however to be of insignificant scale to make a resounding impact on the distribution of gender power relations in ICTs, globally. Unless more concerted action is taken at all levels, the information society will remain the predominant preserve of Anglophone urban, males residing in richer economies and corporations.

This article suggests that in turning the tide towards the empowerment of women, a systemic, societal approach to gender relations in general also needs to apply to an analysis on the digital divide and furthermore, strategies towards gender inclusion, gender equity and women's empowerment through ICTs need to assume the form of system-wide interventions that seek to transform the societal structures that perpetuate gender discrimination.

This requires an understanding of gender as a social construct and an allusion to the power relations between men and women as a function of the social, cultural, economic and political institutions and systems within society. It further requires a consensus among decision-makers, that ICTs are not gender neutral and that gendered power relations are inherent in the way in which the production, distribution and consumption of ICTs take place and perhaps moreover, how these are perpetuated and intensified through the rapid growth and diffusion of ICTs which underscores the globalisation process.

The digital divide has a female face

ICTs are defined in the UNDAW, ITU, UN ICT Task Force report (2003) as a complex and heterogeneous set of goods, applications and services used to produce, distribute, process and transform information. The ICT sector consists of segments ranging from telecommunications, broadcasting, computer hardware and software, computer services and electronic media including the content of the media. For most interventions related to ICTs for Development (ICT4D), there is agreement on a broad definition of ICTs that include both traditional technologies such as radio and print media to high-end new ICTs such as the email and Internet. Further on in the UNDAW report it also makes the point that ICTs are more than an 'instrument' but also a phenomenon. The ILO (2001) refers to ICTs as a *'meta technology'* characterised by their pervasive effects on economy and society as a whole, well beyond the ICT sector itself.

Globally, there are substantial differences between women and men as reflected in women's political participation and their representation in decision-making structures, gender disparities in economic opportunities, access to resources and division of labour. Marcelle, in a lucid analysis on transforming ICTs for gender equality, explains that the rapid diffusion of ICTs takes place through institutional settings where there are '*socially embedded gender relations*' and that a number of processes within the ICT sector contribute to a continued uneven distribution of power between men and women as well as to their unequal access to resources. These processes may be found with the rules, routines and practices of ICT firms, the markets for goods and services and the macro-economic environment in which the diffusion of ICTs take place. (2000:11)

She alludes to the generalised under-representation of women in decision-making positions within ICT firms as a function of their limited experience of science and technology training and to ICT markets as carriers of gender bias in terms of the under-representation of women as consumers of ICTs relative to their proportion of the world population. This has been corroborated by research done by Sanders (2005), Huyer (2004), Margolis (2001) which, although mainly confined to experiences in advanced economies of North America and Europe, suggest that the way in which women and girls are socialised from an early age, discourage their active and confident participation in a masculine sector like science and technology. Margolis (2001) state that in the US research departments of computer science, fewer than 20% of the graduates are female and fewer girls are enrolled in high school programming or advanced computer science classes. She argues that women have lost ground in the world of computing despite its historical coincidence with the rise of the women's movement.

Research conducted by Bisnath (2005), further confirms that women's opportunity for paid work in the services sector has increased over the past 25 years in many countries. However, they continue to be located in the lower and middle echelons of the service sector labour market, again reflecting an extension of their general position in society.

Whilst globalisation may have led to an expanded market for more developed economies and transnational corporations, it has also led to the feminisation of political disempowerment, inequality and poverty and greater gendered social polarisation. (Isaacs and TURP, 1997).

The emergence of *'information poverty'* or the digital divide has become a very real feature of globalisation. In view of the rapid speed of technological diffusion, the digital divide becomes apparent between those economies that are more prepared to manage these changes relative to those who do are not. (ILO, 2001). The digital divide is a broad allusion to the skewed distribution in access and use of ICTs as mechanisms for social and economic development between and within countries. The concept also incorporates *inter alia*, disparities in skill levels in the production and consumption of ICTs, literacy levels in the use of ICTs, varying constraints in enabling environments to promote ICT access and use and the disparities in digital local content particularly in countries with diverse multi-lingual communities. As Hewitt Alacantra correctly asserts (2001), the digital divide is a function of the existing development and socio-economic divide and within the digital divide itself there are further manifestations of social imbalances biased against people in non-Latin language groups, rural communities and girls and women (Hafkin and Taggert, 2001). Because the digital divide relates strongly to levels of educational attainment, perhaps the most gendered manifestation of the digital divide is within education where girls lag in educational attainment relative to boys the world over, particularly in Africa. (UNESCO, 2005). Together with the fact that ICTs like any other technologies are socially constructed and impact men and women differently, reference has been made to a *'gender divide'* within the digital divide which is reflected at various levels not only in the significantly lower numbers of women users of ICTs compared to men but also in the gender-specific structural inequalities, such as education, that constitute barriers to access. (UNDAW et al, 2003).

Integrating a gender equality perspective

Strategies to integrate a gender equality perspective have included the *'mainstreaming'* of gender issues. Gender mainstreaming refers to the conscious integration of gendered concerns from conception to execution of any planning, policy or programmatic process and stems from an understanding that unequal gender relations are often interwoven in the complex fabric of a generalised social inequality which become manifest in planning, policy and programmatic processes as well. Bisnath (2005), drawing on the definition of the ECOSOC in July 1997, states that gender mainstreaming is the process of assessing the implications for women and men of any planned action including legislation, policies and programmes in any area at all levels. It is a strategy for making the concerns of women and men an integral part of the design, implementation, monitoring and evaluation of policies and programmes in all political, economic and societal spheres so that women and men benefit equally and inequality is not perpetuated. The ultimate goal is the achievement of gender equality. Gender mainstreaming acknowledges that there are no gender neutral decisions (Green, 2003).

In addition to the conscious integration of gender issues, gender equality advocates have also promoted preferential action targeted specifically at women and girls in an attempt to promote equal opportunity.

From Beijing to Tunis: how far have we come?

The ILO report (2001) refers to the ICT revolution as a *'steerable revolution'*. Based on the brief expose above, it is evident that steering towards gender equality and women's empowerment through ICTs has to assume a systemic approach, accompanied by as Bisnath suggests, *'a [strong] political will and the availability of a supportive, enabling environment'* (2005:6). In addition strategies that consider both gender mainstreaming and interventions targeted specifically at women and girls have to be incorporated.

To date there has been a sustained attempt at promoting gender inclusion in programmes and initiatives related to bridging the digital divide within the official UN system and beyond. Advocacy for gender inclusion in ICT programmes first gained recognition at the Fourth World

Conference of Women in Beijing in 1995. The recommendations in its *Platform for Action* focused on increased access and participation of women to decision-making in order to overcome negative stereotypes of women in ICT and the media. Since then, a range of new issues have emerged that speak to the increasing ubiquity of ICTs in society and within this, the need for the integration of gendered considerations within an emerging information society.

In 2000 the ECOSOC adopted a Ministerial Communiqué on the role of information technology in the context of a knowledge based economy. In 2000 the Millenium Declaration underscored the urgency of ensuring the benefits of a new technologies especially ICTs, be available to all.

Due to the consistent efforts of various groups including the WSIS Gender Caucus, gender inclusion in the *Declaration of Principles* and *Plan of Action* commits specifically to:

> *"...ensuring the Information Society enables women's empowerment and their full participation on the basis of equality in all spheres of society and in all decision-making processes. To this end, we should mainstream a gender equality perspective and use ICTs as a tool"* *(WSIS Declaration of Principles, Paragraph 12).*

The WSIS official documents also make specific reference to the empowerment of women and girls in education through the use of ICTs and to the removal of gender barriers to ICT education and training. The WSIS *Plan of Action* encourages government to work with other stakeholders in formulating ICT policies that also promotes the participation of women and the development of gender specific indicators on ICT use and needs, and the identification of measurable performance indicators to assess the impact of funded ICT projects on the lives of women and girls. The latter is particularly important in the assessment of progress during the second phase of the WSIS to be held in Tunisia in November 2005. In addition, the WSIS official documents also identified the following issues:

- exploitation, violence against women and sexism on the Internet;
- security restricted to anti-terrorism, protection of information, etc;
- universal access should benefit women as well as men;
- more explicit recognition of the use of traditional communications technologies;
- references to women and/or gender equality in the suggested indicators/targets for 2015;
- specific references to women and decision-making in ICT policy, in additional to the references to "all stakeholders" (Hafkin, 2004).

Whilst many gender equality advocates concluded that the WSIS process and official outcomes represents a watered down version of the spectrum of issues that were raised for inclusion, it nevertheless represents an important reference point for future policy and planning processes. Hafkin (2004) states the significance eloquently:

> *"Without the imprimatur of the global Summit, [gender equality advocates] would have faced an uphill battle to secure a voice in the elaboration of ICT policy and the consideration of gender issues in projects." (2004:7)*

Drawing on this, the ECOSOC report presented at the Forty Ninth Session of the Commission on the Status of Women in March 2005, recognises within the context of an assessment of general progress on women's empowerment over 10 years, that ICTs can be a vital tool for training and empowering women and calls on member states to enhance access to women in ICT-based economic activities in all sectors. (ECOSOC, 2004).

In addition to the official declarations to date, there are numerous initiatives promoting gender equality world wide, at all levels. The UNDAW et al (2003) report reveals a wealth of examples of how, women of varying class, spatial, cultural and linguistic backgrounds, have been able to exploit their access to ICTs to their economic, social and political advantage because they have been supported by such an enabling environment.

Promoting economic empowerment

The UNDAW report shows how ICTs offer economic opportunities for women both in salaried employment and entrepreneurship and that the technologies offer flexibility in time and space which accommodate the interests of women in particular. It states for example, how the State of New York reportedly provides customised computer training tailored to job market opportunities for women living in urban and rural areas. In Malaysia, a group of government ministries provide loans and grants for women entrepreneurs in information technology in order to increase their participation in industry. In India, an inter-city marketing network for women micro-entrepreneurs was implemented by an organisation called the Foundation for Occupation Development (FOOD) in rural Tamilnadu (UNDAW et al, 2003).

Promoting empowerment through education

A number of complex factors influence the dire lack of access to education for women and girls, particularly in the developing world. These include socio-cultural factors, poverty, illiteracy and time. For instance the UNESCO (2005) report reveals that in 46 out of 133 countries, girls are less likely to enter secondary schools than boys. Green (2003) provides a comprehensive overview of interventions in the education sector in Asia and the Pacific that have proven to be very effective. These include examples of how traditional technologies, such as interactive radio instruction, have been applied to promote learning access in countries like Zambia and Papua New Guinea. She also shows that when ICTs incorporate local languages and strong visual imagery, they have the potential to reach women with low levels of functional literacy. Here the example of the Women's International Tribune Centre in Uganda, and their use of CD-roms for poor rural women farmers is a case in point. With reference to gender mainstreaming strategies, Green also refers to the way in which SchoolNet Africa promotes gender issues in its policies and programmes in ways that incentivise its network of African practitioners to take account of the differential effects of their work on girls and boys, women and men.

Engendering national policy

The creation of an enabling environment that promotes the active participation of women and girls in the information society, often refers to the potential of gender-inclusive ICT policies in opening up the floodgates of opportunity for women and girls. Most national policies are generally silent on gender issues and do not address gender equality goals. The UNDAW et al (2003) report provides examples of the very limited number of gender-inclusive ICT policies, stating Guinea (at the time) as the only African country with a national ICT policy that comprehensively includes gender issues. Similarly, the Ministry of Gender Equality in the Republic of Korea developed a basic women's informatisation plan that is targeted specifically at promoting ICT skill development for women. Hafkin (2002) provides a worthwhile table of important policy issues that can incorporate gendered concerns. More recently, a succinct overview of gender inclusion in national ICT policy conducted by Huyer (2005) confirms that where policies have been adopted in Africa, they are generally silent on gender issues; that in some cases references are made to gender equality and women in particular, in the formulation of policy but that in general, policy implementation falls short of the delivery of gender equality and women's empowerment programmes.

Promoting women's participation in governance

There are many examples of how ICTs particularly enable women to participate actively in the effective implementation of service delivery at local community level. One case in point is that of the Women Mayors' Link project based in Romania, which won the Outstanding Multi-Stakeholder Initiative Award presented by the Global Knowledge Partnerships Gender Awards at the WSIS 2003, in Geneva. This project began in 2002, and uses electronic communication to foster co-operation between women mayors and local governments and local women's networks by preparing small projects to improve the quality of life of women and children in local communities. (Hafkin 2004: 6).

Promoting secure online spaces for women

ICTs have also provided secure spaces for women to network and build empowering communities of practice. The Internet allows for the creation of private online spaces, particularly for women, that protect them from harassment and that enable them to enjoy freedom of expression and privacy of communication. The Women's Caucus Gender Justice – an international group with an international board – has been lobbying for the nomination of judges to serve on the international criminal court. (UNDAW et al, 2003).

Grassroots initiatives

Many of the examples of the use of ICTs as mechanisms for the advancement of women are those promoted by various organisations and groups active in the ICT for Development sector. However, often these do not reflect the myriad of spontaneous grassroots initiatives that are spearheaded by women where they appropriate the technologies to advance their interests and that of their communities.

The *Sunday Times* (6 March 2005), a South African weekly newspaper, reported on the establishment of the Township Mama's in Alexandra Township, situated North East of Johannesburg. The Township Mamas is a group of about 30 women aged between 30 and 66 years, formed in 2002 who use their cell phones to monitor and respond to crime in their community. When they receive text messages, they alert the community by sending messages to the local radio station. They also go on patrol at night when they receive the message. In this way they have reportedly helped reduce robberies, hijacks and rape in the area. With the widespread prevalence of sexual violence against women in South Africa, strategies like these go a long way in the struggle for women's empowerment.

ICT as an instrument for women's disempowerment

There are also many examples of the use of ICTs that militate against women's empowerment. Ramilo (2002) states that many organisations have highlighted how the onset of the Internet has greatly facilitated the international trafficking of women and girls, the significant proliferation of pornography and the use of the Internet in promoting violence against women – as well as racism and sexism – that has been of great concern to gender equality advocates.

Many of these issues have been furiously debated within the context of appropriate strategies for Internet Governance. Many have argued that the strategy to promote filters and to censor access to pornographic material and hate speech have been subsumed within strategies that also tend to violate privacy and limit access to education and private online spaces, particularly for women.

The road ahead

The above reveals that the struggle for gender equality appears to have made inroads in the official policy and decision-making agenda to some extent with the WSIS process being a case in point. However it can also be argued that together all the initiatives currently under way appear to be too limited in making a resounding impact on gender relations. For instance, Ramilo (2002) suggests that gender inclusion in ICT policy has been confined mainly to international and regional processes and less on national policy processes.

Such a concerted effort has to include greater clarity on the vision for women's empowerment and gender equality in the information society as well as serious interventions at all levels, including national policy, both in terms of the process and content of policy making and implementation.

Furthermore, there appear to be major gaps in knowledge production and scholarly analysis on gendered experiences in the information society in particular. Sanders (2005) refers to contradictory methodologies and research outcomes with reference to gender and ICTs in education in the US. There remains very limited and highly skewed information with particular reference to developing countries. The production of gender disaggregated data and the development of gender appropriate research methodologies and instruments such as standardised gender specific indicators remain an important area of intervention. Hafkin (2002) has done pioneering work on policy in this regard. Similarly the Republic of Korea has developed women informatisation indicators and the Association for Progressive Communication (APC) developed a gender evaluation methodology, which are all worth considering as part of a more concerted effort in theorizing gendered experiences in the information society.

There also seems to be a disjuncture between development efforts at bridging the digital divide on the one hand and broader social development programmes in general. For instance globally, there are major campaigns under way to challenge the HIV/Aids pandemic while the initiatives on the use of ICTs in awareness raising, prevention and treatment of HIV and Aids appear not only limited but also disconnected from the broader campaigns. The ECOSOC report (2004) provides extensive references to development programmes that advance the empowerment of women with the limited references and connection to gendered ICT programmes.

Substantial work still lies ahead as we move beyond the Tunis Phase of the WSIS in November 2005. The UNDAW report (2003) provides extensive recommendations for action in the area of policy, health, education, economic and social empowerment. Realising these recommendations together with those raised above, would involve a far more concerted, sophisticated global and local effort to turn the tide towards gender justice.

References

- Bisnath S (2005): *Women Take the ICT Leap. Gaining Entry into Service Sector Employment.* ITU.

- ECOSOC (2004): *Measures Taken and Progress Achieved in the Follow Up to and Implementation of the Fourth World Conference on Women and to the Twenty Third Session of the General Assembly with an Assessment of Progress Made of Mainstreaming Gender Perspectives in the United Nations System. Report of the Secretary General.* Commission on the Status of Women.

- Green, L (2003): Gender-based Issues and Trends in ICT Application in Education in Asia and the Pacific. In Farrell C (Ed) *UNESCO Meta Survey on the Use of Technologies in Education.* UNESCO, Bangkok.

- Hafkin (2004): *Gender Issues at the World Summit on the Information Society,* Geneva. Unpublished.

- Hafkin, N., & Taggart, N. (2001). *Gender, Information Technology and Developing Countries: An analytic study.* Washington: USAID, Office of Women in Development.

- Hafkin, N (2002): *Gender aspects of ICT policy issues,* prepared for the Expert Group Meeting, Seoul, Korea, Nov 11-14, 2002.

- Hewitt de Alcantara, C. (2001). *The Development Divide in a Digital Age. An Issues Paper.* The Hague: United Nations Research Institute for Social Development.

- Huyer S (2004): *Position Paper on Gender and Science and Technology from an International Perspective.* Office of Science and Technology of the Organization of American States * Inter-American Commission of Women * Gender Advisory Board – UN Commission on Science and Technology for Development.

- Huyer S (2005): *ICT Policy is Not Gender Neutral.* Unpublished.

- ILO (2001): *World Employment Report. Life at Work in the Information Economy.* ILO, Geneva.

- Isaacs S and TURP (1997): *South Africa in the Global Economy. Understanding the Challenges. Working towards Alternatives.* Trade Union Research Project (TURP), Durban, South Africa.

- Marcelle G. M. (2000): *Transforming Information and Communication Technologies for Gender Equality.* Gender and Development Monograph Series. No 9. UNDP.

- Margolis J (2001) Unlocking the Clubhouse: Women in Computing, in *The Digital Divide,* Spring 2001 Vol 1 Number 2, Graduate School of Education & Information Studies, UCLA.

- Ramilo, C (2002): *National ICT Policies and Gender Equality. Regional Perspectives: Asia.* Prepared for the Expert Group Meeting, Seoul, Korea, Nov 11-14, 2002.

- Sanders, J (2005): Gender and Technology in Education. A Research Review. To be published in Skelton C, Francis B and Smulyan L (eds) (2006) *Handbook of Gender in Education,* Sage Publications, London.

- UNDAW, ITU, UN ICT Task Force (2003): *Information and Communication Technologies and their Impact on and Use as an Instrument for the Advancement and Empowerment of Women.* UNDAW, New York.

- UNESCO (2004): Education For All. The Quality Imperative. Summary. *EFA Global Monitoring Report 2005.* UNESCO, Paris.

- World Summit on the Information Society Geneva 2003-Tunis 2005. *Declaration of Principles, Building the Information Society: a global challenge in the new Millennium.* Document WSIS-03/GENEVA/DOC/4-E, 12 December 2003. Original: English. http://www.itu.int/dms_pub/itu-s/md/03/wsis/doc/S03-WSIS-DOC-0004!!MSW-E.doc.

- World Summit on the Information Society Geneva 2003-Tunis 2005. Plan of Action. Document WSIS-03/GENEVA/DOC/5-E, 12 December 2003. Original: English. http://www.itu.int/dms_pub/itu-s/md/03/wsis/doc/S03-WSIS-DOC-0005!!MSW-E.doc.

The author offers grateful thanks to Nancy Hakfin for her constructive comments on this essay.

Shafika Isaacs is Executive Director of SchoolNet Africa (SNA), one of Africa's first African-led pan-African NGOs that promotes learning and teaching through the use of ICTs in African schools, in partnership with schoolnet practitioners and policymakers in 35 African countries. She is based at the SNA headquarters in Johannesburg, South Africa (www.schoolnetafrica.net). Previously, she worked as a Senior Program Officer, with the International Development Research Centre (IDRC)'s Acacia Program that promotes development in Africa through the use of ICTs – where she supported the SchoolNet Africa initiative as well as youth, women's empowerment and schoolnet projects in a range of African countries.

Ms Isaacs was formerly Director of the Trade Union Research Project (TURP) – a labour research service organisation based at the University of Natal in South Africa. She worked at TURP for 10 years where she specialised in research, training and writing publications on globalisation, gender issues and the impact of changing technologies on the labour market .

Ms Isaacs originally hails from District Six and later, Bo Kaap in Cape Town South Africa where she was involved in youth organisation and education initiatives that challenged the apartheid education system. She was a founder member of the Cape Town-based Primary and High School Schools Tuition Program and the Skills Training and Education Centre. She won the Mandela Scholarship Award in 1996 to complete an MSc in Science and Technology Policy at the Science Policy Research Unit (SPRU) at the University of Sussex. In 2003 she was a finalist for the World Technology Network Award.

She serves on the Steering Committee of the UN ICT Task Force's Global eSchools and Communities Initiative (GeSCI), on the Board of Directors of OneWorld Africa and Ungana Afrika, the Advisory Board of the Southern African Network for Educational Technology and eLearning (SANTEC), the Advisory Committees of the Global Teenager Project and the World Summit on the Information Society (WSIS) Youth Caucus and acts as advisor to the Open Education Resources project of the Global Development Gateway. She is also a member of the Council of the Free and Open Source Software Foundation for Africa (FOSSFA) and a Board member of SchoolNet South Africa.

Ms Isaacs is known for her role in the first phase of the WSIS Gender Caucus where she served on its Steering Committee and as Interim Co-ordinator in 2003. She also served as chairperson of the United Nations Division for Advancement of Women-led (UNDAW) Expert Group Meeting on ICTs as an Instrument for the Advancement of Women. She has also been involved with the New Partnership for Africa's Development (NEPAD)'s eSchools Program.

Contact Details: Ms Shafika Isaacs, Executive Director, SchoolNet Africa
PO Box 31866, Braamfontein Centre, Braamfontein,
Johannesburg 2017, South Africa.
Tel: +27 11 339 2300 Fax: +27 339 5912 Email: s.isaacs@schoolnetafrica.org.

Chetan Sharma and Brig. Y.R. Maindiratta

Datamation Foundation Trust

11.

Putting ICTs in the hands of disadvantaged women for lifelong learning & skills enhancement

Chetan Sharma and Brig. Y.R. Maindiratta

Datamation Foundation Trust

Seelampur is situated in the northeastern part of Delhi, the capital city of India. The eastern part of the city is characterised by low-income groups, high population density and poor civic amenities. Seelampur is inhabited primarily by Muslims. It has a high density of population and family incomes are low. The average monthly family income is US$ 60-80 and the average family consists of eight members. Within Seelampur the area of Zaffarabad (with approximately 90% Muslim population) stands out as a pocket of extreme urban poverty and immensely poor living conditions. There the open drains are clogged with sewage, there are frequent power breakdowns, the houses are dilapidated and the people live in overcrowded lanes. Lack of opportunities in terms of education and employment also mark life for the people here. Formal education has become quite common and thus enrolment is high but dropping out at different grades is a continuing problem. Without adequate education, the possibility of white-collar jobs remains a distant reality for most boys and women. Common occupations are unskilled work in factories, handwork in cloth, etc. Most young women have not completed high school. Usually they drop out of the school after finishing Grade VIII. Datamation Foundation had recently initiated some work in the area particularly with women.

At this time, UNESCO launched a pilot initiative to innovate and research social and technological strategies to put ICTs in the hands of the poor. This seemed a good opportunity in the given context and an ICT centre was set up at Zaffarabad. The initiative seeks to deploy ICTs to address urban poverty and is designed to empower the women of Seelampur.

The cultural settings

The towering minarets of numerous mosques in the area are indicators of the role played by religion and the clergy in the lives of the community. Traditional customs still play a powerful role especially with respect to gender. Women are expected to be good housewives, look after their husbands and in-laws, procreate and take care of children and the house. Education is not considered to be important for them. They are not encouraged to move out of the locality independently and the 'burqa' (veil) system is prevalent. It may be noted that several studies done in India among other religious communities also suggest very strong gender related norms such as on mobility, marriage and education. Many other traditional practices are also still adhered to like with respect to kinship and arts, handicrafts and learning. It was considered that for the initiative to make inroads into the lives of the women it may be useful for the ICT centre to be located in their midst. Thus a collaboration was formed with the Babool-Uloom Madrasa. It is a Madrasa (a place of learning) and Masjid (the place where prayer is offered and is also the centre of other religious activities) headed by the Maulana (refers to leader of prayer, Muslim caliph). The Madrasa is not only a place of prayer but also of learning. The Babool-Uloom Madrasa is a religious residential school providing learning to about 200 boys from humble backgrounds. A majority of students aspire to take up advanced religious studies so as to become Imams (teachers). They lead simple frugal lives, living in dormitories that double up as classrooms. The parents are happy in their circumstances of extreme poverty as the basic needs of the child are taken care of and the child is likely to become an Imam in the future. The Babool-Uloom is also a mosque, where the devout gather five times a day to offer prayers to Allah. Women are not allowed entry into the mosque. However, they do come to the Maulana for advice. He arbitrates on social disputes and religious matters. He is also believed to have healing powers.

Permission was sought to start the ICT centre at the Madrasa and for this purpose space was also requested. The factor that played a positive and decisive role was not that the key people viewed ICTs as important but that they felt a strong need to create some opportunities for women in the area. Indeed, it was much later that they began to understand the utility of ICTs.

The ICT centre provides an open learning space for women. They receive training on computers and Internet and also obtain information on varied topics. Interactive multimedia content is developed and used to support vocational and life-skills training and provide rights-based information on various areas to poor women. The marginalised women use ICTs to learn marketable skills and build their awareness of health issues, their rights and livelihood opportunities. In contrast, the Madrasa has its own philosophy, where it seems to isolate itself from the outside world and the teachings have little influence of the outside, changing world. Movement of the students is restricted; there is no radio and no television.

For ICTs to establish their appropriateness, an overall evaluation is necessary. In an ideal world, universal access to information would create a global information society, yet the mode of interpretation will depend on the culture and traditions of the people and societies. A study (Ryckeghem 1995) shows how information technology and culture interact, wherein culture provides the condition for interpreting the utility of information technology. It is also believed that some 'cultural beliefs' are a hindrance to the adoption of ICTs, though the reverse maybe true in many cases. Computers are a product of industrialised civilisation, not from this particular cultural context. Yet the endeavour in community-based interventions has been to be sensitive to cultural differences, which was also the point of departure for the present initiative. The decision to set up the ICT centre in the annexe (one room) of the Madrasa gave it immediate legitimacy. Appreciating the socio-cultural scenario and the importance of the Masjid and Maulana in the lives of the community helped to harmonise that with the technological tools.

In today's information age of globalisation, computerisation, Internet and a virtual world, there are fears that the global media is fast promoting a global monoculture that denies diverse socio-cultural realities. It is felt that this process of globalisation may swamp the not-so-strong cultures. English is the predominant language of the information age. The majority of the material on the Internet is from the developed and industrialised countries. Thus, there are fears that the local cultures would be eroded so the tendency is to further isolate themselves.

The global village is not global for most of the world's poor nor simply because technology is not available to them, but because with or without these technologies the poor are likely to remain marginalised from the benefits of society if they are excluded from the benefits of overall development. Apart from this is the issue of language and content – because of which, even if computers may be physically available, they may continue to be 'out of reach' in crucial ways. Thus, the intervention was located within this fraught relationship between the modern-global and the traditional. There is an interesting contrast between the possibilities of globalised culture that the computer/Internet represents while being at a place that fiercely protects the local culture. What have been the experiences?

There are the traditional restrictions on mobility. Added to this is the fear of the 'anti-social' elements that prohibits parents and husbands in Seelampur from sending women from their homes outside Seelampur.

ICT adaptations to oral culture and traditions – how the ICT intervention has adapted to cultural values...

It was felt necessary to embed the project in the community, taking into account the existing cultural values. Concrete actions are being taken to preserve the local oral culture and propagate the same. For culture to grow, it must be active, contextual and social. ICTs such as videos, TV and multi-media computer software that combine text, sound and colourful images, are used to provide media for expression acting as facilitator.

The ethnographic action research revealed that the women spend a considerable time at home watching soap operas and Hindi movies on television. Seeing the glamorous people on screen, they too are keen to dress well. They want to dance and sing like them. They are also keen to act. The ICT Centre provided them with a platform and an opportunity to express their talents. At the Madrasa, singing is taboo. So the women sing 'Naats' (odes to God), with their heads covered in reverence. These along with 'Ghazals' (melodies about love and sacrifice), 'Sher-Shairi' (short Urdu couplets), stories, comic skits and plays have been recorded at the ICT centre.

Technological skills have been acquired in the process of expressing talents. Digital photography, downloading on the computer, sound recording are some of the skills learnt in the process. The elderly women are being encouraged to record old songs, lullabies, recipes and home-remedies for illnesses. This initiative is named 'Seelampur Voice'. CD-based programmes of this nature are cablecast for wider viewing by the community. The endeavour is not only to preserve the local culture by recording but also to encourage others to come forward to share their experiences, talent and learning acquired through their elders.

The learning of local art and handicraft is being encouraged in the process of learning computers. The women bring local traditional designs and patterns of embroidery to the centre. These are computerised through the process of scanning or digital photography. Then these pictures are modified, improved and more innovative designs are developed with various colour combinations. Some of the participants download various patterns from the Internet and then evolve their own designs using traditional and modern tools as base. It is the same with the application of intricate Mehendi patterns traditionally made on the hands and feet of women.

Web marketing for the arts and crafts of Seelampur and e-learning....

With the help of the community, a portal (www.seelampurmart.org) has been established for marketing arts and crafts made by the women. The portal provides forward and backward market linkages by providing direct access to portal to the producers. The producers of arts and crafts can register themselves at the portal; showcasing their products with their pricing. The portal administrators subsequently would approve inclusion or otherwise of their products in the portal. There has been brisk sale of the arts and crafts from the portal. The women have been encouraged to access the portal themselves directly to know details of pending orders and how these orders can be served. Entire back end supply-chain management for processing the order is gradually getting transferred to the women; even though Datamation Foundation is required to play a facilitating role significantly. Apart from ensuring quality merchandise for the customers by intensive community linkages, the Foundation has actively marketed the portal world wide as a signature statement; hyper-links with other portals have been requested to help increase traffic to Seelampurmart.

Studies have shown that despite its criticality to the success of information technology projects, culture is the most difficult to isolate, define and measure. From the conclusions of their study, every country must have an information technology policy that recognises its culture and ensures that adoption of information technology does not destroy the cultural heritage. The problem arises when there is a difference between the 'culture of an IT product and the culture of its users'. Hence, every possible effort has been taken to develop local content in Seelampur.

It was observed that the women were keen to acquire certain vocational skills while learning to handle computers. To fulfil this need, more than 50 CD-based vocational skills learning packages were developed in-house where the participants have been actively involved. The packages, with a voice-over option in both English and Hindi, include candle making, liquid soap and phenyl making, henna application and designs, making of soft toys and rag dolls, tailoring etc. Also, based on their traditional skills (such as handicrafts) many new avenues are being explored to make these women have a means for an independent income. Many of the women eagerly want to have an independent source of income after coming to the centre and also, to be able to support or help their families financially.

The Internet, together with eNRICH – a local Web-based browser developed by the National Informatics Centre, a Government of India organization – is being used imaginatively to record and showcase local talent and cultural heritage. At the same time, participants are getting an exposure to other cultures and ideas as well. Thus, computers and the Internet create the possibility for such mutual sharing and learning. Email has opened an avenue to exchanges with people of the same religion, living in different countries. Images from the Internet, coupled with email exchanges are making the participants aware of the cultural differences and similarities amongst Muslims living in countries like Malaysia, Bangladesh, Pakistan, West Asia and the West. Looking at cultural aspects with a sense of enquiry and respect has been a big gain from the ICTs.

Various e-Government services offered by the Delhi Government, such as applying for birth and death certificates, vehicle registration, property registration and few other citizen services, are being accessed by the women from the Seelampur Community Centre. Since most of the participating women from the community have not even completed their upper primary education; there is a keen desire amongst the women to

159

complete their basic secondary education through open distance learning. Consequently the women access various distance learning sites, such as the National Institute of Open Learning (NIOS – www.nios.org), or for those who have completed their school education and are desirous of enrolling themselves for graduation, admissions and learning sites such as the Indira Gandhi National Open University (IGNOU), Manipal-Sikkim Open University, Mysore University, Annamalai University are very popular. The e-Government and e-leaning opportunities offered by these education sites to the Seelampur women and are helping the women get over their 'school drop-out' stigma very rapidly.

How the community and the clergy have also adapted

The centre also observes Fridays as a holiday, as it is a day devoted to offering special congregational prayers among the Muslims (the day is called 'Jumma', when Muslims make an extra effort to go to their local masjid to listen to the khutbah, or community address, from the Imam, or worship leader, and to perform formal worship with their fellow Muslims).

The tutor at the centre is from the same community, so the women feel comfortable. Hindi and Urdu are used along with English to facilitate learning. Some computer based learning programs in the form of vocational CDs have been developed with voiceover and content in Hindi as well as English. This was done for easy comprehension and for the realisation of the importance of English as a link language (especially for using the Internet). Above all there is an informality of atmosphere so that the staff and project team members are open to being approached.

Sensitivity has also been shown to the fact that the women from the community are not allowed to move unaccompanied, especially outside the confines of Seelampur. Consequently, in any event such as the WSIS Gender meeting or the Knowledge Fair at Global Development Network, where the Datamation Foundation was invited to present, or even for the excursion to Agra city that adjoins Delhi, adequate travel arrangements are made and it is ensured that the women are escorted to and fro. Thus, they are not denied the opportunity for the exposure because of these mobility restrictions.

There are the traditional restrictions on mobility. Added to this is the fear of the 'anti-social' elements that prohibit parents and husbands in Seelampur from sending women from their homes outside Seelampur. Sexual harassment of women is quite common in the area and one hears of such cases frequently. The Community ICT Center has gradually emerged as a 'nodal' point of social contact in Seelampur as this is perceived as a safe place. Many women state that they feel very happy coming here and want to stay here for longer periods. Some women have profusely thanked the team at the centre for providing them with an opportunity to 'constructively' interact and socialise. Now, older women and men in these families also support them in this interest. Several opportunities have been created such as picnics and other visits to facilitate their mobility even outside the area.

The centre is on the first floor of the annex to the Madrasa with an independent entry from the lane. The second floor of the Madrasa and the annex are interconnected with a passage like an airbridge over the lane. Generally someone stays at the ground floor of the annex. For some period, there was no one staying in the annex, thus for security reasons the Maulana was not keen to keep the independent entry open. Financial constraints did not allow hiring a security guard. He then allowed the women to enter the Madrasa from a side entrance, go up to the second floor, transit through the dormitory being used by the boys and then cross over to the annex. The women were apprehensive of the arrangements; especially of going through the dormitory, but the arrangement worked. Though women are not allowed into the Masjid they were permitted to transit through the exclusively boys' zone in this instance.

And there is resistance to ICT enabled Education

There are occasions when traditional values are too strong and play a decisive role. In such situations, the women may raise a voice or submit to tradition. The centre was to be formally inaugurated by the Chief Minister of Delhi on 26 June, 2003. The women were enthusiastic and so were guided to organise the centre, make arrangements to receive the honourable guest and present themselves appropriately. The Maulana was the chief co-ordinator. It had been planned that after the formal inauguration of the centre, the Chief Minister would be escorted to a hall that serves as the Madrasa as also the Masjid, where she was to be greeted publicly. After that she was to address the gathering. Yet despite their efforts, because of tradition the women were not permitted entry into the hall.

Often within the kinship context also, age-old patriarchal values may reinforce themselves even if by taking new forms in the face of these changes. Traditionally, women are seen as having a role only within the house and thus, formal education of any kind may not be seen as valuable and may even be discouraged. Recently in Seelampur women are being rejected in the process of spouse selection in arranged marriages on the ground that they know computers so will not 'adjust' in their marital family. Similar instances have also come to light about the boy's family making greater demands for dowry from the girl's family if she is computer literate. Voices are raised in dissent...

The women remain in awe of the Maulana because of his status and traditional standing. During the month of Ramadan, he wanted the centre to be closed down. All through the month of Ramadan devout Muslims keep strict fast. Only before sunrise and after sunset do they take food. Early morning as the call for prayer is heard from the mosques, the boys and men set off to offer Namaz (prayers). Women stay at home and recite the Koran. Fasting during the days of Ramadan normally does not affect their daily routine and they go on with their daily chores. Thus the 29 or 30 days of the month of Ramadan pass and the sighting of the new moon brings good tidings of Eid-ul-Fitur and the end of the month.

The women were not happy with the decision that the centre be closed down for the month of Ramadan. They were enjoying ·the learning experience at the centre. They were encouraged by the project staff to go through the relevant websites to understand the significance and meaning behind the rituals and why Ramadan is observed. Having understood, they gathered courage and went to the Maulana to plead their case to keep the centre functioning. They did that convincingly and successfully. The compromise arrived at was that the centre would close down at 4 pm instead of at the usual closing time of 5 pm. Only a few months ago such a dialogue between the Maulana and the women would have been unthinkable.

Concluding observations

These small steps lead to changing relationships, practices, and adapting of old values to new situations. As we go along, these seemingly small changes may go on to impact the culture. Culture is how we view the events, how we think, how we perceive events, how we react and respond. Culture consists of social norms, group behaviour, respect and authority of decision-makers. This experience shows that while every effort is being made to respect the local culture, the project is also impinging on the participants and the stakeholders, making them think and act a little differently. Earlier there were doubts as to whether the space would continue to be provided by the Madrasa or the centre would have to shift soon. The outcomes of the dynamics are very evident in the fact that now there is a commitment to give the space for the centre for many years to come and an extra room has also been provided for the centre.

The initiative has shown that ICTs, e-learning and e-Governance can be used to understand, preserve, and share cultural heritage, and enhance cultural values. Local culture can be shared with people of different cultures with mutual understanding and respect. Exposure builds confidence in women due to which they are able to articulate their opinions better. The Seelampur Community ICT initiative has been an interesting learning experience for the community as also for the project team.

Chetan Sharma is the founder of Datamation Foundation Trust (a registered non-profit organization) & CEO of the Datamation Group of companies – one of India's most reputable knowledge management companies, employing over 2,500 full time workers from marginalized and deprived communities. Ever since its inception, the mission at Datamation has been to empower the weakest of the weak, specifically women & youth, with the deployment of innovative models in education, health and livelihood opportunities.

Mr Sharma is the Member of the National Apex Committee on e-Governance set up by the Indian Government's Ministry of Communications and Information Technology, a Member of the National Committee of CII on Education, Member of the Governing Council Member of the India Country Development Gateway (a World Bank – Government of India project), and a Member of the Centre for Public Policy-Indian Institute of Management, Bangalore.

He actively works with the United Nations backed Gender & Youth Caucuses of the World Summit on the Information Society (WSIS).

Mr. Sharma has been a University Topper in both MBA and Masters in Computer Applications(MCA) Programs. He has been an active Researcher in diverse development areas such as education, health care, urban infrastructure, tourism, e-governance and gender. He is a regular speaker at national and international seminars.

Contact details: Chetan Sharm, Datamation Foundation Trust,
"Vimal-Shree", B-12 Swasthya Vihar, Delhi -110 092, India
www.datamationfoundation.org
www.datamationindia.com
Tel: +91-11-22167230 Email: csharma@giasdl01.vsnl.net.in.

Professor Tim Unwin

Professor of Geography, Royal Holloway, University of London

12.

Reflections on ability: the use of ICTs to support people with disabilities in poor countries.

Professor Tim Unwin

Professor of Geography, Royal Holloway, University of London

One day, not so long ago, I was in a small town in Ghana and came across the two posters shown below. This essay is about bringing together the notions contained within them.

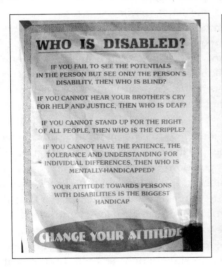

Experiencing information and communication technologies

Societies create and use technologies in a diversity of ways. But how we conceive of their use fundamentally depends on our experiences thereof. Those of us who can see might say that people from different backgrounds look at the use of ICT through different lenses. But for those born unable to see, the concepts of 'looking' and 'lenses' have negligible experienced value.

For those primarily interested in making financial profits, new Information and Communication Technologies (ICTs) have opened up a wealth of potential opportunities. Such technologies can dramatically improve the productivity of labour, and thereby reduce significantly the costs of production. They can also help to open up vast new markets, enabling producers to realise the profits from the production of surplus value much more readily than was the case previously. In short, ICTs can fundamentally alter the ways in which two of the key constraints on capital, namely labour costs and market size, can be overcome (Marx, 1976). Moreover, at an individual level, knowledge of ICTs can dramatically enhance people's employment opportunities. They are a way of getting ahead.

However, there is a completely different way of thinking about technology. Instead of privileging the already advantaged, it is possible to concentrate on ways in which technology can be used to enable the marginalised and least privileged to gain access to the opportunities that were previously only available to their richer or otherwise more favoured peers. Technology can be used as a way of catching up, of reducing differences rather than of increasing them, and of empowering the least privileged among us. New technologies can give people chances and opportunities that were previously unthinkable. All that is required is a will; a different way of being. The problem with ICTs is not technological, but moral. We can choose whether we wish to use our skills and resources to make life better for those who already have much, or whether instead we wish to use them to improve the lived experiences of those who have long been marginalised and excluded.

Such contrasts lie at the heart of debates about the digital divide. On the one hand are those who argue that people in positions of power will always use technology to maintain their positions of strength, control and authority (for a wide ranging discussion on the links between 'science' and 'society', see Habermas, 1978). On the other are those who believe that it is possible to 'bridge the digital divide', and that technology can indeed be used in innovative ways dramatically to transform the lived experiences of the world's poor and marginalised people and communities. The Maitland Commission report, *The Missing Link*, presaged such debates, noting that telecommunications can indeed play a vital role in stimulating economic growth, enhancing the quality of life and creating world-wide networks. In advocating this role, its authors focused particularly on the ways in which the needs of those living in remote areas of developing countries could be met at lower cost (see Chapter 4, paragraph 30). However, they paid scant attention to the needs of communities and individuals that are marginalised socially or ideologically, rather than simply because of where they lived.

Twenty years on, we have seen the enormous contribution that ICTs can make to the lives of those with disabilities and special educational needs

(SENs) in the richer countries of the world (see, for example, Watkins, 2001). However, the potential to use such technology in the poorer countries of the world is all too often ignored, with few donors or international agencies even being aware of the scale of the problem, let alone the potential that ICTs have in helping to enable and empower these most marginalised of people living in poor communities (although see Casely-Hayford and Lynch, 2003a; World Bank 2005).

While we keep detailed statistics on trade balances, government spending, and financial markets, we have little idea of the numbers of people with different kinds of disability in the poorest regions of the world. The first UN workshop on disability statistics in Africa was thus only held in 2001 (see http://unstats.un.org/unsd/disability/work_prog.asp[1]). For Mitra (2004), 'disability' is the hidden side of African poverty, and she emphasises that "despite this link between disability and poverty, there has been an uncomfortable silence among international development organizations about disability issues". For her, "This lack of awareness is triggered by the general absence of reliable data sources on disability in developing countries, which prevent researchers from documenting the two-way link between poverty and disability" (Mitra, 2004).

Information and communication: changing the lives of people with disabilities

In order to understand the impact that ICTs can have on the lives of people with disabilities[2] or SENs, it is helpful to disaggregate the significance of both the information and the communication dimensions of these technologies.

Gaining information

Access to digital information has become an increasingly important dimension of human life in the past 20 years. In many parts of the world, digital information, be it in the classroom, the workplace or home, has thus become so commonplace, that it is often taken for granted. However, for those who cannot see television or computer screens, who cannot hear the ring of a telephone, or who cannot input data about themselves onto a keyboard, this ever more digital world has not only passed them by, but has often actually increased their separateness and marginality.

If technology can separate people in this way, it can nevertheless also be used in exciting and innovative ways to enhance people's accessibility to information. The Web Accessibility Initiative's work (www.w3.org/WAI/) thus develops strategies, guidelines and resources to make the Web accessible to people with disabilities. For those who are blind, screen readers, speech synthesizers and refreshable braille displays can all make information accessed through computers more accessible. For the deaf, web-designers can incorporate captions for audio content. For those with motor disabilities, information can be gained from the Web by using a specialized mouse, a pointing device or specialist keyboard. It is, though, crucial for all those who design Web pages, or develop digital content, to ensure that it is accessible to those with disabilities.

A wealth of specialist information for people with disabilities is now available on the Internet. Good examples of this in the UK, for example, are the sites developed by civil society organisations such as the Autism and PDD Network (www.autism-pdd.net/), the Royal National Institute for the Blind (www.rnib.org.uk/technology/) and the Royal National Institute for Deaf People (www.rnid.org.uk/information_resources/). There are likewise many companies and organisations specialising in the hardware that enables people to gain access to such information (e.g Inclusive Technology www.inclusive.co.uk/, Don Johnson http://donjohnston.co.uk/, and Quality Enabling Devices www.qedltd.com/).

Communication

ICTs not only enable new forms of access to information content, but they also transform the ways in which communication occurs, permitting new kinds of network and interaction. It is now hard to imagine a world without email, and yet it was only in 1993 that large network service providers, such as America Online, began to connect their proprietary email systems to the Internet (www.livinginternet.com/e/ei.htm). In 2005 more than a billion people in over 200 countries use GSM telephones, and yet it was only in the 1990s that second generation (2G) systems began to be introduced, with 3G systems not being introduced until the start of the 21st century (http://en.wikipedia.org/wiki/History_of_mobile_phones).

Many of the initiatives that have used ICTs, particularly in the field of education, have focused primarily on the content dimension, and thus on the information rather than on the communication aspects of the technology. All too often, educational ICT initiatives in poor countries have digitised old-style textbook content, and displayed this on television or computer screens, rather than using the potential that ICTs have to develop radically new means of communication and learning. However, the opportunities that technology offers for transforming the ways in which we communicate are at least as revolutionary as are the types of information that can be conveyed. Digital video-conferencing enables people from different parts of the world to interact synchronously without leaving their offices; web-based discussion forums permit collective learning to take place among groups of students who may be unable to get together at the same time; mobile-telephony enables people to communicate with each other readily across many parts of the world; telemedicine initiatives enable doctors in rural communities to share information about patients with consultants in distant cities. These new means of communication can both marginalise and empower people with disabilities.

This marginalising and empowering character of technology is well seen in the context of those with hearing impairments. At a very basic level, hearing aids can enhance the sounds that people hear, and thus their ability to communicate effectively with other people. Nevertheless, not all digital wireless telephones are compatible with hearing aids and cochlear implants. Governments are therefore having to legislate to ensure that producers and suppliers do indeed make a sufficient number of such telephones compatible (e.g. www.fcc.gov/cgb/consumerfacts/hac.html), so that those with hearing impairments are not marginalised by the advent of such telephony. For those who are entirely deaf, text telephones (TTY - Teletypewriters; also known as TDD – Telecommunication Devices for the Deaf) also offer enormous potential, whereby those who are deaf or speech impaired can type messages back and forth to one another instead of talking and listening[3].

Used appropriately, though, technology can help people to communicate on a much more equal footing, as with the use of email by blind people. When you receive an email, you have no way of knowing if it has been sent by someone who is blind, deaf or perhaps has some motor disability. Blind people can readily use email through voice-activated software; they can simply speak into the computer, and it will then produce written text for transmission. The emails they receive can be read back automatically so that they can hear them. For people with lesser visual impairments, screen magnifying software can be used to help them. But not all computer companies build such technology into their systems. Among the most innovative of the major companies in this field has been Apple with their Universal Access features that permit the following standard accessibility functions:

- *"Switch the screen to black and white, and other contrast enhancements.*
- *Choose to make the screen flash when an alert sound occurs.*
- *Zoom in on the screen image to make it appear larger.*
- *Make the computer read aloud the text on the screen when you move the pointer over an item in the Finder, Dock, or application toolbar.*
- *Make the mouse functions available through the keyboard.*
- *Turn on Sticky Keys or Slow Keys to help you control the keyboard.*
- *Turn on Mouse Keys to control the pointer using your numeric keypad"* *(Apple, OS 10.3.9, Help: About Universal Access Features; see also www.apple.com/macosx/features/universalaccess/).*

It is essential for all hardware and software designers to ensure that the products they are making take such issues into consideration if their technologies are truly to be empowering rather than marginalising.

The use of technology to enhance communication between people of different abilities should not, however, be seen merely as a one-way process whereby technology is used only to help those with a particular disability to communicate with those without it. People who think of themselves as 'able' can, for example, also use technology to learn how to communicate with others who may not be able to hear. Two excellent websites that provide information on signing this are the Michigan State University's Communication Technology Laboratory at http://commtechlab.msu.edu/sites/aslweb/browser.htm and the site for BritishSignLanguage.com at www.britishsignlanguage.com/. Both of these provide imagery and explanations of sign languages to enable people to communicate more effectively together.

Cost issues

Much of the empowering technology that has been developed for those with special educational needs and various disabilities is beyond the reach of most poor people. In a market economy, where supply and demand are the primary arbiters of cost, specialist technology is almost always more expensive than standard equipment. However, governments and technology companies can play a key role in making this balance more equitable. As in the example above, Apple have built their Universal Access capabilities into all of their more recent Operating Systems, and, although only a small percentage of users actually make use of such software, this does mean that people with many differing abilities and competencies can indeed communicate and gain access to information at no extra cost when using their computers.

The challenge is to make such practices much more widespread, and for global organisations as well as national governments to put into place mechanisms and funding programmes that will no longer systematically disadvantage disabled people from poor communities. The work of the Web Accessibility Initiative (www.w3.org/WAI/) is, for example, crucial in helping Web designers across the world craft Web pages that do not disadvantage people with disabilities. However, we need to go far beyond this, and begin to make real inroads into the funding of technology-enhanced initiatives designed to empower people with disabilities. While there has indeed been excellent work undertaken by initiatives such as the Civil Society Disability Caucus associated with WSIS (for example www.dinf.ne.jp/doc/english/prompt/031215_3wsis.html), much of the focus and participation in such events is dominated by representatives from the richer countries of the world. We need to heed Hiroshi Kawamura's (2005) intervention in PrepCom2 of WSIS II, where he argued that "People with disabilities are poorest among the poors in particular in developing countries. Affordable ICTs need to be accessible and usable for individuals with disabilities to guarantee full participation in the community as active partners. So far, ICTs in many cases created new man-made barriers for persons with disabilities in developing countries in terms of affordability, accessibility and usability".

Case studies in the empowering use of ICTs by people with disabilities in poor countries

Despite the immensely empowering role of ICTs, it is remarkable how few initiatives there are that seek to use them in support of people with disabilities in poor countries[4]. In part this reflects the extremely difficult circumstances in which such people often find themselves. This is not the place to explore such issues at length, but people with disabilities are frequently faced with enormous cultural, social and economic obstacles in their lives. In circumstances where national or local governments have only limited resources, what support there is often tends to go to those who are seen as being able to make most use of it, and all too frequently this excludes people with disabilities. There is thus a very important role for those involved in the processes surrounding WSIS, to highlight the great contributions that people with disabilities are indeed able to make through the enabling technologies associated with ICT. Moreover, it is incumbent on donors and civil society organisations to make much stronger efforts than they are currently doing to provide funding support for such initiatives, to help ensure that rhetorics about equal opportunity and human rights are truly delivered upon. This section thus provides brief accounts of some of the innovative ICT activities that have indeed been developed by and for people with disabilities in poor countries. They have deliberately been chosen to reflect not only different kinds of disability context, but also initiatives that have been developed in contrasting parts of the world.

Information on HIV/AIDS: by the deaf, for everyone

The provision of accurate and appropriate information on HIV/AIDS is vital if infection rates are to be reduced. Over half of all the people in the world who are HIV-positive live in Africa, and unless people know and act on reliable information about the disease millions more are likely to die. Deaf young people from the Mampong Secondary Technical School for the Deaf, working with the Special Education Division of the Ghana Education Service and the Ghana National Association for the Deaf, supported by Voluntary Services Overseas (VSO), the British Council and the British High Commission, have therefore worked together on an innovative project to create a video that delivers HIV/AIDS information in Ghanaian Sign Language (see www.britishcouncil.org/ghana-society-community-hiv-aids-education-for-the-deaf.htm). The idea for the video came from a deaf VSO worker at the Cape Coast School for the Deaf[5], and the film itself was created by Remark!, a deaf film company based in the UK (www.remarkfilms.co.uk/). The entire production process, from planning, through to filming and distribution, was undertaken in close collaboration with young deaf people in Ghana. The result is a stunning and emotional film that has been very widely seen and applauded in Ghana. People with disabilities have often been left out of other HIV/AIDS information campaigns, and this video therefore provides an outstanding resource, not only for deaf and aurally impaired people across Africa, but also for their aurally able counterparts. It is a striking example of ways in which deaf people can use ICTs to make a significant difference to their lives.

I don't have sight. However, I have a vision

One of the most widely-cited examples of the innovative use of ICTs for people with disabilities in Africa is the work of the Adaptive Technology Centre for the Blind (ATCB) in Ethiopia, established in 2000. Through the energy and enthusiasm of Tamru Belay, this civil society organisation has begun to show the world how African blind people can not only help themselves through the use of ICTs, but in so doing can also contribute to their country's economic growth. The ATCB's mission statement neatly summarises its work: "The Adaptive Technology Centre for the Blind [ATCB] is a dedicated computer trainer and Braille transcriber centre focusing on the needs of students and professionals in Ethiopia who are blind or visually impaired. Today everybody is a witness that the blind community in Ethiopia, especially those working in offices or any active job participants and students, are totally dependent on the help of others to perform their duties. Therefore, ATCB aims to cut this shackle off our visually impaired professionals and students and make them free and independent so that they also can become the beneficiaries of modern technology" (www3.sympatico.ca/tamru/Purpose.html).

One of their key goals is to empower the visually challenged community through the use of adaptive technologies, and much of their effort is thus spent in helping blind people to learn to operate computers through adaptive technology such as speech synthesizers, magnifying hardware and software, and Braille displays. The scale of the challenges that they face in so doing is immense. It is estimated that there are some half a million totally blind people living in Ethiopia, with many more having visual impairments. In 2003, the ATCB gained the support of both UNESCO and the ITU and were thus able to launch a programme to build a computer centre, train blind and visually impaired students, professional and government employees to operate computers with adaptive devices, and create public awareness that blind people can fulfil their potential to the wider benefit of society through the use of ICTs (http://portal.unesco.org/ci/en/ev.php-URL_ID=15892&URL_DO=DO_ TOPIC&URL_SECTION=201.html). The following year UNESCO announced an even more ambitious programme with ATCB to develop a training curriculum and establish an employment oriented ICT centre for the visually impaired people, that will equip them with skills relevant to Ethiopia's sustainable development agenda.

ICT training for people with disabilities in Central America

It has been estimated that 18% of those living in Central America have some kind of significant disability (web.worldbank.org/WBSITE/ EXTERNAL/OPPORTUNITIES/GRANTS/DEVMARKETPLACE/0,,contentM DK:20200530~pagePK:180686~piPK:180184~theSitePK:205098,00.html). In 2000, the Trust for the Americas, a non-profit organization affiliated with the Organization of American States, therefore developed a programme of activities supported by the World Bank through infoDev (www.infodev.org) and the Development Marketplace (www.developmentmarketplace.org), to provide IT employment training for people with disabilities in Guatemala, El Salvador, Honduras and Nicaragua. Much of the training was provided by Net Corps Americas volunteers from Latin America, Europe and the USA, and they concentrated both on training people in some 44 NGOs in ways of training people with disabilities for employment, and also providing direct IT employment training for people who themselves had some kind of disability. One of the particularly interesting aspects of this programme was that it worked with people who had a range of different disabilities, and thus included some people who were deaf, others who were blind and yet others who were using wheelchairs. One key finding of the work was that a diversity of training approaches was needed so that people with different disabilities and different levels of education could learn in the optimal ways for them. Another significant conclusion was that it was also important to educate potential employers about the skills that people with disabilities possessed, so that they would indeed be able to find gainful employment on completing their training (for more information, see www.iconnect-online.org/Stories/Story.import97).

South Africa's National Accessibility Portal

A very different kind of project has recently been launched in South Africa to address the marginalisation of the 4 million or so people in the country who are disabled and for whom access to information, services and the ability to communicate effectively are key needs. The National Accessibility Portal (www.napsa.org.za) is being designed to be a "one-stop information, services and communication channel that will support everyone involved in the disability field – persons with disabilities, caregivers, the medical

profession, and those offering services in this domain'
(www.africafiles.org/article.asp?ID=8691&ThisURL=./southern.asp&URL
Name=Southern%20Region), and is exploring the following main technical
challenges:

- research and development in text-to-sign language;
- development of Open Source technologies, including a text-to-speech
  screen reader, and;
- African language support for people with disabilities.

The project is being developed by the South African Council for Scientific
and Industrial Research (CSIR), together with a group of disabled people's
organisations and the Office on the Status of Disabled Persons in the South
Africa Presidency. However, the success of this venture, as with so many
ICT initiatives for people with disabilities, will depend not so much on the
technology, but rather on people's willingness to provide sufficient funding.
In late 2004, it was thus reported that funding had only been gained so far
for the initial pilot phase (www.africafiles.org/article.asp?ID=8691&
ThisURL=./southern.asp&URLName=Southern%20Region) and much
therefore remains to be done to turn this vision into a reality.

Conclusion

The short essays that comprise this volume mark the anniversary of the
publication of the Maitland Commission report, and to highlight the
extraordinary enterprise being taken by individuals, communities and
businesses throughout the developing world to harness the benefits of
ICTs. Twenty years ago, that Commission introduced significant challenges
to the worldwide telecommunications community. This essay has sought to
present that same community with one further challenge: to ensure that
we all use our skills and resources to enable people with disabilities in poor
countries to gain from these benefits just as much as other people.

As the examples of innovative ICT-supported activities being undertaken
by people with disabilities have illustrated, it is indeed possible for these
people to shape their futures through the use of information and
communication technologies. However, at least four things need to be in
place to begin to turn this vision into a wider reality:

- First, those of us who think we are 'able" need to return to the poster
  shown at the start of this essay and realise that our own attitudes to
  people with disabilities are often the biggest handicap.
- Second, we need to ensure that the new ICTs that are developed, be they
  hardware or software, do not only enhance the abilities of the more able,
  but instead also provide ways for those with disabilities to gain
  information and to communicate on an equal basis to others. Given the
  cost implications of such an agenda, this may well require a

commitment by the United Nations, other international organisations and global leaders to some kind of regulatory guidelines, but at the very least the WSIS processes should mobilise support for such practices.

- Third, international donors and civil society organisations can play a crucial role in helping to create a more equitable information and communication environment in poor countries by specifically funding initiatives that support the use of ICTs to empower people with disabilities. The costs of implementing such programmes are not prohibitive, and given the claimed commitment of donors to support the most needy of the world's poor people, it is high time that they began to deliver on such rhetoric with respect to people with disabilities. Ghana, for example, has some 20 basic level special needs schools, and it would be perfectly feasible to implement a coherent strategy for using ICTs to support their learning if there was sufficient funding available (Casely-Hayford and Lynch, 2003b).

- Fourth, it is essential that all emerging ICT policies and strategies in poor countries (see for example the work of UNDP, www.undp.org/rba/ict4dev.html) explicitly take into consideration the implications of such strategies for people with disabilities. Instead of being a marginalised afterthought, such agendas need to be at the heart of these strategies. Only then will we indeed be able to say that we have forged the missing link in 'bridging the digital divide'.

References

Throughout this essay I am using a broad definition of ICTs to include all such technologies, from radio, television and video, through to computers and the Internet, as well as mobile telephony.

1. Note that all of the links cited in this essay were accessed between 15 and 20 September 2005.

2. I am using a very broad definition of disability in this essay, as indicated in part by the imagery at the start of this essay. Most attempts to define 'disability' are fraught with difficulty, and I am inclined to be cautious of legal definitions that by including some aspects of human functioning as 'disabilities' thereby tend to exclude others which may be seriously debilitating to some individuals. I take a view that we all have abilities and disabilities, and how these are seen depends in part on the contexts in which we find ourselves. For the International Classification of Impairments, Disabilities and Handicaps see www.who.int/icidh. See also the UK Government's useful disability site at www.disability.gov.uk/legislation/.

3. For a useful discussion of mobile telephony for people with a range of disabilities, see the Nordic Forum for Telecommunication and Disability's (2004) guide; for a review of the use of telephony for deaf people in South Africa, see Glaser and Tucker (2004)

4. For access to wider information on ICT4D and people with disabilities see, for example, www.gg.rhul.ac.uk/ict4d/disability.html, Shambles' work on ICT and Special Needs (www.shambles.net/pages/staff/ITSEN/) and the Third World Institute's Choike project at http://www.choike.org/nuevo_eng/informes/643.html.

5. Helen Phillips recalls what inspired her: "Many of the deaf children did not really understand about HIV/AIDS. Here is an example - one deaf child said to me 'I won't get HIV because I am deaf'. I was so shocked and explained to the child that anyone can get HIV and this child was really surprised about it. There had been lot published on HIV/AIDS awareness but it was all in English but most of them could not read well. It is most important they have access to their sign language". (www.idcs.info/professionals_at_work/teaching_in.html).

- Casely-Hayford, L. and Lynch, P. (2003a) *A review of good practice in ICT and Special Educational Needs for Africa*, London: DFID (Imfundo KnowledgeBank) (available at http://imfundo.digitalbrain.com/imfundo/web/papers/sen/?verb=view).

- Casely-Hayford, L. and Lynch, P. (2003b) *ICT based solutions for special educational needs in Ghana*, London: DFID (Imfundo KnolwedgeBank) (available at http://imfundo.digitalbrain.com/imfundo/web/papers/sen_phase2/SEN%20PHASE%202%20FINAL.pdf).

- Glaser, M. and Tucker, W.D. (no date [c.2004]) *Telecommunications bridging between deaf and hearing users in South Africa*, http://forte.fh-hagenberg.at/Project-Homepages/Blindenhund/conferences/granada/papers/Glaser/GLASER.htm

- Habermas, J. (1978) *Knowledge and Human Interests*, London: Heinemann, 2nd edition.

- Independent Commission for World-Wide Telecommunications Development (1984) *The Missing Link*, Geneva: ITU.

- Kawamura, H. (2005) Intervention on behalf of the Civil Society Disability Caucus to the PrepCom2 of WSIS II delivered on 25th February 2005 at Room XIX, Palais de Nations, http://www.dinf.ne.jp/doc/english/prompt/050225wsis.html.

- Marx, K. (1976) Capital, Volume 1, Harmondsworth: Penguin (First English Edition, 1887; see http://www.marxists.org/archive/marx/works/1867-c1/)

- Mitra, S. (2004) Viewpoint: *Disability – the hidden side of African poverty*, Disability World, 22, unpaginated (http://unstats.un.org/unsd/disability/work_prog.asp).

- Nordic Forum for Telecommunication and Disability (2004) *Mobile telephony for people with disabilities - a guide to choosing a mobile phone* (Nordic Forum for Telecommunication and Disability's (2004) guide at http://www.nsh.se/NFTH-Mobile_telephony.htm)

- Watkins, A. (2001) *Information and Communication Technology (ICT) in Special Needs Education,* Middelfart, Denmark: European Agency for Development in Special Needs Education (see also their ICT on SNE database at http://www.european-agency.org/ict_sen_db/index.html).

- World Bank (2005) Special Report: *Disability and Inclusive Development*, Development Outreach, July 2005, Washington DC: World Bank Institute (http://www1.worldbank.org/devoutreach/article.asp?id=309)

Tim Unwin (born 1955) is Professor of Geography at Royal Holloway, University of London, where he has established an ICT4D collective (www.ict4d.org.uk). From 2001-2004 he led the UK Government's Imfundo: Partnership for IT in Education initiative based within the Department for International Development. This created a partnership network of some 40 organisations and initiated activities in eight African countries.

Professor Unwin was previously Head of the Department of Geography at Royal Holloway, University of London between 1999 and 2001. He has written or edited 13 books, and over 170 papers and other publications, including *Wine and the Vine* (Routledge, 1991; translated into three languages), *The Place of Geography* (Longman, 1992), as well as his edited *Atlas of World Development* (Wiley, 1994) and *A European Geography* (Longman, 1998). He is founding editor of the journals Ethics, Place and Environment, and Journal of Wine Research.

His research has taken him to more than 25 countries across the world, and he has worked on subjects as diverse as the role of banknotes as expressions of national identity, and rural change in central and eastern Europe during the 1990s. His recent research has focused in particular on the use of ICTs for teacher training in Africa, on a critique of budget support mechanisms in international aid, and on the use of partnerships in development practice. The UK's Secretary of State for International Development appointed him as one of the Commonwealth Scholarship Commissioners in 2004, and he also serves as External Examiner for the Institute of Masters of Wine and on the British Council's Education and Training Advisory Committee.

Contact details: Professor Tim Unwin, Department of Geography, Royal Holloway, University of London, Egham, Surrey TW20 0EX, England.
Tel: +44 1784 443655 Email: tim.unwin@rhul.ac.uk.

Dr. Nii Quaynor

Chairman, Network Computer Systems

13.

Style of Internet and telecommunications governance representative of ALL stakeholders

Dr. Nii Quaynor

Chairman, Network Computer Systems

Internet enthusiasts, or Netizens, as they are usually referred to, are undoubtedly inspired by the search for ideal mutual ownership of the Internet by a community; as a right in digital space.

In other words, just as citizens of a community may have rights and protections in real life to exercise the power of electing public interest officers, a similar service is desired in the new virtual world.

The question, however, is whether the expectations of the new world should be governed by similar expressions, in spite of the fact that the norms in real life are governed by a means of representation and expression. Also, would this new world, this promised world in virtual space be capable of fulfilling the future aspirations for representation for every Internet user, directly or indirectly?

These questions should be answered by stakeholders, since for a fact, the Internet would be greatly enhanced if full account is taken of all stakeholders. And for enthusiasts who appreciate the rapidly emerging importance of the new media for the future, the remedy is to ensure as much inclusion of stakeholders as possible. In all these instances, however, it is expected that care would be taken in constituting the stakeholders adequately to avoid the danger of capture of decisions.

In governance, it would be unreasonable to require participants in the new world to wait until all stakeholders are able to participate, but it is also doubtful how decisions could be made for persons who, as it were, have not had the opportunity to input policy positions that may inadvertently favour some economically. It would be holding back innovation and subsequently development.

These in effect explain the tensions around governance and stakeholders, i.e. representation and decisions that provoke issues of equity and values placed on what the Internet brings.

And the remedy should be how well the world evolves a social system with a human face that works in concert with the new media with complementary powers as well as checks and balances where no one stakeholder evokes an over-bearing dominance. That would determine how well governance has accounted for stakeholders.

It may be noteworthy that what needs to be governed about the Internet would evolve from time to time in tandem with changes in the stakeholder community, mindful that governance is interpreted differently by different communities. And mindful also of the fact that the ability to act in whatever governance influencing role and as what stakeholder type, may itself be determined by other environmental factors including economic, social and the educational capacity of the individual, business, community or government.

In the end an attempt to deal entirely with governance and ALL the stakeholders would defy the interest of flexibly evolving an organic system of self governance from its simplest to its most complex incarnations, as is often cited. Given the complexity of ensuring that there is satisfactory stakeholder participation in governance, perhaps a divide and rule approach would improve the chances of governing the Internet.

Where has the multi-stakeholder approach and bottom-up policy development come from?

Prior to the incorporation of the Internet Corporation for Assigned Names and Numbers (ICANN) in November 1998 through its pre-curser IAHC, there were no functioning multi-stakeholder policy development institutions and bottom-up policy development processes. Telco policies had been the preserve of governments in concert with an International Telecommunication Union (ITU) regulatory regime. Sovereignty was generally paramount and civil society and industry did not have decision powers even though they could comment and input in some situations, albeit without obligations.

In that era, the predominant systems of government-led telco policy meant a centralised organisation because the governance system was itself extremely centralised with government at the helm of policy decision, instead of industry or civil society. Their participation was always relegated to giving input only, even though the noted stability of the Internet has come from its decentralised, edge-oriented nature reflected in the existing technical institutions and organisations. The ability to keep the centre of things simple and have the more complex things performed at the edges near where human interaction is desired, enables the networks to scale amazingly, with a management based on the bottom-up policy development processes.

Take the case of ICANN. ICANN evolved out of the workings of the parties who have operated the network system with the participation of multi-stakeholders who desired to ensure that things did not go so wrong as to affect the stability and security of the existing technical policy processes. In other cases, civil society saw an opportunity to address the issue of representation, decision powers and a chance for "democracy" on the Internet and demanded better inclusion, openness and transparency from ICANN.

Thus the growth of the Internet has been through grassroots and peer supporting mechanisms that take knowledge to the frontiers. These have grown largely out of the realm of regulatory control and maintained the advantage of innovation at the edges of the networks. The organisations that provide direct services for the Internet i.e. its standards development Internet Engineering Task Force (IETF) process, its Regional Internet Registries that provide numbers for network use and ICANN, the technical coordination organization, use bottom-up policy development that operates very clear notions of consensus in a multi-stakeholder environment.

This process was also adopted by the United Nations ICT Task Force (UNICTTF) in November 2001 following a partner programem DotForce, which also used multi-stakeholders in the private sector, civil society, governments and multi-lateral organisations. Fortunately, they have been effective in developing an acceptable multi-stakeholder approach and raised the profile of the more inclusive approach to policy development. The multi-stakeholder organisation complemented by the United Nations organisation, enabled UNICTTF to organise thought-provoking and open forums that brought to bear the essence of Internet governance and resulted in Internet governance being on the agenda of many who otherwise might not have paid attention to it.

It may be of interest to point out that both organisations – UNICTTF and DotForce – were not designed for decision making but for presenting recommendations to governments and opening dialogue on sensitive subjects in multi-stakeholder forums. The World Summit on the Information Society (WSIS) process has courted multi-stakeholders but with caution and an urge to decide exclusively.

This is because the resolutions that established the process authorised an intergovernmental preparatory committee to decide on the modalities of the participation of other stakeholders. Consequently, private sector participation was through the International Chamber of Commerce while civil society participated through civil society plenary, a content/themes group and bureau comprising civil society families from the media to NGOs through trade unions to youth volunteers and others.

It is on record that at certain meetings in December 2003, observers such as ICANN were excused from a forum on Internet governance, because governments wanted to deliberate alone without observers. This can only create processes that have little or no knowledge and understanding of policy issue positions. This, in spite of the fact that the follow-on actions from the World Summit on the Information Society (WSIS), the Working Group on Internet Governance (WGIG) as well as the Task Force on Financing Mechanisms (TSFM) were all intended to reflect a multi-stakeholder constitution.

What is Internet governance?

Over the decade, opinion has varied on the commercialisation of the Internet from very narrow views of its technical operation to democracy on the Internet.

The organisation that is most often referenced in connection with Internet governance is ICANN. Yet ICANN has deliberately defined its function in a very narrow, be it technical, manner: technical coordination and technical policy development.

ICANN is internationally organised and non-profit making, with responsibility for Internet Protocol (IP) address space allocation, protocol identifier assignment, generic (gTLD) and country code (ccTLD) Top-Level Domain name system management, as well as root server system management functions. These services were originally performed under US Government contract by the Internet Assigned Numbers Authority (IANA) and other entities. ICANN now performs the IANA function.

ICANN is a private-public partnership dedicated to preserving the operational stability of the Internet; to promoting competition; to achieving broad representation of global Internet communities; and to developing policy appropriate to its mission through bottom-up, consensus-based processes.

Even though attempts have been made to expand this mandate, ICANN has rightly maintained that it does not have the expertise to manage a larger mandate. It also considers the method of managing the complexities of governing an organic system as complex as the Internet too centralised. This has been countered by groups who have offered to do the work of the entire task and subsume the current functions of ICANN, often citing ITU. What this group forgets is that as an organisation, the ITU has its own multi-stakeholder participation challenges. Not surprisingly, other inter-governmental structures have also been proposed.

With an inconclusive debate on governance at WSIS I, calls were made to the UN Secretary General to form a working group, the Working Group on Internet Governance (WGIG), to define and make recommendations towards WSIS II.

WGIG defined Internet governance as the development and application by Governments, the private sector and civil society, in their respective roles, of shared principles, norms, rules, decision-making procedures and programmes that shape the evolution and use of the Internet.

This definition admits the virtues of a multi-stakeholder approach to governance, yet the definition has been so general that one wonders if clear roles for participation by stakeholders and decision making will ever be realised. No respective roles have been defined for the stakeholders in the WGIG report, leaving a potential for conflict based on a probable misunderstanding of roles in the proposed governance paradigm.

WGIG took the position that the Internet governance envisaged includes more than Internet names and addresses, and issues dealt with by ICANN. It also includes other significant public policy issues, such as critical Internet resources, the security and safety of the Internet, and development aspects and issues pertaining to the use of the Internet. This definition departs from the narrow technical definition used by ICANN, RIRs and IETF to a broader definition which is yet to indicate how existing technical functions would be performed. It is, however, doubtful that these technical policy processes can be performed by other groups not familiar with the Internet technology and the technical policy process that has evolved with the Internet.

In addition, there was no definition of "critical Internet resources". The Internet resources are largely abstract and do not really have the kind of limits the WGIG report suggests. All perceived limits on IP numbers have been postponed for a long time by the planned migration from IPv4, a 32-bit number scheme, to IPv6, a 128-bit numbering scheme that makes available huge numbers for network use. Similarly, the quest for more root servers has been satisfied by the new "anycast protocol" which permits a sizeable number of root servers to be operating beyond previously considered limits. Hence, the technical community has continued to demonstrate that these limits, though difficult to move, have indeed been pushed back by the technical policy process as they are abstract resources.

The bottom up policy process that evolves these abstract "critical Internet resources" is guided by technical professionals from private sector. It is also guided by research and academic institutions and generally not sufficiently accessible to the not too technically inclined, who may not have the capacity to understand the science and technology of the Internet. Influence in decision making in this case is more by peers and industry success of technical policies. In other words, a façade of a free market force with direct government or inter-governmental oversight of the world's abstract Internet resources may not be a tenable option.

Fortunately, innovation and the rapid development that has primarily been at the edges and more in the knowledge capacity of the people would be without limits in the next decade.

The other identified purpose of the proposed larger governance process had to do with the security and safety of the Internet. This is very relevant and probably crucial to the development of the Internet. But again, there are forums for developing policy for security and safety issues at governmental or inter-governmental policy levels including technical standards for global development. It would therefore be better to adopt functionally specific organizations that specialise on function-specific policy development.

Acknowledging that development and social issues are cherished, especially within the domain of governments and civil society, it may not be easy to ascertain the need for an inter-governmental body to develop aspects and issues pertaining to the use of the Internet. Perhaps a United Nations Commission on Digital Rights might send a clearer mandate that would complement human rights in the new world.

How then, would the bottom up policy development process – so powerful in the rapid development of the Internet – be reconciled in this large attempt to solve all at once the new proposed approach to the paradigm of Internet governance?

Opportunities and barriers for governance of the Internet by stakeholders

There is ample opportunity for participation by stakeholders in the governance of the Internet. Practically, a good amount of technical policy, and therefore the core governance of the Internet, occur in a global realm, since the Internet is a global communications system and requires co-operation, co-ordination and communication of operators for the system to function as one Internet.

The primary organisations that manage policy technical development are the IETF for standards development, the Regional Internet Registries (RIRs) who manage the use of Internet identifiers and ICANN where much of coordination across the different groups occur. All these three groups are multi-stakeholder in structure and have absolutely no obstacle for any one to participate. In fact, considering the emphasis of the edge as opposed to the centre in the organisation of the Internet, all groups insist that consensus reached through a physical meeting needs to be further strengthened by further discussion on lists.

This removes all obstacles from participation, i.e. one only needs to have access to email and be interested in the subject for one to contribute to the different policy mechanisms. Note that these organisations are technical, which demands sufficient understanding of the technical issues in order to participate properly. This is by far the biggest obstacle for developing countries, in particular for Africa to participate. But this is largely about building technical capacity on Internet technologies and affords the less educated in this technology only a lesser degree of participation.

In addition, in order to effectively influence policy, participation would often require more than the use of email only. There ought to be the wish to participate in some physical meetings in order to appreciate the complexities and conflicts among policy positions. This need for physical participation has often prompted all the groups to schedule their meetings in different locations in the world so as to bring the meetings closer to the community and increase global participation.

Being regional, the RIRs improve access and participation in the policy process of operators. Among other things, they attend each other's meetings to present a global access with regional technical policy development, a sort of a global community with local service – a "glocal" model for stakeholder participation. The membership of the RIRs is based on need for numbers from the RIR and thus derives from all the known stakeholder communities that request for numbers.

To attend these meetings routinely presents several other environmental obstacles that affect the ability to participate. All these obstacles relate to social and economic gaps between the developed and developing countries. It is not unusual to have more than 10 meetings in one year among these three technical communities. Notably however, funding for African operators to these meetings has been a challenge that could explain Africa's weaker participation in these forums. Other geo-political factors also affect the ability to participate – including the ease of obtaining travel documents, visas, and flight schedules.

The awareness of the relevance of the issues in developing countries is often less than developed countries. This is not surprising as the networks in Africa are the youngest and may not be expected to exhibit the same level of awareness as the more mature networks. This is explained by the fact that in order to become part of the human network that continues to work on Internet related technical policy, presence is desired from time to time while attempts are made to maintain contact with the community which, is sometimes difficult for those at the edges of the network.

Admittedly participation may not be officially prohibited, but these obstacles make the ability to participate vary from region to region depending on technical capacity, economics, social and geo-political circumstances.

What has been Africa's response?

In the 1990s there was a drive to liberalise the telco sector and to introduce competition. Liberalisation was thought to be the best means of creating a level playing field to attract foreign direct investment (FDI) and also acquire adequately skilled management to develop the industry. Ghana was one of the first African countries to embrace this philosophy – that enabled the establishment of an independent regulator in 1996 and the privatisation of the incumbent telco in which a foreign investor acquired equity. Alongside the incumbent, a second national telco license was issued to a second operator. This was lauded as a success story that would increase foreign direct investments, and rapidly grow fixed network operations and the general telco sector in Ghana.

The duopoly was considered a particularly expedient approach at presenting a gradual entry into a competitive market development in the telco sector. Several governments examined and studied the policy regime of Ghana and followed with their own version of liberalisation programmes.

Ironically, in 2005 the entire liberalisation process appears to have been reversed, with the government of Ghana acquiring all the shares of investors in the two telcos. In one fell swoop, the government of Ghana assumed direct oversight of policy and regulation as well as becoming the operator of the two fixed networks in Ghana. The entire process of 1996 was reversed to the *status quo ante*, when the policy maker was same as the regulator and the operator – rather like being the referee, lines person and player at the same time, much against accepted industry norms. This inevitably undermines the independence of the regulator who, as it were, cannot easily regulate government.

It is as yet unclear whether other African countries that followed similar incumbent telco privatisation policy programmes as Ghana – including Uganda and South Africa – would follow the path of Ghana, though it is doubtful. Some have argued that the reversal of the telco policy in the West African country was due to a policy failure, while others assume the position that the reversal was more inspired by political motivations than the interest of industry.

With Africa as the least developed Internet region, its concerns regarding Internet governance have often been benchmarked for developing countries. Although Africa joined the Internet expansion late, it is also one of the fastest growing Internet regions, with some enjoying in excess a 100% Internet penetration per year. Indeed, in this community, new members join the community sometimes faster than one is able to build capacity in response to technical policy development processes.

The real challenge has therefore been how to maintain the consensus to build Internet governance processes in such a fast growing community.

Governments and regulators had been involved in technical policy for telecoms decades preceding the emergence of the Internet in Africa. Yet very few governments had been involved in any technical policy development in information technology prior to the Internet era, due to convergence pressures.

Fortunately again, Ghana was one of the few countries that made an attempt to be part of the evolving process, in 1975 when the government of the day enacted two decrees to regulate the IT industry. These decrees were no match for today's discussions on Internet governance but it is worthy of note that they included the establishment of an e-government institution within the civil service and a policy development body identified then as the Central System Development Unit (CSDU). There was also a Data Processing Control Board (DPCB). Among other things, the regime also developed policies for the importation of computers.

Unfortunately, however, the institutions failed to integrate into a convergent technology policy regime. Instead, not only Ghana, but all of Africa found itself embroiled in negotiating the development of national ICT policies – that incidentally has occupied these poor nations during the whole of the last decade. In some cases, the act of generating a national policy became an end in itself, with very little attention being paid to developing the human capacity and infrastructure capable of managing the demands of a fast growing convergent industry.

Granted that some argue that without a national policy, priorities could not be determined vis-à-vis poverty reduction strategies. However, there is the observation that in most cases, policy had become an end in itself and forced developing nations to take their eyes off the target of developing their networks. They only talk and do not live the concepts.

The net effect is heightened concern and fears that Africa may never get it right. That just when the continent has begun to appreciate and acknowledge the relevance of their input to the development of IT, ICT and Internet capacities, and make efforts to address them through policies, a more complex but new distraction of Internet governance surfaces. For a continent like Africa, with grossly inadequate networks, this development and the interests and battles that it would engender can never be of a positive disposition towards its quest.

From the general and specifics stated earlier, the better alternative should be to concentrate on building networks and technical capacity when evolving a policy regime; the explanation being that the fundamental reason for the failure of most regulatory systems in the developing world is attitudinal. The attitude of the regulator and policy system is premised on waiting. "Please wait we are developing policy then you can deploy technology." In essence the regulator and policy makers refuse to abide by the pace of rapidly changing technology. Consequently, they have been unable to acquire the technical and operational capacities needed to engender the development of a new industry at the edges of the global Internet community.

I have sought to develop parallel regional technical communities in Africa through participation in the processes of RIR's, IETF and ICANN as a conscious way of building specialized human capacity. This position was well informed by an American who was obsessed with getting the Internet to the most remote areas, and an Asian academic who had observed the need for Asia, Latin America and Africa to coordinate their efforts. These African institutions would become the training ground and incubator for network engineers, who would build and maintain these systems in anticipation of the high growth rate of the Internet, in a bid to transform the digital gap.

I may also add that given the organic nature of the development of these communities as technical colonies, it would be pretentious to attempt to force issues, except to embark on advocacy and lobby for groups to get together to coordinate activities. At the Benin Internet governance conference in 1997, organisations such as the African Network Operators Group (AfNOG), African Network Information Centre (AfriNIC), African ccTLDs (AfTLD), African ISOC chapters (AfISOC) and African Research and Educational networks (AfriR&E) enjoyed certain privileges. They were all meant to satisfy Africa's particular need for technical capacity in the operation of Internet infrastructure and policy creation through its own bottom up policy process. Fortunately, all the organisations exist in some form but are at different stages of development and largely successful. These institutions have become commonly known as the Af* organizations.

AfriNIC, the numbers registry, has been the most successful and represents Africa's commitment, despite the diverse network and regulatory issues. Consensus was developed after more than a decade of effort to establish a functioning numbers registry accredited by ICANN and therefore joining the community of RIR's of LACNIC, APNIC, ARIN and RIPE. That was an example of consensus building, even though new members arrived faster than the community was able to agree policy processes. As for the school of thought that one could get caught in a whirlwind of continuously re-educating new members, the answer is that the nuances of the technical subject of the Internet would reach a consensus with a true application of the bottom up policy process.

Also, the success of AfriNIC is closely tied to the operator community AfNOG which, is the actual community of operators: commercial, educational, research or civil society, who meet once a year for workshops on scaleable services and backbone routing and who also hold co-ordination meetings and conferences. The technical workshops, which are bi-lingual in French and English, were modelled after ISOC network technology workshops. AfNOG has held meetings once a year since the maiden event of May 2000 in Cape Town, South Africa. AfNOG meetings have since been held in Ghana, Togo, Uganda, Senegal and Mozambique. The AfNOG community was instrumental in working out the consensus process for the establishment of AfriNIC. This community has the expertise to prepare their charges on scaleable services, backbone routing, exchange points, ccTLD operations, root server principles and in general a community of technical resources to guard the development of the Internet in Africa. AfNOG benefited immensely from the experience of senior members of the global Internet engineering community through support and technical assistance from the Network Startup Resource Center (NSRC).

Not surprisingly, a decade later other related organisations emerged, notable among them being the African ISP Association (AfrISPA) which is a regional association of national trade associations of commercial ISPs. It has taken it upon itself to promote the development of Internet exchanges among its members.

The AfTLD sought to bring the African ccTLD Technical Point Of Contact and Admin Point Of Contact into a community where they may share technical best practices and co-ordinate their services regionally. Unfortunately, the appearance of the nation-state on the management of the country code name spaces has diverted some attention from the development of this community.

While appreciating the relevance of the African Research and Educational Network Community for the Internet – though not in as co-ordinated and deliberate a manner – it may attract more than a mere glance given the critical role they would play in future networks. This community has to quickly come up to speed on next generation Internet-works and drive the development of future networks in Africa.

With such a very diffused user community in Africa it may be commendable that Internet Societies in Africa have often been there to articulate and motivate discussion on social issues.

Conclusion

In conclusion, while the urge to be part of the evolution of telecommunication could be legitimate and timely, the same may not be said for a commodity as abstract as the Internet.

With the new world of the Internet, governance could legitimately be achieved through representation and expression if the issue of ability and expertise to manage a system as organic and complex as the Internet was addressed.

That way, the promised new world in virtual space would be capable of fulfilling the future aspirations of *every* Internet user, direct or indirect.

The solution would not be to attempt to apply revolutionary principles to a process as evolutionary as the Internet.

Dr Nii Quaynor graduated from Dartmouth College in 1972 with B.A (Engineering Science) and received a Ph.D (Computer Science) specializing in distributed systems in 1977 from S.U.N.Y at StonyBrook. Dr Quaynor worked with Digital Equipment Corporation in U.S.A from 1977 till 1992 when he retired and returned to Ghana to establish the first Internet Service operated by Network Computer Systems (NCS) in West Africa in 1993.

Over the years Dr Quaynor has served on a number of boards including ICANN and he is currently a member of the UN ICT Task Force. He is the Director of Enterprise Africa, a regional business development organization of the UNDP, chairman of NCS and an Adjunct professor of Computer Science at University of Cape-Coast, Ghana. He has been a founding member of AfriNIC, Africa's number registry and AfNOG, African Network Operators Group(AfNOG) Technical workshop, Meetings and Conference programme and a past Lecturer at the International Center for Theoretical Physics.

Contact details: Dr Nii Quaynor, Chairman Network Computer Systems Ltd, PMB Osu, Accra, Ghana.
Tel: +233 21 779321 Email: quaynor@ghana.com.

Dr. Jean-François Soupizet

Deputy Head of Unit, International Relations,
DG Information Society and Media, European Commission

14.

Fighting the digital divide :
the challenge for small consumers

Dr. Jean-François Soupizet*

Deputy Head of Unit, International Relations,
DG Information Society and Media, European Commission

In the Declaration of Principles adopted in Geneva on 12 December 2003, at the conclusion of the first phase of the World Summit on the Information Society, political leaders agreed to recognise the potential of information and communication technologies (ICTs) in socio-economic development, including their contribution to attainment of the Millennium Development Goals. In this context, the debate on the digital divide is of particular relevance, as was the debate triggered by publication of *The Missing Link* twenty years ago. Against this background, this paper: a) defines the accessibility situation today, b) questions the impact of changing the dominant model for managing telecommunication services from the public to the private sphere in developing countries, and c) explores the reality behind the emergence of new solvent demand from the substantial new expectations of low income consumers. Econometric references developed here are taken from academic research carried out in the Université Libre de Bruxelles on the impact of the ICTs in developing economies.

From The Missing Link to the digital divide

First, the broadly spread introduction of ICTs is a reality in all countries of the world, independently of their development level. Statistical evidence shows that this diffusion has accelerated in recent years, and that in most cases, expansion rates are higher in developing economies than in industrialised ones. In addition, this diffusion includes a broad range of technologies, including satellite, cable and wireless technologies, as well as new services, such as mobile telephony and the Internet. Moreover, international scale projects relating to communication infrastructures have been implemented – for example the SAT-3 submarine cable connecting the

The views expressed here are those of the author and may not in any circumstances be regarded as stating an official position of the European Commission.

African continent or the Thuraya satellite communication service. This has been the experience for every development region: sub-Saharan Africa, Latin America and the Caribbean, North Africa, the Middle East and Asia.

But the question is whether this evolution is powerful enough not only to maintain the pace of growth for industrialised countries, but also to bridge the existing gap between different parts of the world. To assess this evolution, a simple econometric model based on a "digital distance" between different countries or groups of countries has proved to be enlightening.

Bridging the missing link, widening the digital divide

Instead of following approaches adopted in most of the existing literature, based on comparisons between digital indexes, I have developed an empirical measure of the digital divide (method A), using a natural gap between countries, characterized by four variables representing the density per inhabitant of the various means of access: fixed and mobile telephony, PCs and the Internet. The specific statistical method used was principal component analysis, since it offers the advantage of not imposing an *ex ante* weighting of variables in calculation of the gap. On the contrary, the weighting is a result of the method.

Countries have been grouped in four clusters: OECD countries and then three groups classified on the basis of GNP per inhabitant in high medium income, low medium income and low income. In parallel, a statistical observation (method B) was developed on the same groups of countries but taking into account only access to fixed telephony. The result of method A shows an impressive coherence of evolution between countries of a same group and strong similarities between the evolutions of the three groups of developing countries.

Over the period 1988-2000, the method put in evidence three periods. First, gaps between industrialised countries and those in development increase relatively slightly between 1988 and 1993, and then stabilise and decline between 1993 and 1997, reflecting a period of correction relating to fixed telephony infrastructures. But starting from 1998, the gap increased again quickly and by 2000, it was practically a multiplication by three of gaps initially estimated between the OECD and each group of developing countries at the beginning of the period. During the same period, method B, measuring only fixed telecommunication access, showed favourable evolution of the gap as the situation of less developed countries improved and the differences between various categories of countries was reduced.

It is paradoxical to note that the digital divide seemed to be widening when traditional telecommunications was improving and that many specialists considered that the challenge of the "missing link" was partly

198

resolved thanks to considerable improvement in communications access, and in particular to the development of mobile telephony.

This paradox is only superficial. It is explained by the fact that method A broadened the basis of the measure to the various systems of access and led to technical evolution being taken into account. With the shift from "telecommunication" to "information society", we passed from the missing link to the digital divide. The first is still to be partly fixed, the second is still widening.

Did the mobile telephony boom in the South change the deal?

Everywhere, including in the South, the diffusion of mobile telephony is booming. One figure is sufficient to illustrate the fact: in 2002, i.e. a few years after its arrival as a technology for the general public, mobile telephony connected the same number of users as had been connected to fixed networks over more than the previous thirty years. And, specifically, its spread was just as dynamic in emergent countries such as Brazil, Morocco or China, as in industrialised ones. Moreover, to date, the Chinese market constitutes the largest market in the world.

Did mobile telephony represent the answer to the digital divide? I would advocate in favour of a prudent approach, because as has been made clear in the preceding paragraphs, the digital divide is not the result of delay in the deployment of a specific communication infrastructure. It has resulted from the accumulation of delays occurring with the emergence of each successive wave of technological innovation: mobile telephony, Internet, broadband yesterday, Wi-Fi today and WiMax tomorrow.

It is the reduced ability to make use of information and communication technologies in the structural context of successive innovations that makes the difference. In fact, where innovation is a structural factor of change in the information society, this gap threatens to exacerbate all other disparities. Moreover, it would be risky to promise that everyone in the world will shortly have access to mobile communication services, while there remain areas that are badly served in the European Union, the leader in the field. Finally, the Internet, whose economic role is growing, still lags behind mobile telephony as a means of access, even if Wi-Fi and WiMax technologies open very real opportunities in urban areas both for the Internet as such and for voice communication services through the Internet.

In conclusion, mobile telephony appears certain to give numerous citizens worldwide access to telecommunications. However, without technical and commercial modifications, this technology is unlikely to cover rural areas with low population density, nor to give, at an affordable cost, access to the added value services that constitute a basis for economic transformation.

However, it is interesting to underline the reasons for its success: the appropriate technology; the commercial model adopted, in particular the prepaid card that has played a considerable role by making available services to low income consumers; distribution compatible with the socio-economic characteristics of its customers. These are the elements that have made mobile telephony a reality in the South.

Did the shift towards private funding have an impact on the development of accessibility?

A second area for reflection concerns the transformation of the dominant economic model that took place during the decade 1990-2000: the telecommunication sector passed from a public model of financing and management to a private one. In developing countries, the role of the external influence was predominant in this evolution. Financial constraints hanging over the public sector, pressure of demand and the international environment led these countries to adopt a "liberal" model based on private investment, competition and the creation of regulatory authorities.

In this context, a descriptive study of accessibility to telecommunication services confirms that, in the first place, income per capita levels provide an initial explanation for greater distribution. However, the role of income is only apparent because comparisons cover heterogeneous countries. If we segment countries by income level, the relation between income per capita and infrastructure level shows that weak income differences do not have considerable effects on access infrastructures. This suggests that short-term interactions between the distribution of ICT and relative wealth cannot be easily established.

Broadly, distribution of the means of access has accelerated and should continue to accelerate in developing countries at a rate higher than in industrialised countries, although elasticities remain very high in this category of countries. So we find that penetration thresholds have been lowered significantly: levels of per capita annual average income corresponding to a distribution to 1% of the population in 2000 are US$ 330 for fixed telephony, US$ 500 for mobile telephony and US$ 1,000 for use of the Internet. Five years earlier, they were respectively US$ 500, US$ 4,730 and US$ 10,600.

A second key factor is time. Study of the networks' development through time series was carried out by using logistical mathematical models ('S' shape curves). This made it possible to clarify the dynamics of network growth while referring to observations in industrialised countries where these models have significantly explained developments. For developing countries, it appears that below a given deployment threshold of about 5%, progression is not comparable with models observed in industrialised countries. Beyond this same threshold, developments become more regular and logistical models explain them in an acceptable way – although comparisons against the background of industrialised countries are not convincing. Indeed, we could not observe phenomena suggesting saturation, and, in particular, the results proved that inflection points had not been reached. In this context, available observations are compatible with very different values of the parameters used in the models and it is not possible to derive long-term forecasts from them.

On the other hand, this analysis gives a forecast valid within limited time periods. As such it could be possible to "rebuild" a theoretical present, for example without privatisation, by extending the latest trends, and to observe the effects of restructuring the sector. Observations suggest that strategies which combine market privatisation and liberalisation have a measurable positive effect – and that there is a genuine setback on the graphs accounting for the development of accessibility. This method provides concrete examples of the impact of liberalisation, notably in the case of Brazil and other Latin American countries.

An economic model to quantify the impact of market structure

Taking into account the previous studies, I retained three key factors in the development of accessibility: income per capita, time and market structure (competition and private ownership of the incumbent).

To quantify the effect of each factor, a general model was worked out using a base of 90 developing countries, and by using a panel method (see overleaf). For fixed telephony infrastructures, time undeniably appears as the first explanatory variable with an effect of 28%, followed by gross national income per capita at 16%, the effect of liberalisation measures can be estimated respectively at 8.1% for the setting up of an independent regulator and the introduction of competition and this effect amounts to 9.5% for privatisation of the historical operator. The combined effect of both changes is established at 17.6% and it is higher than the effect of incomes. However, this measure could be an underestimate since it takes as swing date engagement of the process of privatisation and of the introduction of competition which, in the majority of the cases, proceeds in several stages.

This systematic exploration of the effect of opening up markets demonstrates that, in developing countries, the introduction of competition and accessibility to capital through the traditional operator had a measurable positive effect everywhere.

This same methodology was extended to the different access variables, with significant results for mobile telephones and PCs. It shows that the effect of time is much more important than simple observation had previously confirmed, and demonstrates the effectiveness of privatisation

General model of development of telecom access with fixed effects, centered variables and heterocedasticity correction:

$$CCLP= B1\ CLPNBT+ B2\ CTEMP+ B3CPRIV+ B4\ CREG$$

LP: Teledensity fixes for a date t

PNBT: GNP per capita for a date t

TEMP: Time of the panel

PRIV (0,1): Binary variable representing the privatisation and indicating the partial or total privatisation of the historical operator.

REG (0,1): Binary variable representing the Regulation and indicating the creation of a regulation authority. In practice, this date coincides with the first step towards the effective liberalisation of the market and the introduction of competition.

In addition C means centred data and L the use of Logarithm.

B for constant terms to be estimated by the model.

Results of the general model on the main lines applied to 90 developing and emerging economies from 1990 to 2000 gave the following estimates:

$$CLLP= 0.16\ CLPNBT + 0.28\ CTEMP + 0.09\ CPRIV + 0.08\ CREG$$

measures and of the introduction of competition on all access methods. However, this impact remains limited.

This coincides well with empirical observations: liberal strategies mean raising the constraints of supply and result in markets developing in which the constraint becomes that of demand. The order of magnitude of this effect is significant, but its amplitude remains limited, and in the absence of data to measure an impact over a longer period, we do not have data to allow us to predict that solvent demand will be sufficient to ensure the basis of a universal service.

In addition, it is worth mentioning that, in the vast majority of cases, mobile telephony developed thanks to private financing. In some countries that had not yet restructured their electronic communication services, it was the first form of competition faced by the traditional operator.

In this context, the role of regulatory frameworks favourable to competition in developing countries is highlighted. This position is even re-emphasised by the Statement of Principle adopted by the UN's World Summit on the Information Society.

Developing countries and threats against the model

A pro-competitive regulatory framework has shown significant positive impact on access but might not be enough to bridge the digital divide and there are threats against the fund raising scheme for the development of telecommunication infrastructures in developing countries. This model of organisation of the telecommunications sector held "motorboat high-speed" during the 1990-2000 decade and corresponds to massive engagement of the private sector in the financing of telecommunication infrastructures.

But after a 'golden age' of private investment in access infrastructures, in particular during the high point of privatisation of telecommunication operations in the decade 1990-2000, comes a period that begins with far less impetus. Indeed, analysis of privatisations already achieved shows that foreign direct investment played a key role in these developments. Prevailing conditions on capital markets are less favourable to ICT: on the one hand, the most attractive privatisations have already been completed; on the other hand, the sector has been through a financial crisis that reduced financial availability.

Moreover, international communications revenues, which constituted a source of income for developing countries, threaten to dry up, and this is jeopardizing investments. By and large, the General Agreement under the WTO is changing previous arrangements for sharing international traffic revenues. In addition, the benchmarking order adopted by the US administration in 1997 limits payments made by US operators for call termination costs to their counterpart in developing countries. Finally, the rapid development of communications on Internet networks, including voice over IP, is changing the distribution of charges. On a traditional international phone call, revenues are shared between the different countries involved; in an IP communication the Internet user from a developing country is charged by his Internet service provider (ISP) for the totality of the cost (outgoing *and* ingoing communication). These changes are gradually transforming countries that were service exporters into net importers. They may dramatically reduce the revenues from international communications, making it more difficult for local investment in the sector and making telecom operators less attractive to foreign investors. It is clear that the mechanisms which allowed the rapid development of infrastructures in the last decade of the 20th century may be not sustainable in the 21st century.

How to foster the emergence of solvent demand: the low income consumer

In this context, national solvent demand constitutes the key factor, because it is the only area that will attract the levels of investment necessary to deliver accessibility. There is also a real problem of demand in developing countries: prices are too high to ensure distribution to the whole population, and difficulties of use remain important obstacles. However, note that the 'killer applications' remain email and voice telephony.

The central question becomes the following: under what stable economic conditions can a new solvent demand emerge? First, it is clear that existing technologies are compatible with other methods of organisation and it should be possible to offer basic communications services to very large markets in emerging and developing economies. This market would be made up of innumerable low income consumers who could benefit from accessibility in order to improve the determining factors of their situation. If we consider that out of 6.5 billion human beings, a little more than one billion are already connected, this concept is also referred to as the next two billions. This idea echoes work and projects from another field, carried out with micro-credit. It is moreover interesting to note the synergy between the two approaches carried out by NGOs active in the field.

Recently, collective accessibility has developed in several countries, according to various models and in particular, that of 'telecentres'. A study of this means of accessibility, based on case studies of the various experiments conducted both in the North and in the South, demonstrated that price and contractual conditions for interconnection are the determining elements for durability of service supply. This outcome is backed up by a more theoretical approach based on the instruments of vertical integration analysis. In this context, a competitive environment for telecommunication operators would be beneficial for the development of telecentres. However, in many cases, telecom operators prefer to obtain a dominant position via contractual clauses rather than by carrying out vertical integration through absorption of these centres. Regulation certainly has a role to play in offering a status for micro enterprises offering collective access and to compensate to some extent for excessively unbalanced bargaining power between the players.

Subject to this provision, collective access currently represents one of the most promising ways of developing affordable accessibility. Besides, it illustrates the reality of alternative access methods and the potential of markets for consumers with low incomes.

These same characteristics are found in other alternative ICT access models, such as collective access through mobile phones in Bangladesh, (known as the Grameen Phone and developed by a joint venture between TELENOR and the Grameen Bank), cyber-cafes, low cost computer projects such as the simputer, or alternative technologies.

In this respect, these models are also likely to contribute towards bridging the digital divide and beyond, to reaching some of the Millennium Development Goals. Offering a genuine service at an affordable cost could mean new perspectives for users and, in turn, become a central factor for bottom up economic development.

Numerous examples show that ICTs are a factor for genuine progress, as explained by President Wade of Senegal at the opening session of the preparatory Conference of the World Summit on the Information Summit.

Developing accessibility involves, therefore, a broad transformation that includes both the relevant sector context and other elements such as availability of use and the relevant contents. Such policies have been designed in the European Union and taken up by numerous developing countries under the strategies concept (Toporkoff, 2001). In this context, regulatory aspects play a key role. This is not only true for large companies and worldwide markets: some of the key principles may also apply to local markets for the benefit of small consumers.

However, this market will not emerge spontaneously. It can do so only by means of a different approach in which the private sector must adopt a new attitude and identify the potential of growth of these new markets and the conditions to develop them in a sustainable way. To the same end, members of civil society probably have a key role to play in ensuring takeup, notably through the creation of relevant content – equally important in the diffusion of technologies and their uses.

In this respect, initiatives taken in preparation for the World Summit on the Information Society (WSIS), which aim to incorporate the three stakeholders as recommended by the DOT Force, reflect well the political importance attached to the generalisation of access to the networks of electronic communication services, i.e. fighting against the digital divide. Without a massive improvement in accessibility, it is probable that the impact of information technology in developing countries will be limited.

JEAN-FRANÇOIS SOUPIZET is Deputy Head of Unit, International Relations, DG Information Society And Media at the European Commission, with particular responsibility for the World Summit on the Information Society and issues related to the digital divide.

Dr Soupizet is an economist specialising in international relations and global issues in the field of information and communication technologies. Before joining the European Commission, he occupied positions in the French Administration and the Intergovernmental Office for Informatics (IBI) – based in Rome under the aegis of UNESCO. A graduate from the French National School of Statistics and Economic Administration in Paris, he is Doctor of Economic Sciences at the *Université Libre de Bruxelles*, and a member of Futuribles International, a French think tank. He has published several papers on ICT and development, notably *The Information Society and Developing Countries: the European Contribution* (Communications & Strategies edited IDATE, Sept/Oct 1998) and *Prospects for Universal Access in Developing Countries* (*Cahiers Economiques de Bruxelles* No.166, 2000). Jean-François Soupizet is editor of *Nord et Sud Numériques* (Hermes-Science, Paris, Feb 2002) and author of *La Fracture Numérique Nord Sud*, (Economica 2005).

Contact details: Jean-François Soupizet, Deputy Head of International Relations for the Information Society, European Commission
Av. de Beaulieu 24, 1160 Brussels, Belgium
Tel: +322 2968964 Fax : +322 2968970 Email: jean-francois.soupizet@cec.eu.int.

Leonid E. Varakin

Member of the Maitland Commission,
President of the International Telecommunication Academy,
Professor, Doctor of Technical Sciences

15.

The Maitland Commission:
the digital divide decrease

Leonid E. Varakin

Member of the Maitland Commission
President of the International Telecommunication Academy,
Professor, Doctor of Technical Sciences

My work in the Maitland Commission began in 1984 when I was invited to the USSR Ministry for Telecommunications and was informed of my appointment to the position as Head of the Soviet delegation for participation in the work of the International Independent Commission for World Wide Telecommunications Development. I was under the direction of the Ministry for Telecommunications as Rector of the All-Union Telecommunication Institute by Correspondence.

I was informed that the level of the Commission was very high – ministers of telecommunications, bankers and presidents of major companies. I was sent to the first meeting alone as there was not enough time to register my assistant and interpreter. The meeting had to be held in Leeds Castle in England. I could not find a town with such a name on the map of England. In the Ministry I was informed that Leeds Castle was situated near London. The Commission's representatives met me at Heathrow Airport, set me in the limousine and took me straight to Leeds Castle. It was dark by the time we approached a building. People came out to meet us, took my luggage and we entered... a Palace. The walls were covered with pictures by Old Masters and old Persian carpets; magnificent bronze sculptures and china vases stood all round. While going upstairs, I asked the attendant:

"Sir, could you please tell me the cost of the room in this hotel?"

And the answer was: "Sir, you are a guest of Her Majesty the Queen?"!

Leeds Castle turned out to be a castle for English Queens. This is how my work in the Maitland Commission started. And I have unforgettable memories about Leeds Castle – truly a castle for English Queens – and other wonderful places where the meetings of the Maitland Commission were held. Munich in Germany, Dar es Salaam and Arusha in Tanzania, Jakarta and Bali in Indonesia – always there are happy memories.

The structure of the Maitland Commission was indeed unique.

Representatives of seventeen countries of four continents were included in it: five from Asia, five from Europe, four from Africa and three from North America. Practically all world regions, major countries, military-political blocs were represented in the Commission. There were elevcen ministers and senior diplomats, two presidents from among the world's largest corporations (AT&T, NEC) and four professors representing scientific and educational organizations. The author of this essay belonged to the last group. Time showed that, on the one hand, the structure of the Maitland Commission was highly representative, and, on the other hand, small enough to get a final document – the report *The Missing Link*. Undoubtedly, in forming a Commission, the Administrative Council of the International Telecommunication Union (ITU) and the ITU Secretary-General Richard Butler in person did everything in their power to make the work of the Commission efficient and effective.

As chairman, Sir Donald Maitland was the Commission's engine and supervisor. A professional diplomat, top-manager, highly educated and intelligent person, he could attentively listen to opposite views of the Commission's members, suggest compromise (consensus) settlements, strictly follow time-limits of the meetings and lead the commission to complete its task – publication of *The Missing Link*. All of the Commission's members were lucky to have such a Chairman. That is why the Independent Commission for World Wide Telecommunications Development has been called the Maitland Commission afterwards. It is worth mentioning also the well-coordinated work of the Commission's Secretariat, with John Gilbert at its head.

Publication of *The Missing Link* in December 1984 received a positive welcome, as a result of some very specific elements. Firstly, the Report was the first international document that considered how telecommunications in developing countries was fall behind industrial countries. As a matter of fact, the Report as well as the work of the Commission, had a political orientation.

Secondly, the real state of telecommunications in developing countries was reflected in the Report. One phrase – that "there are more telephone sets in Tokyo than on the Africa continent with its population of 500 million people" – became a key to the whole Report, as it showed the poor state of telecommunications in developing countries.

Thirdly, suggestions on technology development, manpower training and financing for telecommunications progress in developing countries were given in the Report.

Fourthly, recommendations developed by the Commission were also addressed to international organisations, heads of states, equipment manufacturers and telecommunications operators' representatives.

Since its publication, time and again I have found links to the Maitland

Commission Report in professional literature in the work of the telecommunication community.

In fact, the Maitland Commission and *The Missing Link* were forerunners of the World Summit on the Information Society. And although the words "digital divide" do not appear in the Report, what we now know as the digital divide between industrial and developing countries is the key question dealt with by the Maitland Commission.

My work in the Maitland Commission was first of all political. On the one hand, being the Head of the Soviet delegation it was essential that I actively discussed all issues of the Commission's agenda. In my speeches I sought to confirm the position of the Soviet Union in supporting developing countries and lend countenance in their attempt to telecommunications infrastructure development. On the other hand, it was necessary to attentively treat suggestions of other delegations, to ensure that the Commission would not make any decision against the interests of my country. The fact is that there was a complicated political situation in the world at that time. Fortunately global politics did not interfere with the Commission's meetings.

My main work in the Commission went according to my practical activity in the field of manpower training and scientific research. That is why I took an active part in discussions and statement of recommendations on telecommunications technologies and manpower training. At my urgent request the cellular concept of frequency assignment and other suggestions on wireless communications for setting networks in rural and remote areas were written down into the Report (p.31). The fact is that cellular communications with code division of multiple access (CDMA in modern terminology) was one of my scientific studies at that time. My first scientific work in this field was published in 1973. Apparently this work appeared prematurely. Nevertheless, it is personally rewarding to note that the cellular concept was introduced in the *The Missing Link* in 1984.

In the twenty years since the Maitland Commission, there have been significant changes both in telecommunications and infocommunications as a whole (infocommunications = informatisation+telecommunications). Worldwide figures on infocommunications for 1982 and 2003 are given in Table 1 (overleaf), based on data from the International Telecommunication Union (ITU), World Bank (WB) and the International Telecommunication Academy (ITA)[1].

In 1982 (the year of the Maitland Commission estimates) there were 587 million fixed telephones. The number of mobile telephones was very small. Thw world population was 4.6 billion people and telephone density in 1982 averaged 13% (or about 13 telephones per 100 people).

In 2003 (according to ITU and World Bank figures) the world population amounted to 6.273 billion people, the number of fixed telephones stood at

Table 1. Basic world infocommunications indicators 1982 and 2003			
Parameters	1982	2003	Parameters variation: 2003/1982
Total number of telephones, millions	587	2547	4.3
Telephone density, %	13	41	3.2
Fixed telephones, millions	587	1148	2
Fixed telephone density, %	13	19	1.5
Mobile telephones, millions	–	1399	–
Mobile telephone density, %	–	22	–
Personal computers, millions	5	589	118
Personal computers density, %	0.1	10	100
Internet subscribers, millions	–	675	–
Internet subscribers density, %	–	11	–
Broadband communications subscribers, millions	–	62.5	–
Broadband communications density, %	–	1	–
Source: ITU, WB, ITA			

1.148 billion, and the number of mobile telephones amounted to 1.399 billion. So the total number of telephones equaled 2.547 billion pieces, and telephone density mounted to 41%. So over a period of 21 years, the number of telephones increased by 4.3 times, and telephone density increased by 3.2 times. The number of telephones on a yearly average grew at a rate of 7%, and telephone density by 5.6%. First and foremost, such a sudden rise in the quantity of telephones is influenced by the rise in the use of mobile telephones.

For the last 20 years there have been sudden changes in mankind's technological structure: personal computers have penetrated into the masses; PCs have become the basis for new wide-ranging means of communication – Internet, broadband communications have appeared etc. All these have been possible due to significant scientific and industrial success in the field of microelectronics and software support. By the middle of 2005 the number of telephones in the world amounted to 3.3 billion (among which there are 1.4 billion fixed and 1.9 billion mobile telephones), the number of personal computers (PC) exceeded 700 million. The number of transistors in PC processors changed from 2890 thousand to 140 million, i.e. have increased by 500 times in the last 20 years!

Distribution of telecommunications resources changed in the world, too. In Africa (which the Maitland Commission estimated had the same number of telephones as Tokyo in 1984) in 2003 the number of telephones exceeded 71 million – totally negating the comparison. At the same time, telephone density in Africa equaled to 8.6% – 4.8 times less than the world average telephone density. This proves that the digital divide between industrial (developed) countries and developing countries still exists today. Not surprisingly, one of the main tasks of the World Summit on the Information Society is development of measures to reduce the digital divide.

The digital divide in the modern world between developed and developing countries remains a reality. The Maitland Commission made international organizations, heads of government and business representatives aware of its existence and suggested a number of measures to eliminate the unequal distribution of telecommunications resources in the world. To my mind the Maitland Commission started the process of reducing the digital divide. The task of the World Summit on Information Society is to take effective measures for the future decrease of the digital divide. But to reduce the digital divide it is necessary to be able to measure it and to continue monitoring its changes. This is one of this author's scientific tasks today.

It is worth saying that we change as the world changes and this author is no exception! After my three years work with the Maitland Commission ended, I was appointed Director General of a major scientific institute – the Central Scientific and Research Telecommunications Institute in Moscow, where I worked for 15 years. Telecommunications economics was among other scientific branches under my supervision (telecommunication technologies, switching, fiber-optic communication networks etc.). Work experience in the Maitland Commission, my acquaintance with problems in telecommunications development as a whole, and in developing countries in particular proved invaluable in my work.

In 1996 my friends and I established the International Telecommunication Academy (ITA) with headquarters in Moscow and branches in Russia, Latvia, Ukraine, Georgia, Switzerland, Germany, and Italy. The ITA unites about 700 academicians from 46 countries. In 2001 the ITA joined the United Nations as a non-governmental organization (NGO), obtained Special Consultative Status with the UN Economic and Social Council (ECOSOC), and became an associate member of the UN Department of Public Information (DPI). The ITA is also an associate member of the ITU and the European Telecommunications Standardisation Institute (ETSI).

The ITA conducts considerable public, scientific and publishing activity including matters relating to socio-economic development. As a result the ITA has published many valuable research books, including the following by this author:

- *Global Information Society: Development Criteria and Socio-economic Aspects* – Moscow: ITA, 2002
- *Distribution of Incomes, Technologies and Services* – Moscow: ITA, 2002
- *Digital Divide in the Global Information Society. The Theory and Practice of Measurement* – Moscow, 2004.

Research into measurement issues relating to the digital divide was started in the first two books and reflected by WSIS in the third book.

To define the divide (both digital and economic) between groups of countries and groups of people within a particular state, it is necessary to use indicators that characterise the level of common weal available to one inhabitant of a particular country. This is telephone density (TD) per 100 inhabitants for the digital divide (which may be evaluated in percentage terms). And it is Gross National Product or Domestic Product (GNP or GDP) for the economic divide. Data for all states should be ranged then, i.e. put in rising order before being integrated and summarised. The cumulative (integral, accumulated) function of parameter distribution between considered countries would be found as a result. The Lorenz curve reflects this function in economics. Such cumulative functions are generally reflected by dispersion curves. We can find a row of indicators which characterize the unsteadiness of considered parameter distribution (inequality) between countries including the well-known Gini co-efficient K_G, extremes ratio (e.g. parameters ratio in 20% "the rich" group to 20% "the poor" group) etc. These questions are considered in more detail in the third book mentioned above. The results of digital and economic divides calculation are shown in Table 2 (opposite). Note that to define the telephone communication dispersion curve in 1982, the data on fixed telephones was used, but the total number of fixed and mobile telephones was used for 2003 (as shown in Table 1).

Table 2 shows that for 21 years from 1982 to 2003, the digital divide has been greatly reduced: the Gini Coefficient K_G fell to 1.27=1/0.79 or to 21%; the extremes ratio «20%/20%» fell to 4.4=1/0.23. This level of digital divide decrease can be explained as follows:

1. The Maitland Commission report and the work of international organisations and national governments
2. Significant development of infocommunication technologies, and mobile communication above all
3. Significant reductions in the cost of infocommunication equipment for the past 21 years.

Table 2. Digital and economic divide 1982 and 2003				
Year	Digital Divide (Telephone Density)		Economic Divide (GNP share)	
	Gini Coefficient K_G	Extremes Ratio 20%/20%	Gini Coefficient K_G	Extremes Ratio 20%/20%
1982	0.7	248	0.64	54
2003	0.55	57	0.68	93
Parameters ratio 2003/1982	0.79	0.23	1.06	1.72
Changes %	-21	-77	+6	+72

Sources: the Maitland Commission Report, ITU, WB, ITA.

As for the economic divide, it has not been reduced during 21 years, but has actually grown: the Gini Coefficient KG grew 6%, and the extremes ratio «20%/20%» – to 72%. This means that despite some decrease in the digital divide, economic inequality between developing and developed (industrial) countries is growing. That confirms the old saying "the rich grow richer and the poor get poorer" once again. This is the main reason for instability in the world and it is a cause for concern.

Finally, it is worth noting that the sharp increase in infocommunication resources (fixed and mobile telephone communication, Internet, broadband communication) and the digital divide decrease have occurred since the Maitland Commission completed its work. However, the decrease in the digital divide is not enough. There are many developing countries with insufficient levels of infocommunication development, and there are many poor people who have no access to information resources.

That is why the world community faces a serious task to reduce the digital divide. And undoubtedly, the World Summit on the Information Society should contribute significantly to this noble affair.

Reference

1. The data were summarized and reported at the 7th International Forum ITA' 2005 "25 Years of Infocommunication Revolution" – Moscow, March 2005. The data for 1982 are given according to the Maitland Commission Report.

Leonid E. Varakin (Professor, Dr. Tech. Sc., ORBL, OBH) is President of the International Telecommunication Academy (ITA).

Professor Varakin is also Chairman of the Moscow A.S. Popov's Science and Research Society for Radio-Engineering, Electronics and Telecommunications, State Prize winner of the Russian Federation in the field of science and engineering, Government Prize winner of the Russian Federation, Honoured Scientist and Engineer of the Russian Federation, State Prize winner of the Ukraine in the field of science and engineering.

He is author of more than 350 published scientific papers in the field of information theory, theory of spread-spectrum signals, CDMA theory, radio-receiving and radar equipment, theory of telecommunication, switching and fiber-optical communication lines. In recent years, professor Varakin has been actively involved in the fields of macroeconomics, infocommunications development forecasting and global information society issues.

Contact details: Professor Leonid E. Varakin,
President The International Telecommunication Academy,
7a 1-st Parkovaya str., Moscow 105037, Russia.
Tel: +7 095 740 3234 Email: varak@ita.org.ru.

David Cleevely

Chairman, Communications Research Network
University of Cambridge

16.

What can technology tell us about the next 20 years?

David Cleevely

Chairman, Communications Research Network, University of Cambridge

No-one who has travelled extensively over the past 20 years can have failed to have noticed two profound changes in communications. One is the widespread use of mobile phones: even the poorest countries' mobile phone penetration is 2 or 3 times that of fixed telephone lines. The other is the Internet café. Someone from 20 years ago would probably not believe the number of places where it is now possible to use a computer to send or receive email or to access the World Wide Web, nor the intensive use to which it is put.

Of course neither mobile communications nor the Internet are ubiquitous: many in the developing world either cannot afford to use either of them, and they are not available everywhere because rural areas suffer twice over – from poverty and from high cost of supply. However, the situation now is radically different from that which might have been expected back in the 1980s. In part this is due to the reductions in cost, and advances in technology, but changes in regulation and innovation in business models have also played a major role. On the supply side, these factors have lead inexorably towards the dis-integration of telecommunications: the ability to pick and choose the products and services which best meet the needs of the customer and to innovate at a faster and faster pace. On the demand side effective use of ICT is demanding more and more knowledge and expertise from the users.

In 1933, H.G. Wells wrote a history of the 20th and 21st Centuries called *The Shape of Things to Come*. Wells looked for long run trends and wove them into a coherent narrative. He thought that the 20th Century would be a violent and unpleasant period, but that, as it came to a close, some fundamental changes would take place which would enable the world to grow and prosper. Wells identified one trend in particular: the increasing role of knowledge in the modern economy, and the importance of sharing that knowledge:

"It is remarkable to note how long mankind was able to carry on without any knowledge organisation whatever.... Nor was there any conception of the need of a permanent system of ordered knowledge, continually revised, until the 20th century was nearing its end.... [To those of an earlier age] our Fundamental Knowledge System...with its special stations everywhere...would have seemed incredibly vast."

It would be hard to match this description of what we now know as the World Wide Web, and written as it was some 60 years before the Web was proposed by Tim Berners-Lee, it must rank as one of the most astonishing forecasts ever made.

Taking the lead from H.G. Wells, we can identify three important long run trends which are likely to continue, and which will have a profound effect on developing countries as well as the rest of the world. These are (a) the continuing fall in the cost of storing, processing and transmitting bits of information, (b) the emergence of new technologies and (c) new services, applications and ways of making money using Information and Communication Technology (ICT). The focus in the following three sections is a description of each trend and its general consequences; a discussion of the implications for developing countries and the nature of the 'missing link' in the future is left to the final section.

Trend 1: Falling unit cost

The unit cost of storing, processing and communicating bits of information will fall by at least a factor of a thousand over the next twenty years.

Let's start with the most obvious: the rate of change of technology. Most of what we have seen over the past 20 years – and which may well continue in one form or another – has been summarised as Moore's Law: the doubling of performance of electronics every 18 months. In fact this observation applies not just to electronics, but also to other components of ICT. The capacity of optical fibres, for example, has been growing at a faster rate. Doubling over 18 or even 12 months seems easy to understand in the short run, but over 20 years leads to changes which are almost unimaginable: computers which run a thousand times faster and networks which will have more than a thousand times the capacity of those we have today – and, crucially, for much the same cost. Each time a new optical fibre cable is laid across the Atlantic it costs roughly the same as cable, but has many times the capacity. The result has been that the cost per bit transmitted across the Atlantic has fallen by more than 100,000 times in the past 15 years.

However, there is another aspect of these technologies which is rarely discussed, but which is equally critical in translating technological improvement into low cost, high capacity systems. If you double the demand for traffic over an optical fibre cable, the extra cost incurred by the operator is relatively small. This is because most of the cost is in laying the fibre in the first place, and much more capacity can be created by adding new equipment (which is getting cheaper all the time). So, for example, a cable TV operator in the UK doubled the capacity of its network by adding extra electronics for 3% of the original capital cost. If that expanded network were fully used, then the unit cost would fall to 51.5% of the network prior to its expansion. In this case it is the demand which is the critical factor: if it keeps on growing then the unit cost will keep on falling. That 'economy of scale' applies to all aspects of ICT: the cost of producing 10 million copies of some software is not much more than the cost of producing 1 million copies, so the cost of a copy is lower, the more copies are used.

Over the past 20 years, improvements in price and performance of technology and the rapid expansion of demand have led to a massive drop in the unit cost of ICT. Whilst the world may be spending more than twice as much as 20 years ago on computers, mobile phones, the Internet and other forms of communication, the amount we are consuming measured in bits of information stored, processed or transmitted has risen more than a thousand times, and in some cases 10,000 times or more. A bit of information is costing us 0.2% of what it did 20 years ago. *In 20 years time it will cost 0.0004%, or 250,000 times less than it did when the Maitland Report was written.*

But we must be careful not to accept this trend as having the same consequences in all circumstances. Much of the fall in unit cost is due to growth in demand, and low demand means higher unit costs. Of course, everyone benefits potentially from the global aggregate demand levels: the consumption of mobile phones has led to low prices for handsets and these low prices are available more or less everywhere. But if the vast majority of a country cannot afford such things, low levels of demand will mean that the cost of provision will be relatively high even in a low cost economy. The implications of this for developing countries are discussed in more detail below.

Trend 2: new technologies

There will be just as few new major technologies in the next 20 years as in the past 20 years, but the number of ways ICT can be combined and used will increase significantly.

Improvements in price and performance and the rapid expansion of demand have not meant just more of the same. New businesses have emerged to take advantage of low cost, high capacity ICT. Old businesses – especially the telecommunications operators – have been subject to competitive and regulatory pressure. The result has been the development of entirely new infrastructure and services (such as the Internet, broadband connectivity and mobile phones) and an explosion in the number of ways in which these can be used.

However, the scope for entirely new infrastructure and services in the next 20 years is probably as limited as it was in the past 20 years. This is due to the time taken to design new infrastructure, the time taken to build it and the time for its use to become widespread.

The design of new infrastructure is probably the biggest barrier to deployment. Communications, in particular, requires standards so that providers of infrastructure can buy from multiple equipment suppliers and so that infrastructure can be connected with other infrastructure and support end to end services. Design and acceptance of standards take time. We are currently in the midst of a boom in the deployment of infrastructure to support the Transmission Control Protocols (TCP) and the Internet Protocols (IP) - the rules which, together, govern how packets of information are sent across the Internet - but the standards were developed in the 1970s. The same is true of mobile phones: the 3G (third generation) phone networks which are now being rolled out are based on ideas first proposed in the late 1980s. In both cases, the Internet and 3G, the time taken for use to become widespread can be measured in years and decades, and the time taken to understand the use of the infrastructure and exploit it fully can be even longer. We may wonder at the speed with which the Internet has spread, but it was 2005 before BT in the UK became the first Telecom Operator (TO) to announce its "21st Century Network", abandoning – amongst other things – the Public Switched Telephony Network which had been in existence in one form or another for almost a century.

So can we expect any major changes in infrastructure over the next 20 years? By major change we do not mean simple extensions to capacity or different ways of using existing services, but radically new ways of communication based on things which are currently the subject of research. What will they be, and what are the implications?

The most important infrastructure change will be in the use of radio. In the past our use of radio has been limited by the technology, to the extent that existing ways of using the radio spectrum – the resource which is used to transmit and receive radio signals – has been highly wasteful. For example, TV broadcasters use a large frequency band to transmit a channel. If the TV broadcaster were able to use a smaller band, then they would be more efficient in their use of spectrum, and this is what is now being implemented with digital TV.

But the size of the frequency band is only one measure of efficiency. The greatest gain in efficiency can be made by transmitting and receiving over a smaller area, because then you can reuse the same spectrum a short distance away without causing interference. This doesn't work with simple broadcasting, because everyone is getting the same channels, but with mobile phones it makes a crucial difference. By providing a channel for the telephone conversation just to one small area and not to a region, the same spectrum can be used in a different place to support another telephone conversation. Mobile radio uses a relatively small frequency band – comparable with one TV channel – over a very small area to support *all* the services.

This means that if you transmit and receive only over short distances, then you can re-use the frequencies in place after place, and so get very high overall use of the radio spectrum. So, for example, the use of Wi-Fi (the IEE 802.11 range of standards) in a small band at 2.4GHz in the radio spectrum has lead to explosive growth in the use of radio for broadband communications. Wi-Fi has restricted power levels and so works only over short distances (more restricted in Europe and other places than in North America). But globally the result is that millions of computers – and even Wi-Fi phones – can use the same spectrum without interfering with each other. And, as we saw above, such large markets bring low unit costs, making Wi-Fi systems extremely cheap.

However, much of the reason for the success of Wi-Fi is not technical, but regulatory. The decision to allow Wi-Fi to be operated without a licence or other restrictions (except of course for power levels) then led manufacturers and users to experiment and develop a wide range of applications. Within a very short time this technology – which relies on a supporting broadband infrastructure to be available – has developed into a multi-billion dollar business.

An extension to Wi-Fi – WiMax – is being promoted as a means of extending the range of broadband radio systems to a few kilometres and to enable it to be used for both fixed and mobile services. The hope is to repeat the success of Wi-Fi in establishing a standard which will enable hundreds of millions of units to be produced, so significantly reducing the cost of broadband radio and connectivity for the last mile. There are some fundamental limitations to WiMax which mean that *it cannot at the same time* do all that is claimed for it: for example, adding mobility means reducing range and capacity. A large range (especially in urban environments) means reducing the capacity for each user. Nevertheless WiMax could bring in an era of lower cost high capacity radio systems which will make it cheap to connect the last mile, which is, after all, the most expensive part of any telecommunications network.

Even in conventional mobile telephony there exists considerable scope. For example, 3WayNetworks is developing a very low cost 3G base station which can provide mobile phone coverage via a satellite back-haul to even the most remote villages, and can provide much cheaper coverage than conventional networks, including urban areas. The technical characteristics of 3G make it perfect for this kind of deployment and, with mass markets in the developing world driving down handset prices, 3G could become a major component of connecting people and businesses in the developing world.

No discussion of radio, especially with respect to developing countries, would be complete without mentioning satellite systems. Communication satellites are subject to the same technological improvements and economies as other forms of technology, and have kept pace with the improvements in terrestrial systems. Whilst the capacity of satellite systems is inherently limited, because they cannot use the 'cell' technique available to terrestrial systems, nevertheless they will have an important and economically effective role to play in filling gaps in coverage.

The next 20 years will be the time when low power, short range radios begin to be widely deployed. There are many ways in which this can be achieved. There will be 'polite' radios which sense the presence of other systems and which will then modify their power output accordingly. Mesh radios – of the kind currently used by the military – will find other radios which they will then use as relays and so send data hopping from one radio to another until it reaches its destination in much the same way as it does over the Internet. Radios will be programmable, so they can operate at different frequencies and with different protocols and be able to make use of unused spectrum, perhaps second by second (an important development, since most of the spectrum is unused most of the time). Some radios will use huge amounts of spectrum but at extremely low power levels over very short distances (Ultra Wide Band) so as to be able to send and receive high quality video within home and offices. The cost of providing connectivity for developing countries is likely to fall significantly as a result of the new radio technologies.

Although we have focused on radio as the area where the greatest changes will take place, there are other important fundamental developments which could affect the price, performance and availability of ICT. Chief amongst these is photonics: the use of optical rather than electronic signals to store, process and transmit information. Photonics provides huge capacity at potentially very low unit cost and so is an obvious candidate for supporting the first trend we identified: but as with all new technologies, the real value may not come with the obvious application. Devices now exist which can use the bandwidth of optical fibres to transmit and receive very large sections of the radio spectrum (one fibre could do this for almost all the radio spectrum commonly used today). It is possible to imagine small cells each with their own fibre, each using huge amounts of spectrum and not interfering with the adjacent cells because the distances and power levels are relatively small. The result would be huge amounts of bandwidth available to a user – effectively ending any thoughts of spectrum scarcity!

Trend 3: new ways of doing things

Arguably the most important issue is neither the cost of technology nor the new infrastructure which could be built; far more crucial is how the technology gets used – both by suppliers and by customers. This is where the greatest challenges for developing countries lie.

Radio – and perhaps photonics – will have a major impact over the next 20 years, providing connectivity for rural and urban areas and enabling new services and applications at low cost. How quickly this happens – and how quickly the benefits of these and other technologies are realised – will depend not on the technologies themselves but on the business models and regulatory environment. The developments in technology have opened up new ways to provide ICT services and applications, and this in turn has led to many new businesses in a sector which had previously been thought to be a 'natural monopoly', in which a government department or a government owned telecom operator was thought to be the best way of delivering service.

This "dis-integration" has crept up on the telecommunications industry relatively late compared to other industries. When the Maitland Report was written, most telecom operators (TOs) were highly integrated businesses selling relatively few products and services such as telephones and telephone calls. Large customers (with equally large budgets) could pay for specialist data services or leased lines, but these were not mass-markets, and the limited services commanded high prices. Now, however, most TOs are expected to sell capacity to their competitors, and competition for (and regulation of) the provision of voice, mobile and data services has cut tariffs and expanded the market. New businesses – including Internet service providers (ISPs) and retail outlets such as Internet cafés - have sprung up, serving unmet needs at very low cost. Voice over IP – the use of the Internet to carry telephone calls – is a good example of this process: the TO may provide the connection to the main network, but an ISP could provide the Internet service itself and the software for making and receiving telephone calls may be provided (free) by another organisation. This is a far cry from the days of one service from one supplier.

This is not a phenomenon unique to telecommunications. Most industries have "dis-integrated", and all for the same reasons. Firstly it may be cheaper and more effective in the long run to buy inputs from specialist suppliers rather than try to provide them yourself. The Ford Motor Company, for example, gave up its rubber plantations in South America and then sourced its tyres from Goodyear (a relationship which

225

lasted almost a century). IBM used to make computers from its own integrated circuits and write its own specialist software to run on them. IBM still does these activities, but mainly uses specialist manufacturers to make the 'chips', has its computers made in Taiwan, and these run industry standard software (mostly supplied by Microsoft).

This process can only happen if three conditions are present. Firstly, there must be an economic advantage in specialisation – whether it be tyres or integrated circuits. Secondly, there must be an 'industry standard' – in other words, a tyre plant can make tyres for any car manufacturer and a FAB plant can make chips for any computer maker (and the instructions for what to make can be conveyed simply and unambiguously between the customer and the supplier). Finally, the organisation can see benefit in focusing scarce resources on its own unique competence: in Ford's case making cars, and in IBM's case systems integration.

All three conditions are present now in many areas of telecommunications – though, it must be said, more in the fixed line businesses than in mobile phone networks and services. There are economic advantages in specialisation, whether it be network providers, service providers, ISPs or Web hosting. The industry standards exist – especially with the emergence of TCP/IP as the way of transmitting across networks – so that an ISP can use a network without having to own it and manage all the technical details, and a company can offer services through the World Wide Web by using an ISP or a Web hosting service without having to manage all the component services. The past 10 years have shown strong evidence of the benefits of focusing a company – whether it be Skype and Voice over IP, or Vodafone in mobile communications. The telecommunications business is dis-integrating, and as it does, it is creating many new possibilities for new services and applications.

But this kind of dis-integration and progress does not come without a cost. In Texas, in March 2005, a young girl tried in vain to phone the emergency services from her parents' VoIP phone whilst an armed raider injured both of them. No emergency services were available over the VoIP connection, so she had to run to a neighbour who had a 'conventional' phone. It is important to recall that there are many services which are taken for granted, but which may need to be dealt with explicitly in a new dis-integrated world. Emergency services, the availability of telephone service even when the electric power is cut, universal service provision and services for the disabled will all need explicit consideration.

What are the implications for developing countries?

It was Arthur C. Clarke, another British writer of science fiction, who noted that people tend to overestimate what will happen in the short run, and underestimate what will happen in the long run. The next 20 years will bring about more profound changes than we recognise today, and the risk is that the developing world will not have the resources, know-how or policies in place to be able to take advantage or to participate.

The magnitude of these changes is likely to be the same or even larger than those we have seen in the past, and even these have been even greater than is perhaps generally recognised. For example, one day in 2003 saw all the international telephone calls of 1972 being made, all the airline passengers who flew in 1975 being carried, all the mobile phones that existed in the world in 1984 being sold, and all the emails of 1992 and all the text messages of 1998 being sent. And the organisations which did all this either did not exist 20 years ago, or the ways in which they do business has changed out of all recognition.

Whatever the precise nature of the changes, it seems likely that the three trends described above : the falling cost of processing, storing and communicating information, the emergence of radio and other new technologies and the 'dis-integration' of telecommunications – will be the dominant forces shaping the future. So what does this mean for developing countries 20 years after the Maitland Report and what are the implications for the policies they should pursue?

Firstly: competition and regulatory policy. No country can afford to be left behind as these changes are taking place, and competition is the main way to encourage innovation and the development of infrastructure, services and applications. But developing countries – particularly the smaller ones – may not be able to sustain the levels of competition seen in the developed world. In such cases the regulatory policies become critically important in helping to stimulate the incumbent and to prevent the emergence of oligopolies. There is also an increased responsibility on the regulator to be aware of international developments and best practice in technology and service deployment, and, as the telecommunications sector in the developed world dis-integrates further – to apply regulatory pressure to achieve comparable sector structures.

Secondly: spectrum. Relaxing the constraints on the use of the radio spectrum is probably the single most important regulatory step a developing country can take, because – just as with the licensing of mobile phones – it will unlock a wave of investment which will benefit not only the urban modern economies but – because of the economic characteristics of the use of radio – will help in connecting the poor and rural areas. We have already seen how 2G mobile phones have revolutionised even rural areas in the developing world. 3G – with the use of low cost base stations such as those now available from 3WayNetworks – could bring broadband connectivity to villages as well as to the business districts. The benefits of radio technology are only just beginning to be realised.

Thirdly: participation and expertise. Today, 20 years after the Maitland Report, the problem of physical connectivity is being solved, mostly (and quite unexpectedly) through the use of mobile phone and other radio systems. A developing country which embraces competition and a progressive regulatory policy, and relaxes the constraints on the use of the radio spectrum may still have significant problems if its businesses and society do not know how to make best use of these technologies. The situation will become more extreme as participation in a modern economy over the next 20 years will depend more and more on the use of ICT. But the use of ICT favours the larger enterprises that can devote resources necessary to fully exploit its possibilities, and the larger economies that can support the sizes of markets which justify the use of ICT. This is a major issue for developing countries and, in an era when technology is developing faster than ever, is crucial for their future prosperity.

In 20 years the problem of the missing link has changed from one of connecting the people of the world to one of ensuring that the right policies are in place and that the appropriate skills and expertise are developed. This is not surprising, as world trade has grown significantly and the commercial attractiveness of ICT has been clearly demonstrated – not least as a result of licensing mobile communications companies who have begun to provide service in even the poorest countries. In 1985, I suggested a fund of US$ 2billion would be needed to help overcome the missing link. Now, 20 years later the costs, technology, business models have moved on. For the next 20 years we need similar ambitious levels of funding, but directed at human capital rather than networks and equipment.

David Cleevely was a contributor to the original Maitland Commission, and is the founder and former Chairman of telecoms consultancy Analysys (acquired by Datatec International in 2004). In 1998, he co-founded the Internet based antibody company Abcam with Jonathan Milner (CEO), and continues as Chairman. More recently he co-founded the 3G pico base station company, 3WayNetworks. He has been a prime mover behind Cambridge Network and co-founder of Cambridge Wireless, was a Director of Cambridge Broadband and was a Director of Bango until shortly after its successful flotation on AIM. He is also a member of the Ofcom Spectrum Advisory Board and the Expert Panel for the Department of Media, Culture and Sport. After being sponsored to study Cybernetics at Reading by Post Office Telecommunications, he joined their Long Range Studies Division. A PhD at Cambridge was then followed by the Economist Intelligence Unit in London. Since selling Analysys he has continued to develop his business and academic interests: he currently holds an Industrial Fellowship at the University of Cambridge Computer Laboratory and is Chairman of the Communications Research Network, part of the Cambridge MIT Institute.

Contact details: David Cleevely, Chairman, Communications Research Network, University of Cambridge, Computer Laboratory, William Gates Building
15 JJ Thomson Ave, Cambridge CB3 0FD, England.
Email: david.office@cleevely.co.uk

An interview with Sir Donald Maitland

17.

An interview with Sir Donald Maitland

Sir Donald Maitland has devoted his life to public service. After wartime service in the Middle East, India and Burma, he joined the UK Foreign Office in 1947 and held a number of posts abroad, including Ambassador to Libya in 1969. In 1970 he was recalled to serve as the late Prime Minister Edward Heath's Chief Press Secretary, a position he held until 1973 when he was appointed the UK's Permanent Representative to the United Nations.

From 1975 until 1979, Donald Maitland was the UK's Ambassador and Permanent Representative to the European Economic Community (now the European Union). Finally, after a couple of years as senior civil servant in charge of the UK's Department of Energy, retirement beckoned.

But it is not in the nature of this energetic Scot to sit and do nothing. In 1983 he was asked by the British Government to represent the country on the ITU's Independent Commission for World Wide Telecommunications Development. He was unanimously elected chairman by his fellow Commissioners.

The list of Sir Donald's activities over the years since completing the work of the Maitland Commission has been characteristically long, focused in particular around his lifelong passion for Europe and for education, including four years as Pro-Chancellor of the University of Bath. Knighted in 1973, Sir Donald was made a GCMG in 1977. He is also a Fellow of the Royal Society of Arts.

In an interview specially recorded for this book, Sir Donald reflected on his time as Chairman of what became officially known as the Maitland Commission.

How did you first become involved with the Commission?
Before retirement, my wife Jean and I agreed I would decline any offer of a Monday-to-Friday job. We knew that Monday-to-Friday could all too soon become Sunday-to-Saturday, and we had other interests to pursue.

But it wasn't long before the phone rang with a message from the minister for industry and information technology. Did I know, he asked, that at a meeting in Nairobi in autumn 1982, the ITU had decided to set up a commission to recommend ways of encouraging the expansion of telecommunications across the world, given the critical role communications played in economic and social development?

The commission was to be formed in May and, since I had experience of the United Nations and developing countries – and had handled technical subjects in the recent past – the minister hoped I would agree to be the British member. Oh, and by the way, he asked, would I also chair the UK's contribution to the UN's World Communications Year? When would that be? I asked. It had already started, I was told.

Was World Communications Year helpful?

It provided valuable context. The UN General Assembly had "recognised the fundamental importance of communications infrastructures as an essential element in the economic and social development of all countries". It was also convinced that "a World Communications Year would provide the opportunity for all countries to undertake an in-depth review and analysis of their policies on communications development and stimulate the accelerated development of communications infrastructures."

This convoluted prose expressed a serious worry. I knew there was a strong feeling in the General Assembly that communications had been given too low a priority in many developing countries.

The UN General Assembly had set two objectives – to offer developing countries increased training opportunities, and to promote greater awareness, especially among the young, of the importance of efficient communications. It seemed to me that both of these objectives were relevant to the work of the new Commission.

What level of briefing did you receive from the ITU?

Richard Butler, the Australian secretary general of the ITU, told me that a characteristic North-South dispute over development aid had threatened to split the ITU the previous autumn. Delegates from developing countries had been deeply concerned over the widening gap in the distribution of telecommunications world wide. Of the 600 million telephones in the world, three-quarters were concentrated in nine advanced industrialised countries. It was said that there were more telephones in Tokyo than in the entire African continent. To redress the imbalance, or at least narrow the gap, developing countries were calling for a substantial transfer of resources. The Commission was a response to those concerns.

The ITU brought together seventeen members to serve on the commission – five from western industrialised countries, two from eastern Europe and the remaining ten from different regions of the developing world.

What were the first actions taken by the Commission?

The first meeting was held in Geneva on 24 October 1983. The first task was to elect a chairman. I was honoured to be proposed and was unanimously elected. Four vice-chairmen from different regions of the developing world were also elected.

We also had to agree what was meant by "telecommunications". We decided to exclude broadcasting and concern ourselves primarily with information transmitted through the telephone system. We also agreed to establish the facts about the situation worldwide, to examine the role new technologies could play, the most appropriate means of organising and managing telecommunications systems, how the sums needed for investment could be raised. And we needed to bear in mind the massive changes that would result from the move towards privatisation that was of increasing interest to governments.

While we recognised the need to anticipate some of the technological changes coming through, we decided it was not realistic to embrace them in our work. Some were still relatively untried – including both cellular telephony and the use of Internet Protocols. It's also worth noting that very few, if any, of the world's experts anticipated that, within 15 years, data would far outstrip voice as the dominant user of telephony systems.

The Commission met in the UK in May 1984, in Tanzania in October and then in Indonesia in November. Was progress as broad as your travels?

It was clear from the outset that, rather than discuss a broad sweep of ideas in general meetings, it would be altogether more productive to start with a draft text. Over the spring and summer of 1984, our secretariat, advisers and others produced outline chapters for the final report. They included a draft from Heather Hudson (a contributor to this volume, see page 00) that firmly convinced everyone of the causal link between investment in telecommunications and economic and social advance.

Abdul Rahman al-Ghunaim, the Kuwaiti member and one of the vice-chairmen, proposed a World Telecommunication Development Organisation. It would seek a balance of telecommunications development worldwide. He envisaged that all members of the United Nations would have shares in the organisation.

We eventually recommended a development body that would contain three elements: the collection of information about telecommunications policies and experience; advice on creating and managing an efficient system; and specific assistance in areas such as preparing specifications for projects, training and management assistance.

We discussed several ideas relating to finance. We considered whether industrialised countries should put some of their revenue from traffic with developing countries into a development fund. We also proposed the creation of a revolving fund, an investment fund, a commercial consortium and investment trusts. We wanted to make it clear that far higher priority had to be given to investment in this sector – not only by the governments of developing countries themselves, but also by donor governments and international organisations, and that developing countries had to create the conditions that would attract foreign private investment.

At our last meeting, in Bali, several members suggested we should commit ourselves to one simple, overriding objective – eventually agreed as "to bring all mankind within easy reach of a telephone by the early part of the next century". As for a title for the Commission's report that would be readily remembered, I suggested the words "The Missing Link".

What happened to the Commission's proposal for a UN-based Centre for Telecommunications Development?

It's true that there was disagreement with the ITU over the form and structure of the proposed Centre. Under pressure, we agreed to revise our original concept and the proposal in the final Report did not represent our original plan. The Centre that resulted was eventually absorbed into the development bureau of the ITU.

That must have been a disappointment, but did it effect the overall impact of the Report when it came out?

No. I presented *The Missing Link* to Richard Butler at a formal ceremony at the ITU in Geneva on 22 January 1985 and evidence soon accumulated, notably from India, the Pacific and Latin America, that the two crucial messages it contained – higher priority for investment in this sector and the need to attract foreign entrepreneurs – had been received, understood and acted upon.

What key messages came out of the Commission's work?

The Missing Link reflected a great deal of intensive study, consultation and debate – and we were left in no doubt that telecommunications has a major role to play in promoting economic and social progress.

Telecommunications are essential to the emergency and health services; they increase the effectiveness of public administration, commerce and other economic activities; they reduce the need to travel. But only if the network operates efficiently.

Less tangible benefits were also available. An efficient network could contribute to national cohesion, enhance the quality of life and distribute more evenly the fruits of economic, social and cultural development. Hence our conclusion, that "no development programme ... should be regarded as balanced, properly integrated or likely to be effective unless it includes a full and appropriate role for telecommunications and accords a corresponding priority to the improvement and expansion of telecommunications".

We proposed action in four areas: to ensure that investment in telecommunications was given higher priority; to make existing networks in developing countries commercially viable; to ensure that financing arrangements took account of the foreign exchange problems of developing countries; and, to improve international co-operation (see complete list of recommendations on page 00). Under each of these four headings we grouped specific recommendations addressed variously to governments in both industrialised and developing countries, international agencies, telecommunications operators, suppliers of equipment and finance houses.

And what legacy do you feel that the Commission has left?

After the press conference for the launch of the Report, I spent many months addressing conferences in every part of the world. For example, in 1986 I addressed the annual conference of Caribbean telecommunications organisations in the Bahamas, followed by a World Telecommunication Forum in Nairobi. And so it continued year after year.

At the Pacific Telecommunications Conference in Honolulu in January 1994, Pekka Tarjanne, Richard Butler's successor at the ITU, reviewed developments over the previous decade. The gap that the independent commission had found unacceptable had been narrowed; the more prosperous developing countries had made substantial progress. But those with low incomes still lagged behind. The gap was still too wide, and much remained to be done. Dr Tarjanne also said that the time had come to abandon the cumbersome title the commission had been given; in future it should be known simply as the "Maitland Commission".

It was an honour to be asked to lead an inquiry into a state of affairs which all seventeen members of the commission regarded as an international injustice. This was the first time that the extent of the telecommunications gap had been acknowledged and defined – and an answer offered that would help fix what became the missing link.

We believed passionately that it was not right, in the last years of the 20th century, that a minority of the human race should enjoy the benefits of remarkable new technologies while a minority lived in comparative isolation. Neither in the name of common humanity nor on grounds of common interest was such a disparity acceptable.

Of course, since *The Missing Link* was published, the telecommunications sector has become part of the information technology revolution. The Internet is changing society in ways that were never imagined by its inventors – and cell phones have removed the tyranny of fixed line communications, particularly in Africa. Are you optimistic for the future?

I've always been an optimist. But there are not still many difficult issues to resolve. I gave an address at Africa Telecom 86 that set out the hopes and the challenges. I am sure they remain relevant today...

> *"The benefits available to developing countries do not begin and end with the contribution telecommunications make to economic and social advance. An effective telecommunications system can be a channel for education and this in turn can enrich national culture and strengthen the social fabric. The linking of the more remote areas with urban centres reinforces the infrastructure, encourages self-reliance and contributes to national cohesion.*

> *"Suppose that instantaneous communication were possible between the great commercial centres, New York, Tokyo, London, and any small provincial town, or even a remote village, in Paraguay, Mali or China. The world would be a single market place. Telecommunications would*

be the new trade routes. New commercial partnerships would be formed. Demand for new goods and services would be stimulated. Standards would have to be set with the world market in view. Design would have to take account of a wider range of physical conditions, usage, aptitude, taste and tradition. Language barriers would have to be overcome. As this happened, ideas about social conditions, wages and the rights of the individual would be freely exchanged and hallowed notions about systems of governance would be eroded.

"The trouble with this scenario is that it is too good to be true. For one thing, not all governments would welcome the free flow of information across frontiers..."

I'm not claiming any particular foresight with those comments. But I think it's fair to say that, 20 years ago, few people anticipated just how quickly we would move down the road to a global village. The discussions and arguments over Internet Governance that have been resurfacing prior to this year's WSIS show that governments and institutions do not let go the levers of power lightly or readily.

But I repeat, I am an optimist. The speed of change across information and communication technologies is such that no economic model for the sector's control can last for long if it doesn't meet the needs and requirements of users. In Africa, the difficulties of wiring the continent are being neatly side-stepped with the explosive growth in the use of cell phones. In developed countries, the best efforts of the established telephone companies to maintain a long-term business model are being thrown into disarray with the arrival of new ventures such as Skype – removing barriers, removing cost, connecting.

The human race is a social species. We depend on our ability to communicate with fellow human beings. When the Maitland Commission was created, a small minority of the world's population had access to the telephone, despite the fact that it had been invented 110 years previously. Today, a Sri Lankan village fisherman will use his mobile phone to check on market prices before deciding where to land his catch. A Masai farmer will do the same with his cattle.

The Missing Link was necessarily addressing the situation as we found it – and was concerned with fixing the missing link with the tools to hand. Such has been the pace of change that many of those tools have become redundant. But the missing link *is* being fixed. That's what matters.

Appendix 1

The Maitland Report : Conclusions and Summary of Recommendations

The complete text of the recommendations made at the conclusion of the Maitland Commission Report, delivered to the ITU on 22 January 1985.

1. The considerations on which we have based the response to our Mandate have been the subject of previous chapters. In this chapter we set out the conclusions we have drawn.

2. The telecommunications situation across the world has certain notable characteristics. Advanced industrialised societies have virtually comprehensive services. In developing countries, services are mainly concentrated in urban centres. Continuing technological advances offer ever increasing efficiency, reliability, and lower unit costs. The level of investment in telecommunications in developing countries is generally low. With certain notable exceptions, telecommunications services in many developing countries are poor or indifferent. In many remote areas there is no service at all.

3. Given the vital role telecommunications play not only in such obvious fields as emergency, health and other social services, administration and commerce, but also in stimulating economic growth and enhancing the quality of life, creating effective networks world wide will bring immense benefits. An increase in international traffic will generate funds which could be devoted to the further improvement and development of telecommunications services. The increased flow of trade and information will contribute to better international relationships. The process of creating effective networks world wide will provide new markets for the high technology and other industries, some of which are already suffering the effects of surplus productive capacity. The interest industrialised and developing countries share in the world wide development of telecommunications is as great as in the exploitation of new sources of energy. And yet it is far less appreciated.

4. We look to governments of industrialised and developing countries alike to give fuller recognition to this common interest and to join their efforts to redress the present imbalance in the distribution of telecommunications which the entire international community should deplore.

5. We have identified several key elements in the joint effort for which we appeal.

   - First, governments and development assistance agencies must give a higher priority than hitherto to investment in telecommunications.

   - Secondly, existing networks in developing countries should be made more effective, with commercial viability the objective, and should become progressively self-reliant. The benefits of the new technologies should be exploited to the full to the extent that these are appropriate and adaptable to the countries' requirements.

- Thirdly, financing arrangements must take account of the scarcity of foreign exchange in many developing countries.

- Fourthly, the ITU should play a more effective role.

6. Our recommendations reflect this analysis of the problem and are aimed at stimulating the actions we consider essential if progress is to be made in creating effective telecommunications networks world wide.

7. First, to ensure that telecommunications are given the priority we believe they deserve, WE RECOMMEND that:

a)   developing countries review their development plans to ensure that sufficient priority is given to investment in telecommunications (Chapter 9, paragraph 9);

b)   developing countries make appropriate provision for telecommunications in all projects for economic or social advance and include in their submissions a checklist showing that such provision is being made (Chapter 9, paragraph 10);

c)   countries and international agencies with development assistance programmes ensure that specific provision is made for appropriate telecommunications facilities in development assistance projects (Chapter 9, paragraph 21);

d)   contributors to and beneficiaries of the UNDP reconsider the importance they attach to the telecommunications sector, and provide appropriate resources for its growth (Chapter 3, paragraph 12).

In addition to these specific recommendations, WE APPEAL to the governments participating in the next Economic Summit to give encouragement to practical measures to improve and expand telecommunications (Chapter 9, paragraph 23).

8. Secondly, to make existing networks in developing countries more effective and progressively self-reliant and to exploit the benefits of the new technologies, WE RECOMMEND that:

a)   telecommunications operators in developing countries review their training needs and resources, and prepare systematic training plans (Chapter 6, paragraph 18);

b)   developing countries use the resources available through the IPDC (Chapter 6, paragraph 19);

c)   industrialised countries organise seminars to improve the qualifications of experts from developing countries (Chapter 6, paragraph 20);.

d)   the ITU supplement the catalogue of training opportunities with information about training opportunities in the private sector (Chapter 6, paragraph 22);

e)   operators and manufacturers consider how they can enhance the training opportunities they offer to developing countries (Chapter 6, paragraph 23);

f)   the major regional and sub-regional political and economic organisations consider as soon as possible how best research and development institutes might be established (Chapter 7, paragraph 15);

g)   the research and development institutes proposed be developed as a source of higher technological, supervisory and managerial training and as co-ordinating agencies for external training opportunities (Chapter 6, paragraph 21);

h) developing countries consider pooling their purchases of appropriate equipment including terminals and components (Chapter 5, paragraph 24);

i) when purchasing equipment, developing countries ensure that the contract includes commitments on the supply of spare parts, training, commissioning, post-installation and maintenance (Chapter 5, paragraph 25);

j) manufacturers and operators be encouraged to develop systems which will enable the needs of the more remote areas of developing countries to be met at lower cost (Chapter 4, paragraph 30);

k) the ITU, in conjunction with manufacturers of telecommunications equipment and components, consider compiling a comprehensive catalogue of telecommunications suppliers and systems currently in use (Chapter 4, paragraph 33);

l) developing countries review the possibilities for local or regional manufacture (Chapter 7, paragraph 22);

m) manufacturers in industrialised countries consider the scope for cooperation with developing countries in local or regional manufacture (Chapter 7, paragraph 23).

9. As an immediate step to improve the present arrangements for assisting developing countries WE RECOMMEND that:

a Centre for Telecommunications Development, with its three components of a Development Policy Unit, a Telecommunications Development Service and an Operations Support Group, be established by the Administrative Council of the ITU during 1985 (Chapter 8, paragraph 4).

WE INVITE the Secretary-General of the ITU to carry out the necessary consultations so that the Centre can be established as soon as possible in the course of 1985 (Chapter 8, paragraph 15).

10.Thirdly, to finance the development of telecommunications WE RECOMMEND that:

a) countries and international agencies with development assistance programmes give higher priority to telecommunications (Chapter 9, paragraph 20);

b) those who provide international satellite systems study urgently the feasibility of establishing funds to finance earth segment and terrestrial facilities in developing countries (Chapter 9, paragraph 22);

c) industrialised countries extend export/import financing and insurance cover to suppliers of telecommunications equipment (Chapter 9, paragraph 25);

d) the IBRD consider including telecommunications in its proposal for multilateral guarantees against non-commercial risks (Chapter 9, paragraph 26);

e) where projects are financed in part by IBRD loans, finance agencies consider cross-default arrangements as a form of insurance (Chapter 9, paragraph 27);

f) member states of the ITU consider setting aside a small proportion of revenues from calls between developing countries and industrialised countries to be devoted to telecommunications in developing countries, for example to fund pre-investment costs (Chapter 9, paragraph 30) .

With the longer term in view, WE ALSO RECOMMEND that:

g)   governments of industrialised countries review their financing instruments and institutions to ensure that they can meet the financing requirements of extending telecommunications networks in developing countries (Chapter 9, paragraph 32);

h)   member states of the ITU, in collaboration with international finance agencies, study the proposals for a revolving fund and for telecommunications investment trusts as methods of raising funds for investment in telecommunications with a view to putting these into effect by the next Plenipotentiary Conference at the latest. The Secretary-General is invited to report to the Plenipotentiary Conference on the progress made with these studies (Chapter 9, paragraph 35);

i)   the Secretary-General of the ITU, in the light of progress on our other recommendations, study the proposal for an organisation to co-ordinate the development of telecommunications world wide (WORLDTEL) and submit his conclusions to the Plenipotentiary Conference (Chapter 9, paragraph 37).

11.Fourthly, to strengthen the role of the ITU, WE RECOMMEND that:

all international organisations concerned with telecommunications give more favourable consideration than hitherto to assistance for the expansion of telecommunications world wide and that regional cooperation be accorded a high priority (Chapter 3, paragraph 13).

12.Finally, WE RECOMMEND that:

the Secretary-General of the ITU monitor the implementation of all the preceding recommendations, report on progress to the Administrative Council and, where necessary, act to stimulate further progress.

13. Our analysis of the problems and the recommendations we have made show that there is no single remedy. A range of actions over a wide front and at different levels is required. Progress will be made only in stages. But, if the effort is sustained, the situation world wide could be transformed in twenty years. All mankind could be brought within easy reach of a telephone by the early part of next century and our objective achieved.

Appendix 2

Members of the Maitland Commission
with contemporary biographical details

Professor Dr Sukhamoy CHAKRAVARTY, India

Chairman, Advisory Council to the Prime Minister Planning Commission
• Professor of Economics, Delhi School of Economics, University of Delhi • Served as a consultant to various United Nations agencies • Member of the Indian Delegation to the Seventh Non¬Aligned Summit • Chairman of the Indo-Dutch Committee for Research and Social Sciences (1981) and of the Advisory Committee on Research in areas relating to planning (1982) • Member of Planning Commission, Government of India (1971-1977) • Chairman Fuel Policy Committee, Ministry of Steel and Mines (1971-1974) • Visiting Fellow, Netherlands School of Economics (1957-1959), Assistant Professor, MIT (1959-1961) and various professional appointments.

Mr William M ELLINGHAUS, United States

Formerly President American Telephone and Telegraph Company (AT&T)
• Executive Vice-Chairman, New York Stock Exchange • AT&T New York, Vice-Chairman of the Board and President and Chief Operating Officer (1976-1984) • New York Telephone Company, President (1970-1976) • AT&T New York, Assistant Vice-President, Vice-President and Executive Vice-President (1965-1970) • Various posts with the Bell System in telephone companies in Maryland, Virginia, West Virginia and Washington, DC (1940-1965) • Affiliated in the capacity of Director, Co-Chairman, Trustee and Member, to various companies, corporations, councils and orders, as well as educational civil and philanthropic institutions.

Mr Abdul Rahman K AL-GHUNAIM, Kuwait(Vice-Chairman)

Under Secretary Ministry of Communications
• Director of: The Bank of Lebanon and Kuwait; The United Insurance Company Ras Al Khaima; The Merchant Bank Corporation, South Korea • Member of the Board of Governors, University of Kuwait • Member of the Board of Directors, Kuwait Port Authority • Member of the Environmental Protection Council and Chairman of Research Group in Kuwait for Environmental Protection • Member of National Defence Council, Kuwait • Governor for Arab Group III, INTELSAT Board of Governors since 1973. Represented Kuwait as Plenipotentiary and Head of Delegation at INTELSAT meetings since 1969 • Represented Kuwait at various meetings of ITU, ATU and UPU since 1963 • Chairman of INMARSAT for two terms (1978-80, 1980-81) • Deputy Chairman INTEL SAT Assembly of Parties (1978-80) and of meeting of Signatories, 1973 • Served as Director or Chairman of several banks and financial institutions • Assistant Under-Secretary in charge of Telecommunications for five years • Deputy Chief Engineer 1964.

Dr Koji KOBAYASHI, Japan

Chairman of the Board and Chief Executive Officer, NEC Corporation
• President of NEC Corporation, Tokyo (1964-1976), Director (1949-1964) • An officer and/or member of a number of industrial, professional and governmental organisations • In addition to honours awarded by the Emperor of Japan, has received decorations from the Governments of Brazil, Egypt, Jordan, Paraguay, Peru, Poland, Thailand and Madagascar.

Dr Volkmar KOEHLER, West Germany

Parliamentary Secretary of State to the Federal Minister for Economic Cooperation
• Member of the German Federal Parliament since 1972 • Member and Vice-Chairman of the

Committee for Economic Cooperation (1972-1982) • Responsible for management training, Volkswagen Company (1962-1982) • Vice President of the German-Arab Association and of the German-Moroccan Association • Member of the Planning Committee the Konrad Adenauer Foundation • First Mayor of the City of 'Wolfsburg, 1972.

His Excellency Mr Mohand LAENSER

Minister of Posts and Telecommunications
• Head of the Moroccan delegation to the ITU Plenipotentiary Conference, Nairobi, 1982 • Head of the Moroccan delegation to the Baghdad Congress of the Arab Postal Union (UPA), 1980 • Head of the Moroccan delegation Rio de Janeiro Congress, 1979 • Attended the UPU Lausanne Congress, 1974 • Author of diploma thesis on "Town planning and national development policy", 1970 • Previous posts in Ministry of Posts and Telecommunications include: Head of the Budget and Equipment Division; Director of Personnel Budget and Equipment Department; Director of Posts and Financial Services; Secretary-General • Has taken part in various regional and international meetings connected with posts, telecommunications and savings banks.

Mr Louis-Joseph LIBOIS, France

Chairman, Caisse Nationale des Télécommunications (CNT)
• Graduated engineer from Ecole Poly technique and Ecole Nationale Supérieure des Télécommunications • Senior Engineer in telecommunications • Senior Counsellor, Court of Audit • Vice-Chairman of the Interministerial Board for data processing and office automation, chairman of the permanent Committee • Vice-Chairman, FRANCETEL • General Director for Telecommunications (1971-1974) • Chairman of both SOTELEC and SOCOTEL Societies (1971-1974) • Director Centre National d'Etudes des Télécommunications (1968-1971) • Director of the Centre de recherches des Télécommunications in Brittany (1963-1968). Start of the French digital electronic switching system design • Head of the Electronic switching division, Centre National d'Etudes des Télécommunications (1957-1963) • Professor at the Ecole Nationale Superieure des Télécommunications (1953-1957) • Head of the microwave radiolinks laboratory of the Centre National d'Etudes des Télécommunications (1947-1957) • Former Chairman of the Société Française des Electriciens, des Radioelectriciens et des Electroniciens (SEE) • Former Chairman of the France section of the Institute of Electrical and Electronics Engineers (IEEE) • Fellow of IEEE • Commander, Ordre de la Légion d'Honneur.

Sir Donald MAITLAND, GCMG OBE United Kingdom (Chai rman)

• Permanent Under-Secretary, Department of Energy (1980-1982) • Deputy Permanent Under-Secretary of State, Foreign and Commonwealth Office (1979-1980) • Ambassador and United Kingdom Permanent Representative to the European Communities, Brussels (1975-1979) • Deputy Under-Secretary of State, Foreign and Commonwealth Office (1974-1975) • United Kingdom Member Commonwealth Group on Trade Aid and Development, 1975 • Ambassador and United Kingdom Permanent Representative to the United Nations, New York (1973-1974) • Chief Press Secretary to the Prime Minister (1970-1973). - Ambassador to Libya (1969-1970) • Various diplomatic service appointments in the Middle East, North Africa and the Foreign and Commonwealth Office (1947-1969).

His Excellency Mr John S MALECELA,MP, Tanzania (Vice-Chairman)

• Minister for Communications, Transport and Works • Elected Member of Executive Committee of Commonwealth Association,1982 • Elected Chairman of PAPU, 1982. - Minister for Minerals of the United Republic of Tanzania (1980-1982) • Minister for Agriculture of the United Republic of Tanzania (1975-1980) • Minister for Foreign Affairs of the United Republic of Tanzania (1972-1975) • Minister for Communications, Research and Social Services of East African Community • Chairman of Communications Council and Research and Social Council of the East African Community • Elected Vice-President of Emergency Session of ICAO, June 1970 • Minister for

Finance and Administration of the East African Community • Chairman of the Finance Council of the East African Community (1969-1971) • Ambassador Extraordinary and Plenipotentiary Permanent Representative of Tanzania to UN • Elected Vice-Chairman of a 'Seminar of Decolonisation (Committee of 24 - 1966) • Member of UN Mission to Equatorial Guinea (which Mission led to Independence of Equatorial Guinea in 1968) • Elected Chairman of International Seminar on Apartheid and Colonialism in Southern Africa, Kitwe, Zambia • Tanzanian Ambassador to Ethiopia (1964-1968) • Tanganyika Consul to the United States and Secretary of Tanganyika Mission to the United Nations in New York • Regional Commissioner for Lake Region • Chairman of Western Tanganyika Cotton Advisory Committee • Member of Tanganyika Lint and Seed Marketing Board (1962-1963).

Dr Manuel PEREZ GUERRER, Venezuela

Minister of State for International Economic Affairs Venezuela
• President of Interpress Service - Third World since 1983 - Secretary-General of the United Nations Conference on Trade and Development (UNCTAD) (1969-1972) • President of the Economic and Social Council (ECOSOC) (1968) • Minister of Finance, Director of the Department of Planning and Coordination, Minister of Mines and Hydrocarbons (1946-1966) • Various posts within the United Nations system (1946-1968) • Served with the Secretariat of the League of Nations (1937-1940) and the ILQ (1943-1944).

His Excellency Mr Jean PING, Gabon

Director of the President's Office of the Republic of Gabon
• Ambassador Extraordinary and Plenipotentiary, Permanent Delegate of the Republic of Gabon to UNESCO • First Counsellor at the Gabonese Embassy in France (1978) • International Civil Servant, UNESCO (1972-1978) • Member of the Association Nationale des Docteurs Et Sciences Economiques (ANDESE, France) • Member of the Executive Board of UNESCO • Member of the Inter-Governmental Council of the International Programme for the Development of Communications • Chairman of the UNESCO African Group • Vice-Chairman of UNESCO Group of 77.

His Excellency Mr Alioune SENE, Senegal

Ambassador of Senegal in Switzerland and Permanent Representative of Senegal to the United Nations Office in Geneva Senegal
• Former Director in the office of President L S Senghor. - Former Secretary of State for Information • Former Minister of Culture • Chairman of the Diplomatic Conference on the Revision of the Paris Convention (Protection of Industrial Property) • Chairman of the Group of Experts on the Right to Development • Former Ambassador of Senegal in Zaire, Cairo and Beirut.

Professor Dr Alexandru SPATARU, Romania

Head of Applied Electronics Department Bucharest Politechnical Institute
• Head of the Applied Electronics Department, Bucharest Politechnical Institute • Vice-President of the National Council for Science and Technology • President of the Romanian Commission for Space Activity • Scientific Manager, Telecommunications Research Institute • General Manager, Ministry of Post and Telecommunications • Deputy Technical Manager, Romanian Broadcasting Committee • Head of the Romanian delegations to UN Science and Technology Conference and Outer Space Conferences and to ITU, CCIR and CCITT meetings.

His Excellency Mr Achmad TAHIR, Indonesia (Vice-Chairman)

Ministry of Tourism, Posts and Telecommunication Indonesia
• Member of Consultative People's Congress 1983 • Chairman, Indonesian Veterans Legion since

1979 • Secretary-General Department of Communication (1976-1983) • Ambassador Extraordinary and Plenipotentiary to France, concurrently to Spain (1973-1976) • Member of Consultative People's Congress 1972 • Governor Military Academy (1966-1968) • Leader of the Indonesian Delegation to the ITU Plenipotentiary Conference Montreaux 1965 • Deputy Chairman, Indonesian Telecommunication Council (1963-1966) • Leader of Indonesian Military liaison group to the United Nations 1963 • Chief of Staff, Mandala joint command of armed forces for liberation of West Irian (1962-1963) • Military Attache, Indonesian Embassy Rome (1956-1959). - Commander of Military police (1946-1947) • Founder and commander of the 4th division peoples defence army (North Sumatra) (1945-1946).

Professor Dr Leonid E. VARAKIN, USSR

Rector, All-Union Telecommunication Institute by Correspondence Ministry of Posts and Telecommunications
• Professe>r of Technical Sciences since 1973 and Doctor of Technical Sciences since 1970 • Member 0 f Scientific and Technical Council of the Ministry of Telecommunications of the USSR • Member of the Praesidium of the Council of Rectors of the City of Moscow and Chairman of the Moscow Commission of Extra-mural (by correspondence) Education of the Council of Rectors • Member of the local Council of People's Deputies of the VOROSHILOV District of Moscow and Chairman of the Permanent Commission of People's Education • Since 1974 Head of Department of Radio receivers of the All-Union extra-mural Electrical Institute • Since 1963 involved in lecturing activity in the field of commu.nications in the Moscow Institute of Telecommunications • Author of more than 140 scientific works and some books on telecommunications, mobile communications, statistical radio techniques, theory of signals , digital techniques and radio receivers • Publications: "Theory of complex signals" 1970, "Theory of systems of signals" 1978, "Statistical Theory and its application" (co-author) 1979 • Participant in many international conferences on telecommunications.

His Excellency Mr Armando VARGAS ARAYA, Costa Rica (Vice-Chairman)

Minister of Information and Communications
• Appointed Presidential Adviser and Minister of Information and Communications by President Luis Alberto Monge in May 1982 • Involved in activities for the international development of information and communications since 1975 • Founded the Telecommunications Centre for the Third World in 1979 • President of the World Association for Christian Communication (Latin America - Caribbean region),(1977-1982) • Led Costa Rican delegation to ITU Plenipotentiary Conference, Nairobi 1982 • Attended World Administrative Radio Conference, Geneva, 1979. . _ Chaired WCY Seminar Meeting, Region 2, San Jose, 1983 • Attended UNESCO DEVCOM Conference establishing the International Programme for the Development of Communication, Paris 1980 • Vice-Chairman National Infor'mation System Activities (ASIN) • Manager of Latin American Special Services Agency.

His Excellency Dr Faisal ZAIDAN, Saudi Arabia

Deputy Minister of Telephones Ministry of Posts, Telegraphs and Telephones
• Joined Ministry of Posts, Telegraphs and Telephones 1962 • Member of INTELSAT Board of Governors • Chairman of the Board of Directors of ARABSAT • Member of the High Commission on the development of Riyadh City • Former lecturer, King Saud University.